Peter Stansky was born in 19[...] in New York City, and educated at Yale University, [...] Harvard University. He is aut[...] *Strategies*, a study of the leade[...] the 1890s; has edited *The Left*[...] *Party and World War I*; and h[...] *Today*, *Partisan Review*, *Victorian Studies*, and other journals. He is now associate professor of history at Stanford University.

William Abrahams was born in Boston, Massachusetts, in 1919. A graduate of Harvard, he is a novelist and poet whose work has appeared in *The New Yorker*, *Horizon*, *Partisan Review*, and elsewhere. He is West Coast editor of Holt, Rinehart and Winston.

Together with *Orwell: The Transformation* and *Journey to the Frontier* (whose subject was John Cornford and Julian Bell), *The Unknown Orwell* completes the authors' original purpose – a study of three British writers of the early 1930s, and the reasons for their involvement in the Spanish Civil War.

Peter Stansky
and
William Abrahams

The Unknown Orwell

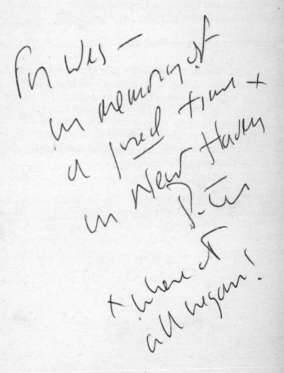

A PALADIN BOOK

GRANADA
London Toronto Sydney New York

Published by Granada Publishing Limited in 1974
Reprinted 1981, 1982

ISBN 0 586 08178 X

First published in Great Britain by Constable and Co 1972
Copyright © Peter Stansky and William Abrahams 1972

Granada Publishing Limited
Frogmore, St Albans, Herts AL2 2NF
and
36 Golden Square, London W1R 4AH
866 United Nations Plaza, New York, NY 10017, USA
117 York Street, Sydney, NSW 2000, Australia
100 Skyway Avenue, Rexdale, Ontario, M9W 3A6, Canada
61 Beach Road, Auckland, New Zealand

Made and printed in Great Britain by
Richard Clay (The Chaucer Press) Ltd
Bungay, Suffolk
Set in Monotype Ehrhardt

To Stan, Marina, and Fay and also to Edward

'The future work ferments in its future author'
Paul Valéry

Contents

Illustrations

Foreword

We cannot exaggerate our indebtedness to Avril Dunn, Eric Blair's sister, and to certain friends and acquaintances of his, who knew him in the years before he became George Orwell. Much of what we have written is based upon their memories of him, and we are deeply grateful to them for their willingness to share their memories with us. Our book would not be what it is without their extraordinary generosity and co-operation – the extent of which will be evident in the pages that follow – and we trust that we have not misrepresented them. Of course, we take full responsibility for errors of fact and questions of interpretation.

When we began to work in the summer of 1962, our plan was to write a study of a number of young English writers of the 1930s, among them George Orwell, who had fought on the side of the Republic in the Spanish Civil War. But that first plan, as so often happens, proved unwieldy and uncongenial. We chose to limit ourselves to Julian Bell and John Cornford; our book about them, *Journey to the Frontier*, was published in 1966. The year before we had already returned to Orwell, intending to study his life and work in the 1930s, from the publication of *Down and Out in Paris and London* through his experience in the Spanish Civil War and his subsequent account of it in *Homage to Catalonia*. As the reader will discover, that book is not the one we have written.

Where Orwell is concerned, the by now traditional formula that the man and his work are inseparable seems to us beyond dispute, yet it leads towards a succession of simplifications and reductions. The work is magnificently there; the man is elusive, simultaneously out of sight and in full view. We found it difficult to begin at the point where we intended to begin. Eric Blair was thirty years old when he published *Down and Out in Paris and*

London and became George Orwell. Were the thirty years of Blair before Orwell to be dismissed as of no consequence? The question was raised and an answer provided by Sir Richard Rees, a friend of Orwell's since 1930 and an ambulance driver with Julian Bell in Spain, whose kindnesses to us extended back to the early stages of *Journey to the Frontier*.

In May 1967 we went to Rees's small house in Burnsall Street to talk about Orwell, as we had done many times before. At some point in that afternoon he remarked, in a characteristically off-hand, diffident way, 'But of course, if you want to understand Orwell, you have to understand Blair' – his way of pronouncing the name was remarkable and cannot be reproduced; he seemed to lengthen it by at least a syllable – 'and to understand Blair – well, there's your book.'

There, certainly, was a book, and we have attempted to make it ours: a study of Eric Blair becoming the writer George Orwell; and we have ended it where we had originally thought to begin, with the publication of *Down and Out in Paris and London*.

Richard Rees died in July 1970. We never had the opportunity to show him any portion of our manuscript, as we had done with *Journey to the Frontier*. We can only hope that he would not have been displeased with this book which a casual remark of his helped to engender.

To Sir Richard Rees, then, and to Mrs Avril Blair Dunn – unceasing gratitude; and what a great pleasure it is to be able finally to acknowledge how much we owe to them – and to Cyril Connolly, the late Mrs Vaughan Wilkes, Miss Ruth Pitter, Denys King-Farlow, Sir Steven Runciman, Roger Beadon, and Mrs Mabel Fierz.

Also, A. L'e. Brownlow, R. M. Cazalet, Francis Cruso, the late Humphrey Dakin, A. Dunbar, James Gibson, A. S. F. Gow, Christopher Hollis, John Lehmann, W. C. A. Milligan, Sir Roger Mynors, the Hon. Michael Norton, C. B. Orr, Professor Richard Peters, R. Gordon, B. Prescott, Lord Rathcreedan, Miss Brenda Salkeld, E. F. Seeley, George Wansbrough, Sir Maurice Whittome.

Our indebtedness does not end here with those who knew Blair before he became Orwell. There are many who knew him after 1933, whether as Blair or as Orwell, who were kind enough to talk with us about him, and whom we hope to have the pleasure of thanking in a later volume.

We are deeply grateful to Graham Bennett, Mrs Valerie Eliot, Lord Harlech, Dr Hamida Khuhro, Alec Livingston, and Jeffrey Meyers, and the Master in College, Librarian, Captain of the School, and Keeper of the Wall, Eton College (1967).

The late John D. Gordan, a valued friend, was extremely generous in making the resources of the Berg Collection of the New York Public Library available to us.

We have had the benefit of editorial advice and encouragement from Benjamin Glazebrook, the Hon. John Jolliffe, and Andrew Mylett in London, and from Robert Gottlieb in New York.

Peter Stansky would also like to express his deep appreciation to the John Simon Guggenheim Memorial Foundation for granting him a Fellowship to work on this study.

Prologue

The making of a writer is a complex process; and who is to say with any assurance where it begins – with his first book, or his first day at school, the day of his birth, or generations back, lost in a tangle of genealogy? History of this kind is difficult to uncover and describe, for beginnings, apprenticeship, and the first stirrings of a talent that has yet to declare itself even to itself, are not infrequently cast aside and forgotten, like a cocoon that has served its purpose, or else lost sight of in the fame of what was afterwards achieved. Certainly this would seem to be the case with Eric Blair, who, in 1933, in his thirtieth year, upon the publication of his first book, *Down and Out in Paris and London*, became George Orwell.

At first Blair found in Orwell a *nom de plume*; then, later, virtually a second self, a means of realizing his potentialities as an artist and moralist to become one of the major English authors of this century. Orwell he became; but he was Blair before Orwell, and there was always in Orwell the residue of Eric Blair. He never changed his name legally. To those who knew him in his early years he remained 'Eric' or 'Blair' – Eric to women and members of his family; friends of his later years called him 'George' or 'Orwell', and he often signed letters as George Orwell. The creation of George Orwell was an act of will by Eric Blair, and it was carried on at almost every level of his existence, affecting not only his prose style but also the style of his daily life. Becoming George Orwell was his way of making himself into a writer, at which he brilliantly succeeded, and of unmaking himself as a gentleman, of opting out of the genteel lower-upper-middle class into which he was born, at which he had only an equivocal success. But the significant result of the creation was that it allowed Eric Blair to come to terms with his world. Blair was the man to whom things happened; Orwell the man who wrote about them.

Much of his life before thirty was an attempt to escape from the system into which he had been born, and which inexorably provided him with an education, an accent, and a standard of judgement that might be turned against him. The system he felt had almost crushed him in his prep school days, and towards the end of his life he left a grim version of them in 'Such, Such were the Joys'. Cyril Connolly, who was at school with him at St Cyprian's, thought him a 'true rebel' there, but in his own mind Blair was sure he was damned, and doomed to failure. Such, he felt, was the judgement of St Cyprian's and by inference of the system. Even after he went to Eton, and from there to the Indian Imperial Police in Burma, he continued to believe that it was an unalterable judgement, and that your place in the world did not depend on your own efforts but on 'what you were'. This mood continued to afflict him until his return from Burma in 1927. It was only then, breaking with the system, that he began seriously to write – and so ultimately to disprove the judgement against himself in the breadth of his achievement; yet his novels early and late alike, down to *Animal Farm* and *1984*, accept the omnipotence of the system while his heroes are its victims.

As George Orwell, Blair made himself a happier man than he had ever dreamed of being, and a writer of extraordinary power. It was here that he was best served by his creation. Much as Orwell in conversation would pick and choose what he would reveal of himself – even to close friends, whom he tended to keep carefully separate, giving each his own quite different share of the truth – so Blair, through Orwell, could select, control and put to use the elements of his rejected past.

Ironically, many of the qualities that contribute to the Orwell personality and style as we are familiar with them in his work are precisely the qualities Blair had thought despicable in his schooldays. Eric Blair saw himself as a smelly, impoverished member of the lower-upper-middle class who, because of his being bright enough for a scholarship and coming from a suitable Anglo-Indian background, had received an inappropriate gentleman's education. But George Orwell was an idiosyncratic Socialist, who, no matter how shabbily he dressed or austerely he lived, would never lose an air of authority – in his life as in his prose – that is sometimes thought to mark a Public School 'old boy'. Orwell could transform the values of the upper-middle class that Blair resented, and infuse them with the egalitarianism he had witnessed among the miners in Wigan and experienced at first hand as a soldier among soldiers in Spain. Eric Blair looked back unforgivingly on the world before 1914 – it was that world that had sent him to his prep school – while George Orwell could believe it was superior to what came after it, and looked back to it nostalgically in *Coming Up for Air*. And if Eric Blair came to disdain the platitudes and hypocrisies at a boys' school in England of the First World War, George Orwell was moved to a simple, intense patriotism during the Second World War when England was endangered.

There were moments when Blair and Orwell were at one: in the comradeship of the Spanish Civil War, and in the inspiriting early years of the blitz when it was possible to believe in a brave new England to come. They were moments of honour and decency, in which Blair and Orwell could participate and feel at ease. But such moments could not last: they would be undone by the Stalinists, as in Spain, or by the thought police, as in *1984*. Then the struggle would be resumed, between the patriot and the radical, the idealist and the sceptic, the sahib and the victim. Out of the tension came the many books that Orwell was to write between 1933 and his death in 1950.

In the churchyard in the village of Sutton Courtenay, where Orwell is buried, his grave is marked by a plain grey-brown stone on which has been inscribed

Here Lies
Eric Arthur Blair
Born June 25th 1903
Died January 21st 1950

The inscription was specified by Orwell himself in the first part of the final sentence of his last will. The will was drawn up on 18 January 1950, three days before his death, in University College Hospital, London, where he had been a patient since the preceding September. Having chosen his epitaph, he went on to conclude the sentence with a request that no memorial service be held for him and no biography of him be written; and then he signed his name, Eric Blair. It was as though the creator were determined once and for all to separate himself from his creation – as though the two were not inextricably bound together. So long as Orwell exists, Blair exists too. Orwell he became. But he had been Blair first.

Part One:
From Bengal to St Cyprian's

I

The complexities of the English class structure are not to be unravelled in a single paragraph. It is nothing so simple as the conventional three categories, upper, middle, and lower; and one is only slightly nearer a resolution when the minimum number of categories is enlarged to five: aristocracy, upper, middle, lower and working class. For it is in the middle classes where socially the nuances lie, and a gulf is fixed between upper-middle and lower-middle class. The most finicking discriminations are constantly being made. To what class does a bricklayer making five pounds a week belong? To what class does a clerk in a bookshop making three pounds a week, whose father is a clergyman, belong, as opposed to a clerk in a bookshop making three pounds a week, whose father is a bricklayer? Or in the latter case, suppose that it is not his father but his grandfather who has been the bricklayer and his father is the clergyman, what then? Or to complicate it another way, think of a clerk in a bookshop whose grandfather was a clergyman but whose father is a bricklayer – a perfectly honest, respectable trade, after all – what class is he?

The question of class in all its ramifications and permutations has fascinated, irritated, reassured, and divided generations of Englishmen, and has provided English novelists, from Jane Austen to the present, with a seemingly inexhaustible subject. It is difficult to think of a single English novelist, even an overt fantasist like Lewis Carroll, who has not been affected by the question, nor has failed to take it into account, directly or by implication, in his work. 'Who is he?' tends to accompany 'What is he?' and sometimes to precede it, and the consequences in life as in art are comic or tragic, or in the great grey wastes between.

Perhaps the luckiest are those at either end of the spectrum, the aristocrat and the working-man. They are recognized and accepted without equivocation for what they are, not least by themselves, and so Who he is and What he is are of no concern to them. But for those in the middle of the spectrum, especially those on the lower edges, shading off downward from one class to another, the borderland of impoverished gentility, these questions are of the gravest import: the answers to them can decide or despoil a life. Orwell knew this at first hand, and as a young writer he was fascinated as well as embittered by the class question: it figures obsessively in much of what he wrote before 1936, in the novels, *A Clergyman's Daughter* and *Keep the Aspidistra Flying*, and in the autobiographical portions of *The Road to Wigan Pier*. It is only in 1937 with *Homage to Catalonia*, his account of his experience in the Spanish Civil War, that he gets beyond it to what would be his principal concern thereafter: human freedom. (And yet at the end of his life he was still settling scores with the class discriminations of St Cyprian's, from which he felt he had cruelly suffered.)

To what class, in fact, does a young writer belong, whose books, articles and reviews do not bring in even the austere minimum of money sufficient for survival; who therefore takes a series of lowly jobs, among them clerking in a bookshop; whose father is a retired colonial civil servant of the middle rank (and a younger son); whose grandfather was a clergyman, vicar of a country parish (and a younger son); and whose great-great-grandfather was a man of property married to the daughter of an Earl? The young writer, of course, was Eric Blair in the 1930s, when he was already writing as George Orwell, and Orwell's answer to the question of his class was a sardonic, finely-shaded 'lower-upper-middle'. Towards the end of his life, when his spirit was no longer so exacerbated by questions of class and money, he wrote in the Preface to the Ukrainian edition of *Animal Farm* that he came from an ordinary middle-class family of soldiers, clergymen, government officials, teachers, lawyers, doctors – in other words, the professional classes, a central group in English society in which money has always counted for less than position, and for whom it was more important to be of 'some service' to the State than to make a fortune, although there was no objection to money should it appear in the process.

Family background and family history play a part in the making of any writer, however rigorously he himself may suppress overt references to them. In Orwell such references are not frequent, but one has a sense of continuity, of parallels and foreshadowings reaching into an earlier age, of family styles and attitudes that presage the kind of writer he was to become. Or, to put it another way, if Eric Blair as George Orwell is the most considerable of the Blairs, the culmination of a line, it is neither startling nor incongruous that it should be so. A glance at the history of the family will confirm this.

Charles Blair, his great-great-grandfather, who was born in 1743 and died in 1802, was a man of considerable wealth, the owner (we learn from his will) of 'Estates, Plantations, Messuages, Lands, Tenements and Hereditaments . . . in the Island of Jamaica', as well as 'Negro, Mulatto and other Slaves'. It would appear that his fortune was increased when he married Lady Mary Fane, the second daughter of Thomas, eighth Earl of Westmorland, for there is a record of an exchange of deeds between his father-in-law and himself in 1765 in Jamaica.[1] (Blairs, probably of the same family, had been prominent in Jamaica since the early eighteenth century; they might also have been associated with the abortive Scottish Darien scheme in Panama of 1698.)

Lady Mary, two years older than her husband, introduces an aristocratic aspect to the background, quite faded out by the time of the fifth, Eric Blair's, generation, yet there are strains in the history of the Westmorland family that are not without interest for the amalgam that made up both Eric Blair and George Orwell. Since the time that the title was created in the Fane line in 1624, the Earls of Westmorland have served the state at the level expected of the aristocracy. Theirs too is a family in which there has been something more than the expected aristocratic patronage of the arts. There have been Fane poets, a Fane playwright, and a Fane composer. The second Earl was joint lord-lieutenant of Northamptonshire in 1660; he left poems in manuscript; his cousin and contemporary was Sir Francis Fane, the dramatist. The seventh Earl served under Marlborough, was installed as

Chancellor of Oxford in 1759, and engaged the architect Colin Campbell to build him a country seat. The result was Mereworth Castle in Kent, one of the great Palladian villas in England, a copy of the Villa Rotonda at Vicenza, and only a few miles distant from the hop fields where Eric Blair was to work for a time as a hop-picker in the 1930s – an irony that would be even more pointed if his kinsmen had still been in possession of the house. The tenth Earl, the cousin and godfather of Thomas Richard Arthur Blair, Orwell's grandfather, was a friend of Pitt's, a lord-lieutenant of Ireland and Lord Privy Seal – he also helped replenish the family fortune by running away to Gretna Green with the heiress of Robert Child, the great banker and owner of Osterly Park. The eleventh Earl served in the Peninsular campaigns, had an active diplomatic career, and was also a composer. One of his sons, Julian Fane, was a diplomatist, translator, and poet. The twelfth Earl had a career in the military, and served in India. (So too, on a lower level, did Richard Walmesley Blair, Orwell's father.) But by then the connection, not to speak of communication, between the aristocratic Fanes and their distant relations, the worthy Blairs, was faint indeed.

To return to the generation when the connection was established. Charles Blair's properties were in Jamaica, but he was an absentee owner, in the style perhaps of Sir Thomas Bertram of *Mansfield Park*, and he and Lady Mary spent most of their married life at Winterborne Whitechurch in Dorset. In 1793 they moved to nearby Blandford St Mary where they leased Down House. In the parish church of Winterbourne Whitechurch, whose chief claim to fame is that John Wesley, the grandfather of the great John Wesley, was its vicar from 1658 until he was ejected for his opinions in 1662, there is a plaque on the north aisle wall on which the vicissitudes of the family are recorded. Four of the children died young: Maria in infancy; Thomas at thirteen; Mary of consumption at sixteen; and Henry Charles Blair, at nineteen, in 1794, in the service of His Majesty at St Domingo, as a Captain in the 23rd Regiment of Foot. (The family's affluence is evident in Henry's military career in the days of purchase: he entered the service at the age of fifteen or sixteen as a second Lieutenant, was a Lieutenant the next year, and a Captain in 1793.)

Charles Blair's will, drawn up in 1801, the year before he died, is preserved in Somerset House. It is a document that might well inspire a novel – others like it already have, in abundance – dealing with matters of entail, primogeniture, and the plight of the younger son. The property was tied up in a trust for two hundred years, to be administered by two relatives of his wife (and their descendants): Francis Fane, and Charles Michel from Lyndhurst near Southampton. The latter was a member of the Michel family of Dewlish, a village very near Winterbourne Whitechurch, and he was related to the Blairs through Lady Mary. The two trustees were to administer the estate in the interest of Charles Blair junior, the oldest surviving son, who was assured an annual income of eight hundred pounds, or more at their discretion. Lady Mary was to receive three hundred pounds per year, the household goods and 'all her paraphernalia Jewels and Ornaments to and for her own proper use and benefit'. There was a twenty-five-pound annual income for a faithful servant, and some provision was made for the wife and children of Charles Blair junior should he predecease his father. But he did not. The same year in which Charles Blair senior died – 1802 – Mrs Charles Blair junior gave birth to Orwell's grandfather, Thomas Richard Arthur Blair. From this epoch of affluence very little appears to have remained in Orwell's family save for a portrait of Lady Mary Blair now in the possession of his sister Avril Dunn.

A step down was taken by Thomas Richard Arthur Blair. With apparently not many material advantages to speak of – revenues were in a general state of decline from Jamaica in the early nineteenth century – he was expected to fend for himself, choosing a career from among the handful of possibilities open to the younger son of a good family: Church, Army, the Colonies. True, he had the spiritual or social advantage of being the godson and cousin of the Earl of Westmorland. But the difference between his own and his cousin's situation was unmistakable, a gap that would have been closed only if he had married exceptionally well, which he did not. As it was, after a year at Pembroke College, Cambridge, where he enjoyed the distinguished rank for a student of a Fellow-Commoner, he went out to serve God and country in the Empire.

He was ordained Deacon in the Church of England by the Bishop of Calcutta in 1839, and Priest by the Bishop of Tasmania in 1843; in 1854 he returned permanently to England to become Vicar of Milborne St Andrew in Dorset. Several years earlier, coming home from India on a visit, he had stopped at Cape Town, where he met and became engaged to a Miss Emily Hare, and then continued on his journey. On the return voyage, he stopped again at the Cape, intending to be married and bring his bride back with him to India, only to discover that she had married someone else in the interim. With great insouciance, he decided that, as Emily was already married, he would marry the next Hare sister, Frances, 'Fanny', who was only fifteen at the time, and he promptly did.[2] The marriage was a happy and fruitful one: there were ten children, the last two born after the return from the colonies.

Milborne St Andrew as a parish has been in existence since 1067. The Pleydells were the great family at Milborne itself, with their hatchments adorning the church, but the parish is connected with the neighbouring village of Dewlish which has its own small church. The same vicar has ministered to both churches since at least the fourteenth century, and it was the family of Dewlish, the Michels, who had the gift of the living – an extremely good living of approximately one thousand pounds annual income. As we have seen, the Michels were connections of the Blairs through marriage. It was Lady Mary's niece's son, Sir John Michel – he too had had the experience of the colonies, having served as a Major General in India and Canada – who gave the living to his cousin in 1854.

In 1935, when Orwell's uncertainties and dissatisfactions were at their most acute, he wrote in a poem first published in the *Adelphi* and afterwards incorporated in his essay 'Why I Write' that he would have been a happy vicar born two hundred years ago. One feels that the life of his grandfather, vicar of a quiet country parish remote from the tensions and disaffections of mid-Victorian industrial England, would also have fulfilled this ideal. (Of course it was an impossible ideal, as Orwell knew: that was the point of the poem, that we are living in 'an evil time' – the phrase and the insight seem to have been in common use among poets of the 1930s, from Auden and Louis MacNeice down – and cannot escape from it into a wish-dream of the past.) The Reverend Thomas Blair was not a diary-keeping clergyman like the Reverend Francis Kilvert, but the texture of daily life in Milborne St Andrew finds its counterpart in the pages of Kilvert's *Diary*. There were the natural joys and sorrows, the pleasures of living in unspoiled countryside, visits back and forth between Dewlish House and the Vicarage. A son, Dawson, was born in 1855. Another son (Orwell's father), Richard Walmesley Blair, was born on 7 January 1857, and was baptized by his father in the church a month later. A daughter, Augusta Michel, died in 1862 at the age of twelve, and was buried in the Dewlish churchyard. So the round of days and years continued – in a sense it is recorded in the church register: births, marriages, and deaths. The last baptism Thomas Blair performed in his church was on 28 July 1867. A month later he died, at the age of sixty-five, having been vicar of Milborne St Andrew for thirteen years, and leaving a large family who thereafter must fend for themselves.[3]

The second step down towards Orwell's 'lower-upper-middle' was taken by Richard Walmesley Blair. Given his circumstances, this was inevitable. He was a child of late middle-age; he was a younger son; like his father he would go out to India to begin his career – unlike him he would remain there. But he was starting out with even fewer material advantages than his father had done; and as for the social advantages of being well-born and well-connected, which in the end had proved of considerable value to his father, he was a further generation on – the great-grandson of the daughter of an Earl – and this rather tended to thin such advantages out. But there he was, indisputably a younger son of good family, and so the traditional careers appropriate to such a young man had to be considered, and it was decided that he should go into colonial service. He hadn't money or education enough to go grandly. On 4 August 1875, at the age of eighteen, he joined the Opium Department of the government of India in the rank of Assistant Sub-Deputy Opium Agent 5th grade.

The opium trade with China had been legalized after 1860, and was carried on under the supervision of the Opium Department. Blair, as a junior officer in the department, was posted to a variety of stations around India during his years of service: to Muzaffarpur; Gorakhpur; Sarsa, Allahabad; Salem; Rai Bareilly; Fuzabad; Shahjahanpur; Etah; Patna; Tehta; Motihari; and Monghyr. From 11 August 1879 to 11 January 1880, he was on deputation as Famine Relief Officer at Bellary. At the time of his retirement from the service in 1912, his rank was Sub-Deputy Opium Agent 1st grade.

Blair married comparatively late – in 1896 at the age of thirty-nine – when he was stationed at Tehta in Bihar. His wife, several years younger than he, was Miss Ida Mabel Limouzin. The daughter of a French father and an English mother, she was born in Penge, Surrey, but from an early age had lived in Moulmein, Burma, where the Limouzins had conducted business enterprises almost from the time that port city had been ceded to the British in 1826. With the marriage two contrasting traditions were joined: the Blairs', English, genteel, dedicated to the idea of serving the state; and the Limouzins', French, bourgeois, dedicated to the idea of serving the family.

The Limouzins were people to reckon with in Moulmein: a street in the city is named after them. They were ship-builders, and teak merchants; and one member of the family ran a distillery. The founder of the business was G. E. Limouzin, who died in 1863. His son, Frank Limouzin, Orwell's maternal grandfather, was born in Limoges, but grew up in Burma, and in the natural course of events took over the business at his father's death. He appears to have been something of an inventor as well as a man of business for he described himself in the *Maulmain Calendar*, a local periodical, as the 'patentee of a life-boat, which is likely to prove invaluable to all commanders of vessels in case of mishap'.[4] He married twice. His first wife, by whom he had one child, died in 1865; his second wife, by whom he had nine children, one of them Ida, was an Englishwoman of impressive character. Over the years she became a power in the town, although towards the end of her life – she died in 1925, ten years after her husband – she was thought (by the British colony) to have gone 'somewhat native' – that is, she chose to wear native dress (though she never learned the language) which gave rise to the rumour among acquaintances of Eric Blair's in the Imperial Police that he was himself part Burmese.

The first child of the marriage was a daughter, Marjorie, born in 1898 while they were stationed at Tehta. On 5 February 1903, Blair was transferred to a new post, at Motihari in Bengal, and it was there, on 25 June 1903, that the second child, a son, was born. His name was Eric Arthur Blair.

2

We have said that Richard Walmesley Blair (hereafter in these pages he will be simply Mr Blair; and Ida Limouzin, Mrs Blair) took the second step down towards the fourth generation's 'lower-upper-middle', but this would not become apparent until after his retirement from the Opium Department in 1912, when he was fifty-five, and had returned to England to live. Anglo-Indian life in the late Victorian and Edwardian period – when the Blairs were in India – has been described in countless memoirs, some fatuous, some estimable, but almost all forgotten, and set for all time by a writer of genius, Kipling, whose work is familiar to most English-speaking readers, and was greatly admired by Orwell himself. The vivid, exotic details are to be found there. It is enough here to note that while military pay and salaries in the civil service were not large, they were sufficient in the officer ranks and their equivalents to allow for marriage and the raising of a family, to provide for many-roomed bungalows and luxuriant gardens, staffed by native servants – the inevitable ayahs, amahs, cooks, boys, bearers, chhokras (to pull the punkahs), gardeners, and their attendant relatives – and for a social life that was centred in the Club. It was a life based on ethnic and national distinctions – to be white and English; rather less on class. However tenuous one's middle-class affiliation in England might be, however cockneyfied one's accent and gross one's manners, when in India, bearing the white man's burden and serving, building, enlarging and defending the Empire, one was privileged, belonged to a privileged class and the Club. (It is all there in Kipling; and since much of the life he described was traditional and resistant to change through at least the first three decades of the century, it would also be in the work of later writers, in E. M. Forster's *A Passage to India*, and Orwell's first novel, *Burmese Days*.)

Anglo-Indian privilege extended from the time of enlistment to the time of retirement. It didn't travel well: sahibdom dwindled away on the P. & O. steamer taking one back to England. There, forced more often than not to subsist on a small, barely adequate pension, one occupied an equivocal and difficult position, especially so when measured against the assurance and privilege of life in India. This was to be the experience of the Blairs.

Eric, their second child, was born in June in 1903 when they were stationed in Motihari, in Bengal. Nine months later, Mr Blair, then a Sub-Deputy Opium Agent, 4th grade, was appointed to a new station and the family moved on to Monghyr. On 30 December 1906, he was raised to 2nd grade, and on 21 May 1907, after thirty-two years of service, to 1st grade. At the end of July 1907, he was granted leave of three months and seven days, his first since 1902, and took his family back to England, to an unpretentious small house aptly named 'Nutshell', in the Western Road in Henley-on-Thames. In November he returned to Monghyr; Mrs Blair – by then expecting their third child, Avril – remained in Henley with Marjorie and Eric. Mr Blair would not rejoin them until his retirement four years later.

The paragraph above contains all the ascertainable facts about Eric's first four years. Perhaps we should add one further fact, a family recollection of Mrs Blair having recorded in her diary (either in India, or on board ship, or after their arrival in England) that Baby (Eric) called things 'beastly'. But because so little is known definitely of this period of his life, it does not follow that it is of no importance. Mrs Blair's diary has disappeared; there is no reason to believe that her husband ever kept one; Eric Blair when he was becoming Orwell, and later as Orwell, wrote a considerable amount about Burma, based upon his experiences there as a young man, but about his earliest childhood in India he wrote nothing. Consciously he appears to have forgotten it all: his declared memories go back no further than his fourth or fifth year, to a day when he dictated a poem about a tiger to his mother, by which time, of course, they were living in Henley, and the tiger, he felt, came from Blake, not Monghyr. Unconsciously, though, the memory of that hot, subtropical, foreign country where he was born, with its spicy smells and pungent flavours, its flamboyant sights and exotic sounds, may well have survived within him: it might well account for the intensity of

31

his response to Burma, about which he wrote in a highly-charged, highly-coloured, sensuous prose that no other subject seemed to elicit from him. Years later, when he was firmly Orwell, he came to distrust such prose and shrugged it off as merely 'purple'. Yet, as Richard Rees has pointed out, 'The descriptive writing in *Burmese Days* is the most elaborate and probably the best he ever did. Neither his evocation of Spain in *Homage to Catalonia* nor his many attempts to express his feeling for Southern England are so vivid and striking as his descriptions of the climate, landscape, trees, flowers, and smells of Upper Burma.'[5]

In any event, there was a dramatic change, a dramatic contrast in his life in 1907 – it was then, very likely, that the sense of resentment and injustice had their beginnings, that he began to call things, 'beastly'. In India the family had consisted of father, mother, older sister Marjorie, and himself the baby. In England, father was absent – Eric would not see him again until he was eight – and the family now consisted of mother, older sister Marjorie, himself, and the new baby Avril. In India too there had been a house full of servants, to free Mrs Blair from time-consuming, worrying domestic responsibilities, and to cosset and beguile a small boy: for him the bungalow and its surrounding garden would have been a full, satisfying world. In England things were very different. There was a daily char to help in 'Nutshell', but Mrs Blair was busy with the new baby; Marjorie, a nine-year-old schoolgirl, was away at school a good part of the day or playing with her friends – Eric, a shy child in a new and unfamiliar world, where one wore bulky clothes, clinging woollen stockings, and heavy shoes, to protect one against rain and damp, the world of head colds and running noses and sore throats and wheezing chests, had difficulty in making friends and felt increasingly lonely. He adored his mother, but he was too shy ever to confide in her what he felt, and therefore felt himself neglected and misunderstood. Such feelings of loneliness, isolation, and resentment are classic symptoms in a literary history, and it is not surprising that Eric, by the time he was five or six, should have *known* that he would become a writer, that classic way of avenging oneself for an unhappy childhood.

He was shy and reticent as a child, and would continue to be so as an adult, even in his closest friendships. In this respect he resembled his middle-aged father. Neither Mr nor Mrs Blair was warmly demonstrative in their affections, or rather, both had that reserve which some might say is natural to the English, and was not uncommon among those who spent much of their time in the East and had to keep up face in front of the 'natives'. But Mrs Blair had her French side, along with her English decorum. She was lively, friendly, and sociable, very much a woman of her time and background, fond of playing golf and breeding poodles, who fitted in well in colonial society, and in the various places in England where the Blairs were to live after their return from India. There is no question that life was more difficult financially, and grew progressively so, when they were living in England, but she was never obsessively worried about money: she had the knack – very French, some might say – of making the most of what there was. If she could not afford the more expensive sorts of food, then the inexpensive would have to do, but she served them with a dash and imagination not usual in the circumstances. Ruth Pitter, the poet, who was to be a neighbour of the Blairs after they moved from Henley to London, recalls Mrs Blair, a handsome woman with her black hair in a bang and wearing long agate drop earrings, bringing to the dinner table cabbage '*en casserole*', deliciously seasoned, very different from cabbage '*à l'Anglaise*', boiled and boiled to the point of tastelessness.[6] She had a flair for managing things: she managed very competently while alone with the children at Henley, and afterwards when Mr Blair had returned. She is the more commanding figure of the two: by contrast he appears a bit pallid and at a loss, the inevitable fate, perhaps, of the retired Anglo-Indian civil servant. In her competent fashion she was devoted to her children, watched over them and cared for them, and was prepared to make considerable sacrifices for them. But Eric, as a small boy, craved for more than this, or else for something quite different, and he nourished a grievance.

This grievance and the unhappiness it gave rise to constitute a significant part, but by no means the whole of his childhood, though it was the part Orwell chose to emphasize when writing directly about Eric Blair. Granting that most writers are likely to have had unhappy childhoods – to make a sweeping, unprovable, Orwellian sort of generalization – these things are relative:

Blair was never to know anything even remotely like the cruelty and neglect that were the lot as children of two other Anglo-Indian writers transplanted early from India to England, Kipling and H. H. Munro ('Saki'). In fact, there was another, equally significant part of his childhood, and it was expressed by Orwell in the nostalgia he would always feel for the world as it was before 1914. This was the world he came to know as a boy in Henley-on-Thames, that most Edwardian of riverside towns, the scene of the great annual regatta, where the river wound its way through the tranquil countryside, and where life, viewed in retrospect, was an unending summer. Anger and nostalgia, the two emotions that animate so much of what Orwell was to write, had their beginnings here.

At five he was ready for school, and Mrs Blair enrolled him at a day school near by, Sunnylands, run by Anglican nuns, where Marjorie was already a pupil. It was an exciting and enjoyable experience for him. (Characteristically, therefore, he never wrote about it, much as he never went into detail about his time at Eton, which he also enjoyed. The compulsion to correct an injustice, to repair a grievance, was absent: the experience had not rankled enough.) He was a bright, intelligent, eager small boy who learned without difficulty, whatever he was taught, a fact in which Mrs Blair took pride (as any mother would) and which was at the centre of the plans for his future she now began to make. Learning to read was the exhilarating discovery of these years. Inspired by the example of Marjorie, who was a great reader and passed on to him books she had outgrown or grown tired of, he began to read avidly, with the passionate indiscriminateness of a child for whom reading – books, magazines, newspapers, advertisements, *anything* – becomes an essential part of his existence. By the time he was eight, he had read, to single out only a few representative titles, *Tom Sawyer, Coral Island, Rebecca of Sunnybrook Farm* (no doubt a legacy from Marjorie), and *Gulliver's Travels*. His attachment over the years to his childhood reading and to authors whom he first read as a child was very strong. In the 1930s he raised the possibility of writing a biography of Mark Twain; the details of R. M. Ballantyne's *Coral Island* remained so clear in his mind that, writing of the book thirty years later, he could recall the telescope, six yards of whipcord, pen-knife, brass ring, and piece of hoop-iron its three boy castaways had had to depend upon to survive on their desert island. He read *Gulliver's Travels* at least seven times at different stages in his life, the first time the night before his eighth birthday. It had been bought for him by his mother as a birthday present, but on the night before, Eric discovered the parcel, secretly opened it, and began to read at once. Thus began a literary attachment Orwell would celebrate in 1946 in one of his great essays, 'Politics vs. Literature'; and two years before, *Gulliver's Travels* had provided a model or example for him when writing his own allegory, *Animal Farm*. Similarly, three other writers whom Blair would read for the first time before he was twelve, Dickens, Kipling, and P. G. Wodehouse, would be made the subjects of memorable essays by Orwell.

His taste was catholic: there was even pleasure to be got from reading advertisements. As a slightly older schoolboy he would pore over *Old Moore's Almanac*, and relish the advertisements promising ways to earn money, stop the drink habit, develop the bust, gain weight, or lose weight. He would amuse himself by writing to these altruistic agencies, asking for information and drawing them out; then simply stopping after they had sent him a flood of testimonials. At one point, as E. Blair, he carried on an extensive correspondence with Winifred Grace Hartland, who guaranteed a cure for obesity, and, on the assumption that he was a she – in fact he was at this time a 'fat little boy' – urged Miss Blair to come to see her before choosing her summer frocks, as her figure would change so. The correspondence went on for some time, while the proposed fee for advice shrank from two guineas to half a crown, until Miss Blair finally terminated it by stating that she had been cured by a rival agency.

All this profuse, indiscriminate reading helped to educate him and to give him the air of a 'wise child', older than his years and familiar with the ways of the world, though his knowledge was entirely theoretical. It also enriched his fantasy life. Shyness hampered him in making friends, and he tended to retreat into himself, conducting conversations with imaginary friends, and telling stories in his head. A few years later Avril would be an eager and attentive listener to his stories, especially during the summer holidays, when Mrs Blair would take the family to spend a few weeks in Cornwall, either in a house she rented, or in the house of Anglo-Indian acquaintances who welcomed them as paying guests. But, for the most part, his was a childhood in which other children played no significant roles: there were no best friends, no confidants. At the convent school he fell passionately in love with a girl named Elsie, who was twice his age and in the last year of the school. It was very much a passion at a distance, never to be expressed, but it was passion nonetheless, and he would not feel anything comparable to it again until, some twenty-five years later, he met the woman he was to marry. Elsie left the school at the end of the year, and Eric lost track of her – when he next saw her he was a sophisticated Etonian, and she a middle-aged woman of twenty-three, hopelessly past her prime he felt. But he remembered her as his first love, and he chose her name for the first love of George Bowling in *Coming Up For Air*, the most sympathetic of his heroes.

At five he made some friends of his own age, the children of the plumber who lived nearby. With them he would go bird's-nesting; with them, too, he played games of a mildly erotic character, of a sort not uncommon among children. But these were children of the working class; their father was a plumber; their accents were vulgar – Mrs Blair intervened and put an end to the friendship. Orwell, recounting the incident in 1936, has only sympathy for her position: as a middle-class parent she could not run the risk of her son growing up with an unsuitable accent. But what Eric Blair felt at the time we do not know. Nor do we know if Mrs Blair learned of the erotic games; in which case, they, as much as the threat of class contamination, might have prompted her to act as she did. We do know that two years later Eric was noticeably prudish, offended by the casual obscenities of childhood, and anything that smacked of lavatories or sex. By then he was accepted on sufferance as the youngest member of a gang of middle-class Henley boys of whom the eldest and leader was a boy of fifteen named Humphrey Dakin. On one occasion he tagged along on an expedition up the Thames, where hooks and lines were brought out, and he was introduced to the art of fishing, one of the great pleasures of his life, as it was also to be for George Bowling. For Orwell that first experience proved unforgettable. He made an important place for it in *Coming Up*

For Air, though there, recreated as fiction, there are some significant differences: George, like the other boys in the gang, comes from a lower-class family; and he is given an older brother, Joe, hefty, virile, immoral and illiterate, who runs away from home at eighteen and is never heard from again. Eric of course was the only boy in his family, but the heroes of his early childhood were young men of the working class: farm hands in Cornwall who let him ride along with them while they sowed turnips, and who on memorable occasions would milk the ewes to give him a drink; and the workmen who built the house next door to the Blairs', from whom he first heard the word 'bloody', a favourite word of Joe Bowling's. Then the taboos of the lower-upper-middle class were imposed upon him: there were to be no more heroes (except in books). The boys of the real gang had appropriate accents and backgrounds, and one of the boys would eventually become Eric's brother-in-law: Humphrey Dakin, who married Marjorie Blair in 1920. Orwell's own estimate of himself as an unpopular child seems borne out by his brother-in-law's recollection of him as he was in 1910: 'A rather nasty fat little boy with a constant grievance.' And he adds, 'it took him a long time to grow out of it'.[7]

At seven the prudishness, which Dakin and the other boys in the gang did not share and disliked, had set in. He was acutely sensitive to dirt and smells; he was repelled by physical ugliness, the paunches, jowls, wrinkles, sagging breasts and stomachs, and flabby thighs and buttocks of adults; he was disgusted by dogs' messes on pavements and horse-dung in the streets; his nostrils caught the whiff of sweat, bad breath, stale beer, and unwashed armpits; he was offended by mortality, the sense of decay made visible when he came upon the carcass of a frog being eaten by maggots. This was the hated aspect of childhood. Against this was the wonder of discovering each day something new in the world; the unfailing pleasures of reading; the love he felt for his mother (alone among adults); the tiny memorable satisfactions – visits to the sweet shop with a penny, street games, street songs, expeditions along the river. Disgust on one side; joy on the other. The tension between them was essential to him as an artist, and found a resolution in his work. But it was to take a long time.

3

When he was eight there was a new grievance, and it was the one to which Orwell would attach the greatest importance. In September 1911 he was sent away to school, the conventional fate of a boy of his age and class, in that time and place. The implications of the event were difficult in themselves to cope with – that he was being thrust from the nest. But as it happened, in one of those ironic coincidences that are so pat as to seem contrived, it was at this time too that Mr Blair came back permanently to his family, some months in advance of his official date of retirement. Thereafter, in that household of women where Eric had been the only 'man' for the past four years, there was Father, and there was 'Father's room', over-heated to a temperature as close as possible to India's, for he was uncomfortable in the chill airs of England.

Mr Blair had been away too long, and came back too late, to play a decisive role in the life of his son, with whom he barely had time to become reacquainted before he went off to school, and whom he would see thereafter mainly in the holidays. There was little *rapport* between father and son. In later years there was a sharp divergence of interests – a taste for fishing was one of the few things they shared* – and always there was a shyness and a reticence on both sides that would have made intimacy difficult. Orwell's chief childhood memory of him seems to be of an elderly gentleman whom he disliked, saying 'Don't' in a gruff voice. Sons tend to deprecate their fathers, much as in their own

* Even the taste for fishing was not a deep bond between them. As Avril Dunn comments, 'Father was never really keen on fishing. He did it at Southwold because some of his cronies fished & it was simply a matter of baiting a hook, slinging it into the sea & then balancing your rod on a rest, & waiting till the little bell rang, that was fixed to the top of the rod. No finesse, no skill needed. Eric was a dedicated fisherman with a genuine interest in various kinds of fish and their habitats.'

fashion fathers tend to deprecate their sons, especially respectable fathers who discover that their sons intend to be writers – that alarming Bohemian possibility. Certainly this proved to be the case, as we will see, with Eric and his father, and it may account for the note of disparagement in Orwell's recollections. It is worth remarking, then, that others who knew Mr Blair in England remember him as rather vague, gentle and charming, but somewhat dry, fond of walking around Henley and later in Southwold on the Suffolk coast (where the Blairs moved in 1921), passing the time of day in shops and on the sea-front, watching cricket matches, chatting in pubs, striking up friendships, and, when he had the luck to come upon an Anglo-Indian acquaintance, reminiscing about the good old days in the warm subcontinent.

During the four years of her husband's absence, Mrs Blair had been the dominant figure in the household, and she continued in the role after his return, in part because he was quite content that she should do so. Where Eric was concerned, there was no disagreement between them: both wanted the best for him, and both had a clearly defined idea of what the best was. It may be argued that as much can be said for any parents who are concerned about the future of their children. But the year was 1911, the beginning of the reign of George V, and the Blairs were parents in England, the greatest, richest power on earth, on whose Empire the sun never set. Also, they belonged, however precariously and minimally, to the upper-middle class. From this conjunction of circumstances it followed naturally that they wanted their son to have a place for himself among the rulers of England, which is not to say that he should become a member of the Cabinet (though that would be possible) or a great landowner, but simply a member of the ruling caste, *one of those who counted*, whether in the legal or medical or political or ecclesiastical or learned professions, the jurists and civil servants and colonial servants, the company directors and bankers and publishers, the officers of the Foreign Service and the officers of the Army and Navy – in a word, the so-called Establishment as it existed in England before the First World War.

The usual passport to this Establishment was to have attended a Public School, preferably one of the 'great' schools, best of all either Eton, Harrow, or Winchester. In 1911 the education to be had at an expensive Public School was likely to be superior to the education one got elsewhere, and its social advantages were undeniable. Fitted out with an accent and manner that were unmistakable and ineradicable – Blair, on the road, was never mistaken by his fellow tramps for one of themselves, but was accepted as an Etonian down on his luck – one was ready to enter an Establishment whose places went as if by right to Old Boys of Public Schools. It is understandable, then, that even those parents of the upper-middle class who could ill afford the expense of such an education were prepared, as the Blairs were, to make considerable sacrifices to obtain it for their children and so secure their future. (In 1911, it was not only possible but usual to think of a secure future, a fixed society, a destined place in life.)

Whatever their advantages as a kind of social 'forcing house', the Public Schools were primarily institutions of learning. Their standards for admission, particularly for a boy like Eric Blair who wished to be awarded a scholarship, were high indeed. So it was not a matter to be taken lightly: too much of a child's future depended on it, whether he would rise to a secure respectable place in the world, or sink down, as Eric was warned would happen to him if he failed his exams, to the level of an ill-paid office boy or a clerk in a shop. Little boys of eight, fresh from their governess or Dame School or convent school in the village, who could hardly be expected to think in such fateful terms, had to be prepared, had to be taught Latin and Greek and otherwise educated for the Public Schools their parents hoped they might at fourteen be allowed to enter. In answer to this need, there grew up yet another unique English institution, the expensive private school where boys between the ages of eight to fourteen were taught, crammed, drilled, and beaten, up to the high standard the Public Schools expected of their prospective scholars. A handful of these prep schools were day schools, located mainly in London, and in Oxford and Cambridge, whose pupils escaped at the end of each day to the protection and solace of home and family; but the greater number were boarding schools, to which, from all over England, Scotland, Wales, and Ireland, came privileged little boys, there to be made miserable.

It was to one such school, St Cyprian's, at Eastbourne, on the Sussex coast, that Eric Blair was sent in September 1911.

Since Mr Blair had not yet returned from India, it was Eric's mother who took the lead in settling his education, although one has the impression that she would have done so in any case. It was she who chose St Cyprian's, and made the arrangements for him to be enrolled there. Anglo-Indian acquaintances had recommended it to her: it was said to do very well in placing boys at the great Public Schools, where Mrs Blair was determined Eric should some day go; but of more immediate importance, it made a practice of taking at reduced fees a few exceptionally bright, promising boys who might go on to win scholarships at the Public Schools, the sons of families of limited means in the Imperial Civil Service, or who were otherwise serving in the Outposts of Empire. That reduced fees would be essential if Eric was to attend a private school, just as he would need a scholarship for Public School later, was understood from the first by his parents: they knew the limitations that would be imposed on them by Mr Blair's pension, down to the last shilling. But Mrs Blair had no doubt that Eric was bright enough and promising enough to deserve reduced fees, so, in the spring of 1911, she went down to Eastbourne to present her case to the headmaster-proprietor of St Cyprian's and his wife, Mr and Mrs Vaughan Wilkes.

The school was situated on the outskirts of that much-frequented resort town, beyond the seaside promenade and the last of the grand hotels. At the point where the coast road begins its winding ascent to the top of Beachy Head, the immense chalk cliff overlooking the Channel, another road veers off to the right, down into a kind of sheltered bowl, and there, at the entrance to what is now a well-mannered suburban street, were the buildings and grounds of St Cyprian's. They consisted principally of a playing field for cricket and football, and two large houses in the late-Victorian style that accommodated dormitories for the boys, classrooms, library, dining-room, offices, living quarters for the seven masters and the matron, and on a grander scale, for the headmaster and his wife and their growing family. From the upper storeys of both houses one had an uninterrupted prospect of the Downs, which began virtually across the street from the school property, and rose up steeply the quarter mile towards Beachy Head. For the boys it was a prospect of freedom: certainly Eric was happiest at St Cyprian's when he could escape from its disciplined precincts and wander over the Downs as he pleased, alone or with the one close friend he made among his schoolmates, Cyril Connolly.

The Vaughan Wilkeses welcomed Mrs Blair in the drawing-room of 'The Lodge', the house nearest to the street, and conversation was conducted over tea.*

In 1911 St Cyprian's was in its twelfth year with an enrolment of approximately seventy boys: by contrast to an historic Public School such as Eton (founded in 1440 by Henry VI) it had barely begun to exist. But private schools, not being foundations, are private enterprises and sometimes do not continue beyond the life span of their proprietors, who are usually headmasters, as was Mr Vaughan Wilkes, and often responsible for much of the teaching – Mr Vaughan Wilkes, for example, took the boys in 'Classics'. By 1911, in spite of its brief history, St Cyprian's was already recognized as one of the better as well as one of the more snobbish and expensive of private schools. The larger number of its pupils were drawn from the affluent upper-upper-middle class, with a smaller number from the middle-upper-middle, and smallest of all, the group each year who were on reduced fees, the bright, promising products of the lower-upper-middle. Then, as exotics (and threatening to lower the high moral tone, for they tended to be sexually precocious) there were a few sons of South-American millionaires; and, as a source of particular pride to the Vaughan Wilkeses and proof that the school was coming on, a tiny aristocratic minority, boys whose fathers had a handle to their names – even, in Eric Blair's time, a boy or two who had a

* It was in the same room that the authors of the present work were received by Mrs Vaughan Wilkes. She had then been a widow for some years, but continued to live with a companion in 'The Lodge', all that survived of St Cyprian's. The school had ceased to exist during the Second World War, and the other house had been destroyed by fire. The drawing-room was virtually a museum of school history: the walls, the mantle over the large fireplace, the tops of the glassfronted mahogany bookcases, the numerous tables, all were covered with photographs, framed and many of them signed, of old St Cyprianites. Sherry was offered, Mrs Vaughan Wilkes's massive scrapbooks, crammed with fifty years of memorabilia including Eric Blair's lost, first published writings, were produced; and conversation began.

handle of his own, authentic lordlings. It would have been in keeping for Mrs Vaughan Wilkes, over tea, to let fall such a name, giving full value to the handle.

Let us acknowledge, at the risk of some exaggeration, that snobbishness was rife at St Cyprian's – for so it would appear in the memoirs of the school written by 'old boys' who went on to become writers: E. W. Meyerstein, Cyril Connolly, George Orwell, Cecil Beaton, and Gavin Maxwell. In that respect, then, as in much else, St Cyprian's was representative, or symptomatic, of the epoch. England in 1911, that halcyon period 'before the war' that Orwell, in one mood, would look back on with so much nostalgia, was itself rife with snobbishness: it did not make even a pretence of egalitarianism, either social or political. It was a time when half the adult population was denied the vote, when a Duke was 'better' than a baronet, just as a clerk at Harrods was 'better' than a lorry driver, and so down, down to a coal miner in Wales who was no 'better' than anyone except, perhaps, a French or German coal miner. It was a time when the division between the classes seemed unbridgeable, and 'only connect', the motto of E. M. Forster's novel, *Howards End*, published the preceding year, seemed an ideal impossible of fulfilment, always assuming that one would want, like the Schlegel sisters in that novel, to 'connect' with someone in a class lower than one's own. By 1911 these assumptions had acquired the status of enduring natural laws, subscribed to by a majority of good, sound Englishmen from the lower-middle classes up. (The Schlegel sisters were not sound; neither were the miners and railway men out on strike; neither were the suffragettes, whose behaviour and aspirations were so unladylike.) But the age of almost undiluted privilege was without knowing it approaching its end: the terminal date was to be August 1914. And while privilege would be reconstituted in different forms after the war, it would never again be as pervasive or self-confident in its assumptions, nor as unbegrudgingly accepted, deferred to, or even tolerated, by those not qualified to enjoy it.

Mrs Blair was not a snob; certainly she did not adulate people who were better off or better placed than she, and rather tended to disparage them; but she would not have bristled when the Vaughan Wilkeses introduced the names of illustrious parents whose children were then at St Cyprian's. It would have confirmed what she had already been told by her Anglo-Indian friends, that the school attracted the 'right sort' of boy. Similarly she would have been reassured to hear that many 'old boys' were now at Harrow – a favourite St Cyprian destination – and also at Eton, Wellington, and others of the great schools: clearly the Vaughan Wilkeses got results, they gave value in return for money received. For their part the headmaster and his wife were impressed favourably by Mrs Blair. She was obviously 'one's sort' and it followed therefore that her son would be the right sort of boy for the school, especially since he had been doing well at his studies, was a bookish child, a great reader, from whom good things could be expected. This brought them to the question of fees.

Here again the headmaster and his wife were impressed and sympathetic: the Anglo-Indian background, the thirty years of colonial service, the approaching retirement, the pension that, it went without saying, would not be generous – all this established the Blairs as a family of the sort to whom the Vaughan Wilkeses would feel obliged, would feel it right, to make a concession. It would be consistent with their own notions of service, which were as firmly engrained in them as in other members of their class who had grown up in the heyday of Empire. Readers of Kipling who believed in him, they preached the ideal of service to their pupils, and instilled it in their own children, one of whom became a missionary, another the headmaster of a Public School, and who distinguished themselves in uniform during the Second World War. So it was settled, as the interview drew to a close, that Eric would be accepted at half fees, and that he would enter the school in the following September.

Orwell's account of his time at St Cyprian's, which he called 'Crossgates', was written some thirty years later, but with an astonishing immediacy of detail, as though his experience there is an open wound he has refused to allow to heal. He can see in the Vaughan Wilkeses' concession no trace of altruism, merely a plain piece of business speculation: that they were taking him at reduced fees because they expected him to win a scholarship at one of the great schools, which would redound to the credit of St Cyprian's, which in turn would make the Vaughan Wilkeses richer, and their business a success. It is true that St Cyprian's was owned by the Vaughan Wilkeses, that their livelihood depended upon it, that a record of boys admitted to top Public Schools was essential to their continuing success. Yet their willingness to take boys at reduced fees was not inspired wholly by calculation. Ambitious though they might be, they believed at the same time in the ideal of service – it was a responsibility of privilege, an English version of *noblesse oblige* – which they instilled not only in their own children, but in many of the boys who came to St Cyprian's, even, perhaps, in Eric Blair. Cyril Connolly's account of the school, which he called 'St Wulfric's', was written eight years before Orwell's. In two brilliantly ironic paragraphs he suggests how easily – how inevitably – idealism and worldliness could co-exist there without conflict:

The school was typical of England before the last war; it was worldly and worshipped success, political and social; though Spartan, the death-rate was low, for it was well-run and based on that stoicism which characterized the English governing class and which has since been under-estimated. 'Character, character, character,' was the message which emerged when we rattled the radiators or the fence round the playing fields and it reverberated from the rifles in the armoury, the bullets on the miniature range, the saw in the carpenter's shop and the hoofs of the ponies on their trot to the Downs.

> Not once or twice in our rough island's story,
> The path of duty was the way to glory

was the lesson we had to learn and there were other sacred messages from the poets of private schools: Kipling, or Newbolt.

Muscle-bound with character the alumni of St Wulfric's would pass on to the best public schools, cleaning up all houses with a doubtful tone, reporting their best friends for homosexuality and seeing them expelled, winning athletic distinctions – for the house rather than themselves, for the school rather than the house, and prizes and scholarships and shooting competitions as well – and then find their vocation in India, Burma, Nigeria and the Sudan, administering with Roman justice those natives for whom the final profligate overflow of Wulfrician character was all the time predestined.[8]

Mrs Blair had reason to be pleased when she returned to Henley: the concession she had obtained at Eastbourne was large enough to permit Eric's going to private school; and to go from St Cyprian's to a great Public School was a logical sequel – so that the respectable, gentlemanly, appropriate future she and Mr

Blair had envisioned for him seemed assured. Even so, it would not be managed without their making some quite stringent sacrifices. The Blairs would be paying ninety pounds a year at St Cyprian's, a not inconsiderable part of their income. In addition, there was the expense of outfitting him properly. Cecil Beaton, a contemporary of Blair's at St Cyprian's, noted some years later (1923) that 'When preparing for this school, my mother was horrified at the length of the prescribed list: 12 pairs of socks, 6 pairs of pyjamas; school cap; blazers; 3 pairs of football shorts; 1 serviette ring and 1 Bible.'9 And there were a good many other items, all of which Mrs Blair faithfully assembled before Eric's departure in September: in this respect he would be indistinguishable from any other arriving St Cyprianite. (His mother had not told him of the reduced fees when she brought home the news from Eastbourne; he was not to learn of his special status until his third year at the school, and then from the headmaster.)

Whether or not Eric was pleased at the news, we cannot say: his own account of St Cyprian's begins in the second week after his arrival. We do know that he was already an avid reader of P. G. Wodehouse's cheerful Public School novels, and he may innocently have imagined that life at boarding-school would be as glamorous as it is made to appear there. In any event, September was still some distance away: by children's time, far enough in the future not to be immediately threatening. In June there was the excitement of his eighth birthday, made unforgettable by his mother's giving him *Gulliver's Travels*; later there was the return of his father from India; and the family holiday at Looe in Cornwall. But at last it was the day for him to leave. His parents took him up to London and saw him on the specially reserved Pullman for St Cyprianites. Inside, peering out, frightened, bewildered, already homesick small boys; outside, on the platform, parents smiling bravely, especially fathers (who have been through the whole experience themselves), mothers surreptitiously reaching for their handkerchiefs – a familiar, painful, classic scene, 'The Departure for Boarding School', which figures inevitably in autobiography, biography, and fiction of growing up in the upper level of English society. Then the train begins to move: he catches a last glimpse of Them. Thereafter he is alone.

What follows, just as inevitably, is Unhappiness, the common fate of boys at boarding-school. We know that Somerset Maugham was unhappy at his school, and Winston Churchill at his, and Osbert Sitwell at his – but the catalogue of victims is interminable: an anthology of the miseries of life at prep school could be quickly assembled, and additions made to it seasonally, for the tradition is long-lived and production vigorous.

The new school my parents chose for me was on the East Coast. At first I was miserable there and cried night after night.

This could come from any one of such memoirs. In fact, it is the opening of the chapter 'White Samite', in Cyril Connolly's *Enemies of Promise*, and in the very next sentence the author's voice becomes unmistakably his:

My mother cried too at sending me and I have often wondered if that incubator of persecution mania, the English private school, is worth the money that is spent on it or the tears its pupils shed. At an early age small boys are subjected to brutal partings and long separations which undermine their love for their parents before the natural period of conflict and are encouraged to look down on them without knowing why. To owners of private schools they are a business like any other, to masters a refuge for incompetence, in fact a private school has all the faults of a public school without any of its compensations, without tradition, freedom, historical beauty, good teaching or communication between pupil and teacher. It is one of the few tortures confined to the ruling classes and from which the workers are still free. I have never met anybody yet who could say he had been happy there. It can only be that our parents are determined to get rid of us![10]

One might think that after such a trumpet blast, the walls of Jericho would have fallen at once; but of course, nothing of the sort occurred, and one can discover an explanation for the continuing durability of the private school as an institution in Connolly's bland admission in his next sentence that St Cyprian's 'where I now went was a well-run and vigorous example which did me a world of good'. Orwell would have found little to take exception to in his old school-friend's sardonic opening reflections, but the good-humoured tolerance and sense of 'fair-play' implicit in the acknowledgement of their old school he would have found intolerable. At no time, early or late, would he believe that it had done him anything but a world of harm, and when he finally wrote of it, when he was already world famous as the author of *Animal Farm*, he did so with an unrelenting seriousness. The passage of more than a quarter century had not made him indulgent: in 'Such, Such were the Joys' nothing was to be recalled joyfully.*

The title came from a line in 'The Echoing Green', one of Blake's 'Songs of Innocence' which his mother had read aloud to him when they were first living in Henley. It is a poem of the mingling of the generations:

> Such, such were the joys
> When we all, girls and boys,
> In our youth time were seen,
> On the Echoing Green.

Then, at nightfall, the gathering in:

> The sun does descend,
> And our sports have an end.
> Round the laps of their mothers
> Many sisters and brothers,
> Like birds in their nest,
> Are ready for rest,
> And sport no more seen
> On the darkening Green.

In its child-like cadences, it idealizes the cohesiveness and protectiveness of family life, which a boarding-school by definition is meant to supplant. The contrast was painful. Fugitives from the nest, the little boys alighted at Eastbourne. Behind, the comfort and affection of home; ahead, the bare dormitory with its hard beds; the dining-room with its meagre portions of evil-tasting food; the lavatories smelling of drains. Children might well believe that their parents wanted to get rid of them – how else to explain their being there? – but it did not make them miss them any the less.

Homesickness, which was epidemic, expressed itself usually in tears. 'During those first days at Eastbourne,' Cecil Beaton recalls, 'I blubbed at the most unsuitable times of day and night.

---

* The piece was written at Connolly's suggestion, and was originally intended for publication in his magazine, *Horizon*, but Orwell decided it was probably too long for magazine publication and certainly too libellous, as he had written it, and put it aside. It was published for the first time, after his death, in *Partisan Review*, in 1952.

I would suddenly be overcome by waves of homesickness and burst into tears in the middle of a sentence . . . I got into the habit of waking early so that I could go to the lavatory and weep alone.'[11] Cyril Connolly, as we have seen, 'cried night after night'. Such boys, one feels, being able to express their unhappiness in uninhibited fashion, were luckier than Eric Blair, who was as unhappy as they, but who could not weep, being too shy, too reticent, too proud. And it is curious that in 'Such, Such were the Joys', with its almost unremitting emphases on unhappiness, cruelty, snobbery, and disgust, and its numberless provocations for tears, Orwell should admit to having wept only once.

Mrs Vaughan Wilkes, who was then a woman in her mid-thirties and the mother of small children, made it a point that the boys should call her 'Mum', and her attitude towards them was richly and complexly maternal, that is, it was not only benevolent, kindly, concerned, and doting, but also demanding, scolding, shaming, reproachful, capricious, and temperamental. Reading of her, one has the impression at times that the role of 'Mum' was being played by Sarah Bernhardt as Queen Elizabeth. Her own view of herself was as a mother to the boys, and a good number of them enjoyed the substitute relationship – or so the many photographs affectionately inscribed to 'Mum' in the sitting-room of The Lodge would suggest. Others did not enjoy it. Eric Blair did not. (And Orwell, in his memoir, will not even accept the use of 'Mum' as a familiar form of 'mother', but as a variant on 'Ma'am', by which the wives of housemasters at posh Public Schools were addressed.)

Mrs Vaughan Wilkes set to work briskly to cure homesickness – as the mother of small children she felt herself better qualified to do so than the staff of seven bachelor masters, and over the years had developed a number of techniques for coping with it. On the first day of the term she came upon Eric Blair, in his green jersey and corduroy shorts, standing apart, eyes dry but downcast, shoulders drooping, his whole expression woe-begone: the familiar symptoms of homesickness. She knelt down, put her arms around him, and drew him close to her. What she expected was the familiar response: that he would rest his head on her bosom, or say 'Oh, Mum', or merely weep, and so be over the worst of it and make the first step to recognizing that he was not 'alone' at St Cyprian's. But he did none of these things. She felt him stiffen, strain to get free of her. 'He was not an affectionate little boy,' she remembered. Undiscouraged by this first rebuff, the next day she had resorted to a favoured technique, and took Eric, and another of the new boys in need of encouragement, along with the one of her children closest to them in age, for a picnic on the Downs. The boys were allowed to wander about freely; they explored the winding chalky lanes; they picked wild blackberries; afterwards there was a feast of cake and sand-wiches. But Mrs Vaughan Wilkes got no further in bringing Blair out, in winning his confidence or affection, than she had the day before. 'There was no warmth in him,' she decided.*

He had such control over his emotions that he would not weep, or rage, or otherwise give outward expression to the unhappiness he felt. So it remained within him, unexpressed. Then one morning, after he had been at the school for about a week, he woke up to find that he had wet his bed during the night, some-thing he had not done since coming from India to England to live four years before. Such a reversion is not uncommon among children at a time of emotional crisis – which for Eric this assuredly was – and now, presumably even at a conservatively-run boarding-school, it would be dealt with psychologically. But we are writing of 1911, and of a school dedicated to 'character, character, character': the remedy for such unmanly conduct was to exercise self-control and stop it; otherwise, one would have to be soundly caned on the bottom, again and again, each time one behaved like a messy baby until, finally, one stopped. Poor Eric. Waking up in the morning to sopping sheets and the smell of urine, he felt guilt, shame, fear, and disgust. At night, before going to sleep, he prayed fervently that it should not happen again. But it did. Prayers failed him; so did his own resolutions.

* This account is based on the authors' interview with Mrs Vaughan Wilkes. Orwell makes no mention of the picnic in 'Such, Such were the Joys'. When Gavin Maxwell came to the school as a new boy in the mid-1920s, he was taken by Mrs Vaughan Wilkes for a similar outing on the Downs. 'It ought to have been a wonderful start,' he writes, 'and I don't see what more she could have done, but it didn't work because I was outside my environment and I behaved as an animal does in the same circumstances. I couldn't produce the right responses, and so I shrank.'[12]

By the third acrid morning, it was evident that he was lacking in 'character': he would have to be punished.

He had been warned, in circumstances that, as Orwell records them in 'Such, Such were the Joys', mingled elements of the grotesque, the comic, and the plausible in the manner of a nightmare. Apparently it was the custom for the boys to be served tea under the supervision of Mrs Vaughan Wilkes. On this occasion she was entertaining a visitor, a woman of masculine appearance and threatening presence who wore – oddly, it might seem, for tea at a boys' school – a riding habit, or what Eric thought to be a riding habit. When the boys had finished their tea, they were allowed to leave the room, all but Eric, who was summoned to the table where 'Flip' – her nickname among the boys – formidable herself, sat chatting with the even more formidable stranger. No introduction was made, as he had naïvely expected. Instead, he was simply and humiliatingly described as the little boy who wet his bed every night. The stranger stared with an expression of disapproval and distaste. Furthermore, Flip continued, if he did it again, she would have him beaten by the Sixth Form. But Eric, too frightened or shamed to hear correctly, misunderstood her, and, with the plausibility of a nightmare where nothing is to be questioned, thought she had said 'Mrs Form' rather than 'Sixth Form'. And Mrs Form, he thought, equally plausibly, must be the disapproving lady in the riding habit. It was she, then – his imagination raced ahead – who would have the pleasure of punishing him, and she would do it with a hunting whip. He stood there, a small boy 'almost swooning with shame', incapable of saying a word, before those powerful, scornful women. The fear of punishment, the pain of being beaten, counted for less, much less, than the humiliation he suffered on that afternoon in September 1911, and would remember virtually until the end of his life and never forgive: that he had been exposed in his uncleanness, that another person (the more shaming that she was a woman) had been told of his disgusting sin.

It was an appalling experience, to undergo and to remember – emblematic for Orwell in its juxtaposition of humiliation and disgust – and its effects upon the boy Eric Blair and the man he became can hardly be over-estimated: they are discernible at a number of crucial points in the narrative of his early life. The immediate effect, not surprisingly, was that he wet his bed that night, and in the morning he was beaten, with a riding crop – not, however, by Mrs Form, or the Sixth Form, but by the headmaster in his study.

There was a ritual in these matters. First, Eric must 'own up' to his offence, which he did – 'owning up' being an important part of the code of behaviour and training for a boy of his class – then the headmaster must deliver the expected short homily on his misdeeds, which he did, and then the crop was applied, with only moderate severity. On both sides the forms of the ritual were being observed; and as such it was a characteristic encounter between a wielder of authority and one who was being brought up to wield authority in his turn.

(Often the forms themselves are carried on from schooldays into adult life. We are reminded by Harold Macmillan in his memoirs that the House of Commons is like a Public School writ large in its tendency to react favourably when a Member 'owns up'. He quotes a passage from Trollope in which one Member explains to another that if he 'owned up' to the murder of his grandmother in a modest, apologetic way, the House would probably forgive him, and might even quietly cheer. This sort of honesty – 'I did it, and I am sorry, and I am willing to accept my punishment' – is indoctrinated early. One learns to deal with authority face to face, so to speak, as part of one's training to wield it. Rather than, as would likely be the case with a working-class child, to keep as far away from it as possible.)

There was always something equivocal in Blair's attitude towards established authority, something at once submissive and defiant, and so it proved in this first encounter of his with it. The proper form would have been for him to leave the headmaster's study with a chastened and repentant air (however angry and unrepentant he might feel) as though to acknowledge the gravity of the offence and the justice of the punishment. But Eric emerged into the ante-room, grinning victoriously, and reported to the boys who happened to be gathered there, that the beating hadn't hurt. It was not the sort of thing one said in the presence of Mrs Vaughan Wilkes, whom he had not noticed in the ante-room, and she, indignant at this proof of an unchastened spirit, ordered him back into the study for a second beating. This time, as Orwell remembered, the headmaster lost control and laid it on savagely: he was beaten for what seemed to him to be a period of five minutes, terminated only by the riding crop's snapping in half. The bone handle, he tells us, flew across the room. (It is a surprising detail – presumably the headmaster would be grasping the handle, and the lower half of the crop would sail free.) For this mishap, too, the boy was blamed – apparently it had been an expensive crop.

He fell into a chair and wept. (It was the only time that a beating, whether at St Cyprian's or Eton, would bring him to tears, and the only time in 'Such, Such were the Joys' that he describes himself as actually weeping.) That night, in spite of having been punished, and as though to prove to himself the impossibility of his being good, he wet his bed again, and the next morning he was beaten again. One might have expected (certainly Eric might have expected) that the cycle would go on indefinitely; instead, from that night forward the incontinent bladder recovered its control – the bed-wetting immediately and permanently ceased. The traditional, no-nonsense application of corporal punishment to curb a defect of character had served its purpose.

The psychological cost, however, was considerable. When Eric had wept in the headmaster's study, it was not because the pain was unendurable, for the second beating, in spite of its length and intensity, appears not to have hurt much more than the first. He wept, in part out of a sense of obligation, a belated recognition that this was expected of him; in part out of repentance, for he never doubted that it was a sin to wet his bed; and in part, the greater part, out of a sense of abandonment and isolation, that he was alone in a system whose demands he could never possibly satisfy. He had sinned by wetting his bed: it was an action over which, so far as he could tell, he had no control, it happened in spite of him. But this did not excuse him from punishment: he was flawed, which was provocation enough. It followed therefore that punishment was one's lot in life; life made one a victim. So early, then, a crucial note was being sounded: the system makes its demands, which he is congenitally unable to meet; hence he is unworthy of its rewards. He is not at ease in the system, not the popular boy, the handsome boy, the favoured one. He had already had some sense of this in Henley; the experience of his first weeks at St Cyprian's confirmed him in his premature pessimism. As a sinner he felt the need of expiation, before he was aware of what he needed to expiate. In dealing with this bed-wetting episode, Orwell is finely aware of the difference it makes that he should be writing of it years later, when much of the ordinary life of his schooldays (the happier aspect, usually) has eluded his memory: but he would argue that what remains is what matters. After allowance is made for the expected distortions of the psyche, the Unconscious misremembering or altering as it must, it is evident here (as in all his work) how subtly Orwell captures the relation of the victim to authority – that one is to be blamed not only for the wrong that one does, but also for whatever difficulties authority may have in enacting its role in the relationship. So Eric was unquestioningly ready to feel guilty rather than jubilant about the breaking of the headmaster's riding crop with which he was being beaten. It was as though he were responsible for it; indeed, by a kind of perverse logic it could be made to seem so – if he had not wet his bed, he would not have had to be beaten; if he had not been beaten, the riding crop would not have snapped in half – therefore, the fault was his. It was this attitude, so early formed, that would allow him many years later to speak for the passive victims of society.

4

Eric was not the sort of boy to tell his parents that he had wet
his bed and been beaten for it, or that he was homesick and
unhappy, or that the food was vile and the drains stank, or that
he hated the headmaster and his wife – so there are not even
veiled allusions to these matters in the letters he wrote to his
mother during his first four terms at St Cyprian's, from September 1911 to December 1912. It is possible, of course, that
these letters were written under the supervision of Mrs Vaughan
Wilkes or one of the masters, inhibiting him from a frank outpouring of what he felt. But the number of uncorrected mis-
spellings seems to argue against this having been a regular
procedure. His own reticence, shyness, and pride explain more
about what he left unsaid than possible intimidation. Quite
simply, a frank outpouring would be as inconsistent with Eric
Blair at eight or nine as it would be thirty years later with George
Orwell. In any case, these letters – all that are known to survive
from his schooldays – are of greater interest for what they
include than for what they omit, for they help to fill in one of
the conspicuous blanks in 'Such, Such were the Joys', the greater
part of which deals with Eric's last three years at St Cyprian's –
from the time he entered the scholarship class and learned that he
was at the school on reduced fees. Of his first two years there
Orwell tells us virtually nothing. After the traumatic bed-
wetting episode, there seems to have been a relatively tranquil
period; it is from the later period that he assembles most of the
evidence for his indictment.*

* Orwell's letters to his mother from St Cyprian's are now in the possession of
his sister, Avril (Mrs William Dunn), who has very kindly made them available
to us.
   'Such, Such were the Joys' is invaluable as Orwell's interpretation of Eric
Blair's childhood, but it is less satisfactory as a biographical account. Written

If one had just the letters to judge from, Eric would strike one as an ordinary young boy – there is no evidence of literary precocity, no hint of the writer he was to become. It is the ordinariness of the schoolboy life described in so ordinary a fashion – with a full quota of jolly chaps and ripping games of footer – that enlightens us. At one level, at the level where art begins, Eric suffered a profound humiliation of the spirit and the flesh – never to forget the sight of the turd floating in the swimming bath – but at another level, he fulfilled the daily round at St Cyprian's like any other little boy there, preoccupied with studies, games, and his stamp collection, and was not unhappy. The letters, in a handwriting that has not yet found itself but varies between the sloppy and the excessively neat, are addressed at first to Dear Mother, or My dear Mother, and upon his return from the Christmas holiday, thereafter to My darling Mother, and they are signed in a formal Victorian style, Eric Blair, or Eric A. Blair, or E. A. Blair, but always with love, or with much love, or from your loving son, and sometimes with a long row of kisses. Sometimes too they are illustrated with drawings – of boats or animals, and once of a pudding and once of an aeroplane. (Aeroplanes were a subject of great interest at the school that winter – some of the boys were building models for a competition, and in February there was an expedition to see a real one, but Eric and a lot of other chaps played footer instead. His own hobby was stamp collecting: in September he had written to his mother to send him his album, which she promptly did.)

His letters reflect the chief preoccupations of St Cyprian's: studies and games. In his first year Eric had classes in Latin, French, History, English, and Arithmetic, and hardly a letter passes without a report on his standing: in each class he was at the top or near it. Mrs Vaughan Wilkes would confirm this: as she said, 'he was a very bright little boy', and she knew it at first hand, since she took the classes in History and French, and

with admirable directness, those straightforward sentences create effortlessly an air of candour and intelligence, and lead one to believe that one is being told everything. In fact, Orwell has written a highly selective and purposive work of art, an 'indictment' of the cruelty inflicted on children in the name of boarding-school education, and whatever will lessen the force of the argument has been omitted.

also taught Scripture. (The school was run on traditional Anglican lines: there was daily chapel, and the plunge each morning into the icy swimming bath.) At games he made up in enthusiasm what he lacked in skill. He played football vigorously – once, as goal-keeper, he fought off the opposing chaps who came at him, he told his mother, like mad dogs; he took part in swimming races, starting last and ending up third (but he was hampered by a bathing dress that was too tight); and he rejoiced in St Cyprian's victories over its rivals, The Grange, St Christopher's, and Kent House.

For the most part the daily round consisted of studies and games, and the spaces between were filled with the characteristic private interests of a small boy. We catch a glimpse of them in Eric's requests to his mother. At various times he asked for his stamp album; for newly-issued penny stamps; for some of the duplicate stamps he had left at home to give to a boy named Moreno who was not English but wanted English stamps badly; for draughts; for dried peas to use as ammunition in a toy cannon belonging to one of the boys; and for cigarette cards. Occasionally there would be departures from the routine. These were events. On a hot, summerlike day in October the boys were taken to swim at the Devonshire Baths, a public pool where the water was pumped in directly from the sea, and Eric thought it 'simply lovely'. (Orwell would remember the pool as it was in mid-winter, murky and cold, when swimming was an ordeal not a pleasure.) On 1 December it was Mrs Vaughan Wilkes's birthday, in celebration of which the boys were allowed to play games throughout the house; afterwards they walked in a crocodile across the Downs to Beachy Head. The next week, on Saturday evening, there was an end-of-term entertainment: some of the boys danced, others sang, and Eric recited a poem.

His mother had kept him in touch with happenings in Henley. The family pets were a source of interest and concern: the well-being of the cat Tojo; the possibility of acquiring a guinea pig – what colour? – the bird Virey; and the reappearance in the house of a small family of white mice, suitably caged: Marjorie's. Eighteen days before the end of term (on 2 December) he says he is sorry to hear that the smelly white mice are back, but that he won't mind them so much if they're *not* smelly. Actually seeing them over the Christmas holidays seems to have softened his feelings towards them: when he is back at school in February, he writes to ask if the mice have had babies – if they have, then his mother must see to it that Tojo doesn't eat them.

February was mid-winter, season of snow, ice, head colds, and stuffy sickrooms. The playing-field was frozen (so there could be no football) and some of the boys went skating, but Eric was confined to the sickroom again with a head cold, his second that winter, along with a younger boy named Leslie Cohen. The reward of illness for a bookish boy like Eric was to have lots of time to read, but Leslie, who is earlier singled out in the correspondence as being especially naughty, gave him no peace; in the end Eric had to put his own book aside and read to him. A week later (11 February) he was out of the sickroom and back in classes, where he was second in everything, but it was not until the next week that he was judged well enough to play footer again.

February had its happier events. There was a 'lovely' lecture on the moon by one of the masters, who gave a demonstration of an eclipse – a football topped with sugar served as a model. And there was also a ripping lecture on how things were made, the manufacture of steel, penknives, soap, and so much else Eric hadn't time to list them in his letter home.

On 2 June, replying to a question from his mother, he wrote that he would like a gun-metal watch for his birthday. On 25 June, his ninth birthday, he wrote to thank her for the various presents that had arrived from Henley, not only the ripping little watch that was her special present to him, but also a book from his father, and a knife, a box of toffee, and a cake that he had not yet tasted – presumably it would be shared at tea – but which he thought to be a seed cake.

Only a few letters survive from the new term in 1912, the beginning of his second year at St Cyprian's. It was a time when the family was making the first of the moves that were to be so characteristic of them in the next fifteen years, as though the pattern set in India, of moving from one post to the next, had to be unconsciously re-enacted in England. This first move was to the nearby village of Shiplake, where the Blairs rented a house called Roselawn, in the Station Road. Roselawn, set in an acre of lawn and garden, was a larger and more spacious house than Nutshell; and Shiplake, though only a few miles from Henley, had a much more 'country' feeling. Above the village was Binfield Heath, waiting to be explored during the holidays; and in the woods beyond Roselawn a pool in an abandoned quarry waiting to be fished, that Orwell (it seems fair to assume) would draw upon for *Coming Up for Air*, though 57 High Street, Lower Binfield, the Bowlings' house in the novel, is of a very different order from the Blairs' house in Shiplake.

The contents of these letters from his second year at the school (the last of them is dated 8 December) are much as before – studies and games – but his handwriting has become larger, clearer, and more disciplined, and won him a compliment from his mother.

The 'events' of the term occurred on two successive evenings early in December. The first was a lecture illustrated with magic lantern slides. The second was the end-of-term entertainment which the boys attended in fancy dress. Costumes ranged from the simple to the extravagant. There was a pirate, there were revolutionaries (shirt open at the throat, sash at the waist), there was a Puss in Boots, a frog, and a sunflower. Resplendent among them was Eric, who came as a footman in a red velvet coat, lace frill, white silk flowered waistcoat, red silk trousers, black stockings, and a powdered wig.

It is a last, lovingly detailed glimpse of him in the letters he wrote to his mother from the school – the correspondence does not survive beyond 1912 – and, of course, very different from the picture of himself as a schoolboy that he chose to record in 'Such, Such were the Joys'.

5

In the autumn of 1913, at the beginning of his third year at St Cyprian's, there would be a significant change: the reason for his having been sent there was brought into sharp focus.

He was ten years old, taller, wiser, and tougher than the sad-eyed bewildered small boy with whose homesickness 'Mum' had tried to cope. That was two years in the past. Since then he had survived homesickness in his own fashion; and the cold and damp, to which he was peculiarly vulnerable, suffering from head colds and chest colds, sneezing, coughing, and wheezing bronchially through the winter months. He had even survived the dreary institutional food of which, no matter how unappetizing it might be, there was never quite enough to curb one's hunger, it still being an article of faith among headmasters that a boy's mind was more easily crammed if his stomach was not.

The unhappiness Eric had felt as a new boy had hardened into a stony resentment. Virtually to the end of his life resentment and anger would be at the base of his feelings for St Cyprian's. While he was there, his experience provided him with a variety of reasons for disliking it, and he forgot none of them and continued to dislike it, up to the day he left for good in December 1916, and beyond that to the day some thirty years later when he began to set down his recollections of it.

In his first two years Eric had done more than well enough to justify the expectations of his parents and the concessions of the Vaughan Wilkeses. Therefore, in autumn term 1913, he was placed in the scholarship class. He became one of the small group at St Cyprian's, some from wealthy families, some not, who would be intensively prepared for three years to sit the examination for 'scholars' at one or other of the great Public Schools;

while the rest of the boys would be brought along more leniently towards the less exacting common entrance exams. (To win such a scholarship – to be made a King's Scholar in College at Eton, for example – was a distinction that bore no taint of charity. Financial need was not taken into account. The scholarship was a reward for braininess as it showed to advantage in a set of formidably difficult exams. But it was also the one way for a brainy boy whose family had little money to get to a Public School and so begin a career in the Establishment.)

The boys of the scholarship class were worked hard. In term-time the pressure was unremitting; during holidays it was only a little less so – for then there were hundreds of lines in translation to be done at home, and, on at least one occasion, as the exams drew near, the Vaughan Wilkeses arranged for Eric to stay at the school for an extra week to be tutored by one of the masters. The scholarship boys were taught in the approved, traditional manner that accomplished what it set out to do: their minds were crammed, drilled, force-fed – what feats of memorization were expected! – with a store of facts and received opinions that would allow them to show to best advantage in the exams. Like show dogs they would go through their paces. Everything was subordinate to the exams; and the fateful consequences of failure, especially for a boy like Eric whose parents could not afford to send him to a Public School, were luridly evoked. If one failed, one disappointed one's parents, let down the school, and put himself outside the pale, doomed to the grey world of clerks and drapers' assistants. In the circumstances, the possibility of finding pleasure or interest or significant meaning in one's studies was irrelevant: they were not meant to be enjoyed, but learned. History was reduced to names, dates, 'events', sonorous phrases and illustrative tableaux (The Princes in the Tower; the Field of the Cloth of Gold), all highlights and no relation. English Literature was a pantheon of hallowed names, suitably tagged, from Chaucer to Shakespeare to Tennyson (by way of Keats) and forward from the Laureate to Sir Henry Newbolt. 'Classics' – Latin and Greek – were lengthy, strategically chosen samplings from the approved authors, that one was made to read, parse, summarize, and memorize, that had turned up in exams in the past and were likely to turn up there again.

Drill and memorization were basic techniques of this pedagogy, but at the root of it was fear – in Connolly's phrase, the boys learned 'as fast as fear could teach us'.

Fear was an orthodox, schoolmasterly method for counteracting sloth, inattention and daydreaming, that classic trinity of schoolboy vices. The exam itself, though constantly invoked and made fearful to contemplate, was yet too remote (until the last month or two) to be of much use in the day-to-day struggle waged at St Cyprian's against lassitude and boredom. One had to be hectored, scolded, shamed, cajoled, and threatened. Besides this, there was a steady rat-a-tat of physical punishments and indignities. The headmaster, who took the boys of the scholarship class in Classics, had a silver pencil (it grew in Orwell's memory to the size of a banana) which he would apply smartly to the skull of a boy who hadn't a correct answer ready to a question. Or he would kick a boy on the shins, jolting him awake. Or tweak his ear, pinch him, pull his hair. Or, as a last resort, after a repeated error in translation perhaps, he would order a boy from the classroom into the study, there to be caned with a springy rattan cane – the successor to the split riding crop – after which, master and pupil would return to the classroom, and the lesson would be resumed.

Physical punishment was painful and therefore to be feared, but its psychological counterpart was perhaps even more effective, for Mr and Mrs Vaughan Wilkes were very skilful at stirring up feelings of guilt, shame, inadequacy, and unworthiness. Which brings us directly to Eric's situation as Orwell remembered it. It was not until his third year at the school that he understood the special circumstances of his being there: that he had been taken as a pupil at reduced fees. It appears that his parents did not tell him of this concession made on his behalf, nor did the Vaughan Wilkeses when he came to the school. But from the time he entered the scholarship class, the headmaster and his wife made use of the concession to intimidate him. It was the final psychological weapon (far more painful than the silver pencil or the rattan cane) to be resorted to when he was slack at his work, when his performance fell below the standard that was essential if he was to win a scholarship.

The headmaster's way was direct: he bluntly reminded Eric of the shameful secret. (For it was thus, as a shameful secret, that

Eric regarded it, and while one might cavil at shameful, a secret it undoubtedly was, and it was perfectly kept.*)

He would summon Eric to his study for a reprimand or punishment, depending on the gravity of the offence, and presently the boy would be reminded that he was there at his bounty – a no less humiliating way of saying that he was a charity boy. Was this how Eric chose to reward him for his kindness, by being inattentive and lazy, by not preparing his lessons etc., etc.? Did he *want* to fail? Consider the alternative that loomed ahead: to fail the exam, which meant to go down to the depths of degradation, to be cast out from the charmed circle and end as a scruffy little office boy at forty pounds a year. There were times when it seemed, even to himself, that Eric was deliberately courting this fate, wanted nothing more than to go down and out – *not to go to a Public School*. Day after day he would be deliberately idle, as though asking to be punished, could not bring himself to work: this idleness too was a kind of torment. At such times Mrs Vaughan Wilkes would add reproaches and exhortations of her own. Unlike her husband she would not speak directly of the shameful secret. She merely alluded to it, a delicacy that proved even more guilt-inspiring. She would speak pityingly of Mrs Blair, so proud of her son and making such sacrifices for him; was it decent, was it playing the game, was it straight of him, therefore, to be an idler, to throw his chances away? And as a final stroke: was it fair even to the Vaughan Wilkeses, who did so much for him – he knew how much, did he not? Oh yes, he knew. It was not necessary to spell it out: it was all there, to his guilty conscience, in the way she looked at him and in the way he could not meet her gaze straight on. The worst of it was that Eric felt that the indictment was deserved, or felt that that was what he ought to feel. So the guilt was compounded and the grievance deepened. The judgement of the adult world was unanswerable. Not even his parents would excuse him: he could not expect to win their approval by disappointing them. Here his intuition was sound, for however different their motives might be, the Blairs

* 'Perfectly kept' is Cyril Connolly's phrase. Mrs Vaughan Wilkes told us that a boy's being on reduced fees was a confidential matter between his parents and the headmaster and his wife, and was never made public. Connolly, who of all the boys would have been the most likely to know and who was a member of the scholarship class, had no knowledge of Blair's special financial arrangement until he read about it in 'Such, Such were the Joys'.

and the Vaughan Wilkeses were alike in wanting the same end for him: not down and out but up and in.

That winter, the winter of 1914, a new boy, Cyril Connolly, came to the school, and entered the scholarship class. This was a significant event in Eric Blair's history, for Connolly was to become his first close friend – before then his only intimacy had been with his mother and sisters – as well as confidant, literary colleague, and fellow critic of the established order at St Cyprian's. The two boys were of the same age, but each, in a different fashion, seemed older, precocious intellectually, quasi-adult in his way of looking at the world – Connolly remembered Blair as 'one of those boys who seem born old'. Cecil Beaton, who knew Blair only slightly but was another of Connolly's close friends at St Cyprian's – it was characteristic of Connolly that he should have several close friends there, just as it was characteristic that Blair should not – summed up Cyril as 'of all the boys . . . certainly the strangest, most fascinating character to me. He seemed so grown-up.'[13] Cyril was the more worldly, but also the more romantic; Eric was the more sceptical and unillusioned. Beaton writes of Connolly, 'We admired one another, though I got a bit of a shock when I discovered how much he knew about life. A few of us vaguely realized that someone's parents were rich or titled, or had a large motor-car. But Cyril knew which of the masters had a financial interest in St Cyprian's, and which were only there on sufferance. He said it helped you to know how to behave towards them.' This worldly wisdom was of no use to Eric in smoothing his way at St Cyprian's – Cyril was noticeably better at it – for then as later he was 'incapable of courtship'; but it did allow him to objectify his dislike of the school. The favourites, the boys who were petted and made much of, who were allowed to go unpunished no matter how stupid or lazy, were now recognized to be those whose parents had pots of money or handles to their names, or came down to visit them in expensive motor-cars. Whereas boys like himself, whose parents were deficient in these crucial attributes, were subjected to punishments and deprivations, were not 'in favour' with Mrs Vaughan Wilkes, were not loved. The moral to be drawn reinforced him in his premature cynicism: you were no good unless you had a hundred thousand pounds; and, as a corollary to this, which he felt his own experience of the school bore witness to day by day, those without money were those who had to work hardest. His sense of the unfairness of life deepened.

Of course he could not present this to Connolly except in the most generalized way, for to illustrate with the particulars of his own experience would have meant revealing the shameful secret, and this he was too proud (or too humiliated) to do. There was always a line drawn as to how much one would confide: this was true for both boys, though for different reasons. Eric was invincibly reticent; Cyril was a good deal more open, but he had his several friends, who played different roles in his life, and to each he distributed the confidences appropriate to the role. For Connolly Blair represented 'Intelligence' (Beaton, 'Sensibility'), and 'Intelligence' was an alternative to 'Character', that shibboleth of St Cyprian's and all the other expensive, snobbish, character-building schools like it in Edwardian England. Intelligence, of a precocious kind, made both boys alert to the pretensions of the school and dismissive of them: this set them apart, a club of two. It was not, however, the sort of intelligence likely to endear itself to the Vaughan Wilkeses. Both boys, properly curbed and held to a tight rein, might well go on to win scholarships – and so, as advertisements, justify the time and effort spent upon them – but neither would be likely to emulate Kipling and write that 'Of all things in the world there is nothing, always excepting a good mother, so worthy of honour as a good school.'

Connolly's people had more money than the Blairs; he was at the school as a regular paying pupil; he went home for the holidays to London, to a house in Brompton Square. The ambience of his childhood was much grander than Eric's. His great-aunt, the Countess of Kingston, lived in Mitchelstown Castle in Cork, 'an enormous eighteenth-century Gothic affair . . . with some thirty thousand acres', and his visit to her there, when he was five, 'left a deep impression'. His aunt Mab, his mother's favourite sister, 'had married a rich man'. (Mrs Blair's favourite sister had married a teacher of Esperanto.) 'Aunt Mab was very beautiful but she also had special smells, smells of furs and Edwardian luxe . . . Wherever we went with Aunt Mab there were presents and large houses [she owned four] and the appeal her wealth made to an imaginative child was irresistible.'[14]

Yet there were interesting resemblances too. The Connollys were Anglo-Irish; the Blairs, Anglo-Indian. Eric's father had been in the colonial service, stationed in India; Cyril's father was an army officer, who had been stationed in South Africa. Both boys had as background memories or impressions the exotic, foreign, unEnglish landscapes from which they had been sent back to England to be schooled, Edens in contrast. At seven, Cyril adored his mother 'but lived otherwise in a world of his own'. Eric, at the same age, it will be recalled, loved only his mother and was already making up stories. Each boy was an insatiable, passionate reader, and the passion for reading – good and indifferent books, and books that Mrs Vaughan Wilkes would certainly have disapproved of – was one of the strongest bonds between them. Studies, games, and the noisy conditions of school life hardly allowed for time enough during official waking hours for them to read as much as they liked; so each would take a book to bed at night to have it ready to begin reading as soon as he woke up, especially in the bright summer mornings: it meant a satisfying hour or two before the dormitory was ordered up at seven and down to the icy swimming bath. Blair had a vivid recollection (which he omitted from 'Such, Such were the Joys') of stealing into the silent dormitory, one summer morning at 4 a.m., and making off with the copy of H. G. Wells's *The Country of the Blind* that Connolly, still asleep, had put beside his bed.

Wells was a favourite author; so were Kipling, Wodehouse, Swift, Shaw, and Thackeray, all of whom they read while at St Cyprian's. Orwell's loyalty to these writers was virtually unwavering throughout his life. When, during the Second World War, he wrote an attack on Wells as a liberal optimist, he admitted to feeling like a 'parricide'.[15] What he valued in Wells was not the later polemicist, but the novelist whose evocation of certain aspects – the anti-St Cyprian's aspect, one might say – of life in England before the First World War recalled to Orwell comparable experiences of his own. He and Connolly would leave the school grounds and set out across the Downs to Beachy Head, or far along the plunging leafy roads that led deep into the Sussex countryside, to villages that might have figured in a Wells novel: Eastdean and Westdean and Jevington. They would pause in each, and buy from the little old lady who kept the village shop, penny sweets and various fizzy drinks: lemonade, cherryade, and cherry fizz. They might have been a world away from St Cyprian's. (Perhaps it is worth noting here that, in an area full of prep schools, St Cyprian's was one of the few that let its boys wander about on the Downs alone, or take prodigious walks by themselves into the countryside.) This was the plain, decent bread-and-sun-lit world that Orwell recalled so nostalgically the further it receded from him; but even the visionary works, such as *Country of the Blind*, which he and Cyril found enthralling, left their mark upon him. Eventually he would write Wellsian novels of both kinds, in *Coming Up For Air* (a re-creation of the past) and *1984* (a vision of the future).

Passionate readers, the two boys were also apprentice authors. As we know, Orwell felt very early – at five or six – that he would grow up to be a writer. At nine, before coming to St Cyprian's, Connolly was already inventing sketches in the manner of Stephen Leacock. There, both boys wrote playlets, skits, stories, light verse and serious, none of it (except by hindsight) promising that these clever schoolboys would become two of the outstanding writers of their generation. It was a further bond between them: manuscripts were exchanged and commented upon, and sometimes, not without calculation, were shown to Mrs Vaughan Wilkes. It was a way of securing her favour. Approving of what they wrote (or, at least, of what they allowed her to see), she found a place for it in her voluminous scrapbooks, and even in her memory – fifty years later she recalled that Blair had written poems while at school and drew attention to them.

So, too, when Eric came home for the holidays that summer, Mrs Blair was pleased with the poems he showed her and encouraged him to write more. No mother whose son would have to support himself would want him to grow up to be a writer – too risky an enterprise – and it is unlikely that the thought even occurred to Mrs Blair; but she was proud of Eric, and saw his writing as another aspect of his cleverness, further proof that he deserved, as she believed him to be getting, the best possible education.

In August the family went as usual to Cornwall for their holiday. It was a happy time for Eric, who did his best to forget the lines of translation he was supposed to bring back to St Cyprian's, bathing, rock-climbing, playing with his sister Avril (to whom he would sometimes tell stories) and the children of family friends, also on holiday. Nostalgia does not need to be added to the experience to make it seem idyllic – as anyone who has spent childhood summers at the seashore can testify – and Avril is speaking matter-of-factly when she says, 'Really we used to have a lovely time down there.' But of course this was not to be the usual summer: on 4 August came the thrilling news that England was at war with Germany. Even for a six-year-old girl the event – as it reached her from the grown-ups – was memorable, and her first conscious memory of Eric dates from 'the day war broke out . . . He was sitting cross-legged on the floor of my mother's bedroom, talking to her about it in a very grown-up manner. I was knitting him a school scarf . . . and I think the school colours were either dark blue and green or dark green and blue. Anyway, it was one of those terrible garments that starts off very narrow and in some mysterious manner suddenly becomes terribly wide.' A vignette for which one is grateful; and she concludes it on a very Blair-like note: 'I don't suppose he ever wore it.'[16]

We do not know what Eric was saying in his 'very grown-up manner' about the war to his mother on 4 August 1914; we do know what he was writing about it soon after. It must be borne in mind that in August 1914 the vast majority of Englishmen (and their wives and children) were intensely, unquestioningly patriotic, proud, excited, and confident. The mood would find its most memorable expression in the war sonnets of Rupert Brooke. Three years and eight hundred thousand deaths later would come the poetry of disillusionment, from Siegfried Sassoon and Wilfred Owen and Robert Graves. Scepticism only gradually made itself felt as the war which was to have been won by Christmas went on year after year: this was very different from the pacifism that a minority had professed from the very beginning. We are speaking now of a progression of thought among adults, not schoolboys; but schoolboys, especially those who are precocious and questioning in spirit, will often parallel and sometimes anticipate a change in thought in the world outside, an attitude that runs counter to and will finally overturn orthodoxy. Eric's scepticism about the war – of which we will presently quote a famous example – was still some years in the future. In August 1914 he was very much the patriotic schoolboy.

Patriotism inspired him to verse. Before the month was out he had written a call to arms in three quatrains which he entitled:

Awake! Young Men of England

Oh! give me the strength of the lion,
    The wisdom of Reynard the Fox,
And then I'll hurl troops at the Germans,
    And give them the hardest of knocks.

Oh! think of the War lord's mailed fist,
    That is striking at England today;
And think of the lives that our soldiers
    Are fearlessly throwing away.

Awake! oh you young men of England,
    For if, when your Country's in need,
You do not enlist by the thousand,
    You truly are cowards indeed.

Debased Kipling or Newbolt, it has no claim to literary interest except as the first published work by a famous author. But it is not without documentary interest: in a generalized way for what it tells of the England of 1914 and of the training and education a schoolboy of the upper-middle class would receive that would make him want to write a poem such as this and equip him to write it; and in a particular way for what it tells of Eric Blair. The intense and rather primitive patriotism – very different from jingoism – that inspired this poem written at the beginning of the First World War was to prove an essential and ineradicable strain in his character.

His parents were delighted with the poem – it echoed their sentiments perfectly – and when the family returned to Roselawn, Mrs Blair sent it off to the local newspaper, the *Henley and South Oxfordshire Standard*. It was published there on 2 October 1914, with the author identified as Master Eric Blair, the eleven-year-old son of Mr R. W. Blair. By then he was already back at St Cyprian's. His mother sent him copies of the paper, and he had the exhilarating experience of seeing his work in print for the first time. Mrs Vaughan Wilkes, to whom he presented a copy, was generous with her praise. For a few days, at least, he was among her favourites. She determined that he should read the poem aloud to the assembled school, and accorded it a place of honour in the scrapbook.

But Eric was incapable of being in favour for long. Being out of favour was the more usual state of his relations with Mrs Vaughan Wilkes. It was a relationship unsatisfactory to them both – more to him than to her, for he after all was only one among the hundred boys under her charge, while she had the power, as one of the boys noted in his diary, to make life 'not worth living' – and it would have a decisive effect upon him while he was at school and for many years afterwards. Simplifying the relationship to its irreducible element, one can say that he wanted her approval and never got it, she wanted his affection and never got it. The pattern was set in Eric's first weeks at the school and it continued so to his last day there. Years later Mrs Vaughan Wilkes's chief memory of him would be of a cold and unloving little boy who stiffened in her arms when she tried to console him; and Orwell remembered her as the woman who, on his last day at school, though she shook his hand and called him Eric rather than the customary Blair, made it clear by the expression on her face and the tone of her voice that she did not approve of him.

All the recollections of the school that old St Cyprianites have written agree that Mrs Vaughan Wilkes played the dominating role. We know from Cyril Connolly that it was she 'around whom the school revolved'; from Cecil Beaton that 'she had more influence than all the masters put together'. Gavin Maxwell, who was there a decade after Connolly, Beaton, and Blair, has described the school as 'a strictly matriarchal culture and the existence of an assertive male at the summit would have been unthinkable'. At the summit was 'Mum'. (They 'loved their "Mum",' she recalled fondly, as an old lady, and some of them evidently did, to judge from the inscribed photographs they sent her when they went on to success in the great world.) She was headmistress, task-mistress, teacher, business-woman, hostess to parents, social arbiter, dispenser of rewards and punishments (which were carried out by her husband). She was also very much a woman, in temperament, and in physique (the boys were nervously, gigglingly aware of her full bosom, and it explained their nickname for her of 'Flip'). As the only woman in a world of males she queened it over them: the school became a court in which the boys vied for her favour. Queenly smiles alternated with queenly displeasure. Connolly's witty summary is extravagant-sounding but accurate: 'On all the boys who went through this Elizabeth and Essex relationship she had a remarkable effect, hotting them up like little Alfa-Romeos for the Brooklands of life.' Gavin Maxwell quotes this with approval, adding that he himself appeared to be 'unhottable' and 'unpromising material for her particular techniques'. Orwell too brings in Elizabeth – seemingly the inevitable comparison – along with Essex and Raleigh and Leicester, about whom he had read very early. In short, a queen to be taken seriously, to whom it was impossible to be indifferent, and whose favour one wanted and courted.

(These memoirs, of course, were written years later by men who had known Mrs Vaughan Wilkes only when they were schoolboys. One wonders how she would have appeared to her contemporaries, this woman in her early thirties whose husband was headmaster of a boarding-school and who was herself the mother of young children. As formidable as a queen? It seems unlikely. We know that Mrs Blair was favourably impressed, and she was not a woman to suffer pretensions gladly.)

One wanted to be in favour. This was as true of Blair as of any other boy in the school. Favourites were boys notable for Character, or Prettiness, or Intellectual Prowess, or Charm, or an Affectionate Nature, or they were boys who came from aristocratic families that were very rich. One of these qualities in itself was not usually enough: a combination was desirable. The more of them one had to offer, the more secure one's favour. Connolly had Intellectual Prowess, but decided he lacked Prettiness and as a substitute would work on Charm, which he did, successfully. Gavin Maxwell had a strong plus in being a grandson of the Duke of Northumberland, but it was cancelled out by the minus of his not having an Affectionate Nature. Whereas the only other boy of his time at the school 'whose parents had what Flip called, with varying intonation "a handle to their names"' ... chanced to be a boy of such stupefying good looks as to present Flip with the irresistible combination –

like certain TV-advertised detergents he was the best on the market because he was the only one to have *two* ingredients *never* combined before.' Then there were special categories: for example, pretty Scottish boys who could be dressed up in kilts for the Sunday parade into Eastbourne for church were almost certain candidates for favour.*

In the long run, the indispensable quality was an Affectionate Nature, or the ability to simulate it. Eric had Intellectual Prowess but not much else to assist him to favour – his face was too flabby to qualify for Prettiness; his grown-up, sardonic manner, the remarks he delivered in a 'flat, ageless voice', would not be thought Charming; and he could not pretend to an Affection he did not feel. There was an art to playing the courtier that he never mastered. Connolly did better. So too did Beaton: 'Generally I remained her angel, for I knew how to suck up to her and curry favour. I pretended to read books that might impress her with my good literary taste. I even mowed the school lawn, and painted Christmas cards for her. In fact, I became such a positive favourite that she often took me down into the town of Eastbourne on her domestic shopping visits, and gave me a mid-morning coconut cake.'[17]

Eric was not above trying to suck up, but he could never achieve the blend of enthusiasm and deference that was desirable, only a servility he was thoroughly ashamed of even as he persisted in it. Still, he had his periods of favour. At such times he was given the run of Mrs Vaughan Wilkes's own library – there, at eleven, he read *Vanity Fair* for the first time; and he was allowed to serve at table when old boys and parents came to Sunday-night supper – a privilege much sought after for one could claim the scraps: as Connolly observed, the waiters were 'in a position to stuff their pockets with potato salad when they took it out'. In each instance, favour followed upon some conspicuous evidence of Intellectual Prowess, as when he wrote 'Awake! Young Men of England', or verses to order to mark a special occasion, or when he won the Harrow History Prize, for which

* A detail that surely contributed to Orwell's long-standing dislike of Scotland, and of books about 'the Highland, Celtic, or romantic side of Scottish life'. Scotland was where the parents of rich boys at St Cyprian's went to shoot in the holidays and play the laird. Towards the end of his life, however, he overcame his dislike and went to live on the island of Jura, off the coast of Argyll.

the school competed each year, or the prize that Mrs Vaughan Wilkes awarded for 'the "best list" of books taken out of the library during the term'. (Connolly won both prizes too. Their library lists were top-heavy with impressive books – e.g., Carlyle's *The French Revolution* – but when they were caught out with Compton Mackenzie's novel of Oxford life, *Sinister Street*, which Blair had brought back after a holiday, they were banished from favour, for it was thought to be rather 'fast' and certainly not the sort of book a boy with Character would read.)

Intellectual Prowess won Eric his periods of favour but they were imbued with the feeling of a transaction, something earned; and rather than liberating him drew him back even more tightly to the Exam, to the pressure to work – he would work harder at St Cyprian's than he ever would again – to the hateful awareness of his status as a charity boy. He was brought back to the shaming reminders from Mrs Vaughan Wilkes that his family was making sacrifices for him, and so he must not be extravagant with the spending money his mother sent him (but which the school took charge of and doled out to him more meagrely, he felt, than to other boys). So that his being in favour never was a comfortable thing; it was too closely related to the anxiety attached to his special status. Meanwhile he saw with jealous, cynical, and deprecating eyes that other boys – boys of an invincible stupidity who were never made to work and who would nonetheless pass as smoothly as strawberry fondant into a Public School – these boys were being petted and favoured for reasons having nothing to do with Intelligence, and everything (as he felt) with Money: their families, unlike his, were rich. All this was in accord with the spirit of the age: Vanity Fair brought up to date in the heyday of Empire, and until recently presided over by jolly, fat King Tumtum. The sons of the plutocracy thrived at St Cyprian's much as their fathers did in the great Edwardian world, of which it too was the product. There were occasions when the plutocrats would descend upon the school, on the way to or from a weekend in Brighton, to visit their heirs. Money was made visible then: in the Daimlers in which they drove up, in their uniformed chauffeurs, and in their wives resplendent in velvet and furs and smelling of parma violets. While Mrs Vaughan Wilkes welcomed these visiting parents – and such a visit ensured a boy's being in favour – Eric felt the more apart, resentful and cynical, for his own parents had no automobile and could not motor down to see him. He arrived at an economic explanation of affection and of society. The loved were rich; the unloved were not. Being rich was something over which you had no control: you were born rich, or not, and if not, were doomed to be unloved. Again, it was something over which you had no control: to be unloved was like having a birthmark or wetting your bed. Of course, if one did well in the Exam, or wrote patriotic verses, one would be praised, called 'old chap', be smiled upon – even so, one would be doing no more than was expected of one, the maximum achievement turning out to be equal to the minimum requirement: working as hard as possible, being as clever as possible, never letting up pressure for a moment, in order simply to survive on the fringe of that world that the beautiful, the well-born, and the rich, but especially the rich, took for granted as their own, and to which they gained entry without effort. They had the credentials: it was a matter of what they were, as much as, or even more than, what they did. And what they were, Eric early decided, he by definition was not: accordingly, he was damned.

This was the side of Edwardian life – the snobbish, opulent, mammonistic side – that Orwell despised, and it was irrevocably joined in his mind with St Cyprian's. But there was another side – all simplicity, good-heartedness and decency, a Wellsian side, so to speak – that he would always value, and associate with growing up in Henley. Orwell, when writing of his childhood, does tend to reduce it to overemphatic blacks and whites – as in a grim fairy-tale – and his self portrait as an ugly, smelly, friendless schoolboy is a feverish exaggeration. But fairy-tales have a truth of their own, and the polarization he imposes on his childhood is a close approximation to what he felt: black for St Cyprian's and white for Henley. Or to adopt the conventions of a fairy-tale: at school he was a scullery boy; at home, Prince Charming. In fact, this was to be literally the case during the Christmas holiday of 1914.

The Blairs, habituated as they were to a 'nomadic' life in the colonial service in India, had little difficulty in uprooting themselves from one place and putting down roots in another. Returning to England, they had quite soon established themselves in Henley and afterwards in Shiplake, and were on friendly terms with a number of local families. Among these were the Nortons of Bellehatch Park, a country house in nearby Harpsden, where Mr Blair, an ardent golfer, was secretary of the local golf club. Mr Norton, who shared memories of India with Mr Blair, was at that time a Member of Parliament and assistant Postmaster General; in 1916 he would be created Lord Rathcreedan. When Eric came home for the Christmas holiday in 1914, he learned that Mrs Norton had proposed a family pantomime be put on at Bellehatch Park, and plans for it were already under way. The piece chosen was *Cinderella* in the version by Lady Bell. Eric was cast as Prince Charming – with his schoolboy's awkwardness and flat high voice he was not altogether persuasive in the role; Marjorie Blair played the cruel stepmother, Avril a page, the Norton brothers the ugly sisters, and their sister, a schoolmate of Marjorie's, Cinderella. Bellehatch Park was not a fairy-tale castle, but a handsome old house whose earliest parts dated back to the Tudor period, and whose front had been refaced in stone and sash-windows inserted in the eighteenth century. At the end of the large drawing-room a curtain was hung and a stage improvised, and there the first performance of *Cinderella* took place before an audience of some fifty people, family, friends, and servants. It went so well that a second performance was given 'for the public' in Harpsden Village Hall, and a third in the Henley Town Hall, which had been converted into a hospital for wounded soldiers. The latter occasion is very much in the spirit of the times – St Cyprian's too would devise entertainments for patients in an army hospital near Eastbourne.

Cinderella 1914 sheds a further light on the quality of the Blairs' life in Henley, which does not appear to have been unduly circumscribed; and as for Eric at home, one has a sense of good times, of an absence of pressures and duties, of affection freely given, rather than as the reward in a transaction.* This was the

* Jacintha Buddicom, a few years younger than Blair, and her brother and sister Prosper and Guiniver, saw a good deal of him in Henley during his holidays from Eton. In 1971 Miss Buddicom published a charming memoir 'The Young Eric' – in the symposium *The World of George Orwell* edited by Miriam Gross – in which she set down her impression of Blair as she knew him more than a half century before during the period of their friendship,

polar opposite, of course, from his life at St Cyprian's, where the inexorable daily question would be, What had he done? Had he done what was expected of him? On the whole, yes, but he saw himself as 'scholarship fodder', a drudge rather than a favourite of fortune, and his cynicism deepened. Connolly writes, 'I was a stage rebel, Orwell a true one.' Orwell, however, writing his own memoir of the school almost a decade after Connolly's, wants to make it clear that he was a rebel only by 'force of circumstances'. In any event, at St Cyprian's, and for a dozen years afterwards, his was an entirely inward rebellion. Outwardly Eric conformed to the codes of the school, worked hard, did well in his studies, won prizes, lived up to expectations: the appropriate conclusion to all this was that in the winter and spring of 1916 he took the scholarship examinations for two of the great public schools.

Eton was his prime objective – to be awarded a scholarship there, to be one of the King's Scholars living in College.* But it was also the objective for scores of other boys from prep schools all over England with whom he would be competing for the very small number of places available. It was a sensible precaution, the Vaughan Wilkeses felt, to have an alternative to fall back on. For Eric the alternative decided upon was Wellington College, and that winter he sat the scholarship exam there successfully. Cause for rejoicing: it meant he no longer need fear the possibility of becoming a scruffy little clerk at forty pounds a year. But although a scholarship at Wellington was a good thing, one at Eton would be even better: the difference between being at the top and the

from 1915 through 1921. 'I knew plenty of boys to compare him with,' she writes, 'and in such a comparison Eric would rate a very high score. He may not have been quite so good-looking as the handsomest, or have achieved a place in a cricket XI or rowing crew; but among all the boys we knew, Eric was one of the most interesting, the best informed, the kindest, the *nicest*.' The total effect of Miss Buddicom's memoir is to evoke in its own particulars the impression of an essentially happy life away from school which Avril Dunn has emphasized in her recollections of her brother.

* To live in College at Eton College is not the tautology it may at first appear to be. King's Scholars are housed in the oldest buildings of the school (College), some of which go back almost to the time of the Foundation (1442) – hence it is literally the case that King's Scholars are 'in College'. The other boys at the school, paying its expensive fees, live *outside* College, in varying proximity to it in the town of Eton (and so are known as Oppidans, 'men of the town') in dormitory-like houses presided over by Housemasters.

very top. In the late spring, therefore, he travelled to Eton (accompanied by Mr Vaughan Wilkes) to submit to an elaborate series of exams that went on for two and a half days. They included Greek verse composition, a French oral exam, and on the last day, a *viva* conducted in the Headmaster's division room in which he was questioned by three or four senior figures, drawn from among the Provost, Vice-Provost, Headmaster, Master in College, and Fellows.[18] It was a formidable experience for a thirteen-year-old, but Eric carried it off very well, a tribute to him and to the training of St Cyprian's. Precisely how well he had done, however, he would not know until the list was published early in June, so there was a period of some anxiety. (Yet even that was lessened by his having Wellington safely in reserve.)

Traditionally, the list of boys who have qualified to become scholars at Eton is arranged in order of merit. Usually it contains more names than there are places immediately available. There are never more than seventy King's Scholars in College. No more than ten to thirteen, comprising an Election, are admitted at a time, and the size of an Election depends on how many places among the seventy are vacant. Thus, the boys at the top of the list are certain of admission; those further down must wait for a vacancy. As (and if) it occurs, they are given the opportunity to enter.

The list was published in *The Times* on 10 June 1916. Blair's name was fourteenth, not quite high enough to include him in the Election that would be entering College in the autumn. On the other hand, there was good reason to expect that, if he were patient, there would be a place for him later. It was a very creditable performance, and Mrs Vaughan Wilkes declared a whole holiday for the school to celebrate his having done so well. Such occasions were usually reserved to mark her birthdays, so Eric was truly a conquering hero. And the event was all the more remarkable because only a few days before, the school, like all of England, had been plunged into mourning for the death of Lord Kitchener.

It is one of the curious aspects of Orwell's memoir of the school that he should make no specific references to his having been there during the first two years of the war. Perhaps because he chose to present St Cyprian's as it embodied the aspect of

Edwardian life he hated, and because that era was swept away in 1914, the life he evoked and condemned is largely pre-war. Yet the war was pervasive in England: a boys' boarding-school, intended to train future proconsuls, would not be indifferent to it. War heightened the physical discomfort of daily life: the food appreciably worsened, although some of the things Orwell complained of, the bluish milk and the rancid margarine, were common beyond St Cyprian's – Mrs Vaughan Wilkes complained of them too – and shortages of coal meant that the radiators in winter gave off even less heat than before. Character and Patriotism were at a high pitch. One had to make sacrifices. The boys drilled on the playing-field; pinpointed the famous battles on maps in the classrooms; visited army hospitals and gave out Woodbines; listened in chapel as new names were added to the Roll of Honour – in all, 155 old St Cyprianites would serve in the First World War, an impressive total from a small school that had been in existence only a dozen years. It was in such circumstances that the secret guilt of a generation of survivors was implanted: the schoolboys who came of age too late to take part in the war in which a generation of older brothers was decimated.

'Your country needs YOU' – this was the message of the recruiting poster designed by Alfred Leete in 1914; above the message appeared a luxuriantly-moustached, stern proconsular face, too famous to be identified: the face of Kitchener of Khartoum, one of the great heroes of the late-Victorian epoch. In 1914, at the age of sixty-four, he was brought into the government, a larger-than-life-size idol above the demands of petty politics, to become Secretary of War. His performance was woefully inadequate, and, as his biographer observes, 'Kitchener's power to give unity to the Government vanished when his colleagues lost confidence in his judgement. But he continued to the last to give unity to the country, and to provide a façade behind which soldiers and politicians, Liberals and Conservatives, and the rival advocates of an eastern and of a western strategy conducted their disputes and intrigues.' It was the façade, encrusted with fame, going back to the great days of Empire, that the vast majority of English knew and revered and presently were to mourn. On 5 June 1916, Kitchener sailed on the cruiser

Hampshire, bound for Archangel, and beyond that for the Russian Front which he had been invited to visit by the Czar.

At approximately 7.40 P.M., when about a mile and a half off Marwick Head, the *Hampshire* struck a mine which had been laid by the German submarine U.75 . . .

It heeled over to starboard, settled down by the head, and sank within a quarter of an hour. Some dozen survivors only reached a wild and inhospitable coast with cliffs rising sheer out of the sea; and they gave no coherent account of Kitchener's movements during the few moments which elapsed between the explosion and the sinking of the cruiser. Kitchener, who was seen by one survivor in the gunroom flat immediately after the explosion, was extremely sensitive to cold; he probably kept on his heavy greatcoat and choked to death among the first in the angry waters. Fitzgerald's body [he was Personal Military Secretary to the War Lord] was washed ashore, but Kitchener's was devoured by the Atlantic.

The news reached London on the morning of 6 June and was published at about midday. The journey to Russia had been a closely-guarded secret; and a sense of awed numbness gripped the land.[19]

The event did not pass unnoticed at St Cyprian's. Melancholy it might be, but how rich in those elements of Character and Patriotism the school exalted, and Mrs Vaughan Wilkes made it a set topic, to be dealt with in prose or verse.

In July Connolly was writing to his mother: 'I enclose a poem(?) I made up about Lord Kitchener a few nights ago. I got the chap who is considered the best poet to critisise (I know I've spelt that word wrong) it, which he did on the other side. He did a very good poem which he sent to a local paper where they took it . . . Think that there is only one more Sunday here!!'[20]

The 'best poet' was, of course, Blair. At the bottom of the page on which Connolly had written out his poem he had added:

Stern Criticism Please
Dear Sir I think your poem(?) is

Blair, ready to 'critisise', turned the page over and ignored the parenthetical question mark. He thought the poem 'dashed good'. ('My dear Blair!!' Connolly interjected, 'I am both surprised and shocked.') And while he took notice of some repetition and ambiguity, he found the scansion excellent, the epithets mostly well chosen, and the poem as a whole 'neat, elegant, and polished'.

It is unlikely that either of the thirteen-year-old poets was deeply moved by the death they were asked to commemorate, although Mrs Vaughan Wilkes was very good at getting the boys 'to mind' about Kitchener. But the poems they produced reveal some interesting contrasts. Connolly's is much the more romantic, musical, and melancholy. The particular circumstances of the event, death by drowning in the North Sea, struck a responsive chord which outweighed other considerations:

> No honoured church's funeral hath he,
> The silent hero of a nation's fame
> No drone of muffled drums can greet his soul
> No last post blown in sadness o'er the sea.
> The time-worn rocks alone can mark his tomb,
> His epitaph the roar of breaking waves.
> No human mourner follows in his train
> The wailing seagull chants his death song through.
> None but the lonely curlews on the moor
> Bewail a mighty empire's tearful loss.
> > 'Bury him not in an abbey shrine
> > Midst tablets of stone and coffins of pine
> > But let him be where no light can shine
> > And the north sea waves rush on.'

Perhaps what is most striking about this mournful exercise is the absence of even one perfunctory allusion to those qualities summed up in Character and Patriotism. It was as though, in writing his poem, Connolly had held himself aloof from the code of St Cyprian's: it would be difficult to find an uplifting moral lesson here. By contrast, Blair's 'Kitchener' is much more the official poem, as was his earlier 'Awake! Young Men of England'. The particular circumstances and setting of the death are not alluded to, only the unexceptionable public sentiments they have inspired:

> No stone is set to mark his nation's loss,
> No stately tomb enshrines his noble breast
> Not e'en the tribute of a wooden cross
> > Can mark this hero's rest.

> He needs them not, his name ungarnished stands,
> Remindful of the mighty deeds he worked,
> Footprints of one, upon time's changeful sands,
> > Who n'er his duty shirked.

Who follows in his steps no danger shuns,
Nor stoops to conquer by a shameful deed,
An honest and unselfish race he runs,
    From fear and malice freed.

How many of the qualities that were valued at St Cyprian's Blair
has managed to include in his last five lines: never to shirk one's
duty, to be brave and honourable, honest and unselfish, and free
from cowardice and malice – for the second time within the
month he had done the school proud. He himself was sufficiently proud of the poem to send it to *The Henley and South
Oxford Standard*, where it was published on Friday, 21 July
1916. For this second appearance in print he was no longer
'Master Eric Blair' but simply E. A. Blair.

A copy of the published poem went as by right to Mrs Vaughan
Wilkes and so to her scrapbook. But there is no reason to think,
therefore, that its sentiments represent an act of calculation. It is
true that Connolly tells us that Blair rejected 'the war, the Empire, Kipling, Sussex, and Character', and he quotes from a conversation in which he said to him, 'Of course, you realize,
Connolly, that, whoever wins this war, we shall emerge a second-
rate nation.' Originally, Connolly placed the conversation at St
Cyprian's; but he has since come to believe that he dated it too
early, and that it belongs to a year or two later when he and Blair
were at Eton. This would be entirely consistent with what we
know of Blair as a fifteen-year-old – by then his cynicism, as it
expressed itself in conversation, had become open and pronounced. It is also consistent with the progress, or lack of progress, of the war and its effect upon public opinion in England.
In the early summer of 1916, when the boys of St Cyprian's (and
other schools) were writing their tributes to Kitchener, confidence had not yet been shaken: the campaign along the Somme
was in its opening phase – surely it would lead to victory. In the
autumn, when the campaign ended, victory was no nearer than
before, and there had been four hundred thousand British casual-
ties. The old assurances, confidences, and slogans began to be
questioned. 'Your country needs YOU' under the moustachioed
face of Kitchener had been sufficient in 1914 to recruit an army;
now it was deemed necessary to conscript one.

Having said this, it is not an injustice to Blair, at thirteen, to
say that he would have had to be even more precocious than he

was, more prescient and more concerned with world affairs, to have allowed the war to dominate his thoughts in the summer of 1916. In fact, and as one might expect, he was chiefly taken up with the problem of his own immediate future. His situation at St Cyprian's had dramatically altered. No longer would there be lines of translation to take home for the holiday; no longer need he fear the banana-sized silver pencil, or humiliating reminders of his status, or any of the other devices the Vaughan Wilkeses had resorted to in urging him forward to his goal. The goal had been achieved. Whatever he had been before his success in the exams, he was now undeniably an object of value, proof positive that the school got results, and the Vaughan Wilkeses would have been content to have him remain there until a place became available for him at Eton. But he was already assured of a place at Wellington: should he not take it up immediately? It was a decision to be made by his parents, though his own wishes would not be ignored. For him it was simple: he wanted to be off to Public School at the earliest opportunity – therefore, Wellington. The Blairs recognized the greater prestige that would be conferred upon him as an Etonian; at the same time they had to take into account a practical consideration. The expense, even at reduced fees, of Eric's continuing at St Cyprian's while waiting for Eton would not be negligible in a family budget already strained. (War-time inflation was affecting Mr Blair's fixed pension. In the latter part of 1915 the family had moved from Shiplake back to Henley, to a semi-detached house in St Mark's Road. This new house though comfortable was noticeably smaller than Roselawn, and so may have appeared to Eric as 'the sacrifice' that was being made on his behalf by his parents. He was twelve years old then and impressionable and surrounded by the sons of the top three per cent; at such an age and in such circumstances the 'step down' from Roselawn – say from the top five per cent to the top seven – would have greater weight with him than the undoubted fact that in St Mark's Road the Blairs were still living better than the majority of Englishmen.) In the end, the practical consideration prevailed. Mr Blair wrote to Vaughan Wilkes to say that they had decided Eric should take up his scholarship at Wellington at the end of the year.

In December his last day at St Cyprian's finally arrived – and it was truly his last day, for he would never, except in memory, return there again. Decked out in a new silk old school tie, he presented himself to Mrs Vaughan Wilkes to say goodbye. She shook his hand, called him 'Eric', congratulated him, wished him well. It ought to have been a happy moment, and yet . . . In her face and expression, Orwell tells us, he read a message of irony and condescension: that he had not been worthy of her, that he was not truly the right sort. As for Mrs Vaughan Wilkes, she remembered that she had not been able to 'reach him', and she was aware that he was glad to be leaving. Orwell concludes his account with what is virtually an aria to Failure, the word itself turning up five times in a twenty-one-word sentence. He had failed in the past; he would fail in the future – that was the message he believed he took away with him from his prep school. In fact, he had succeeded. He had got from St Cyprian's exactly what it was intended that he should get. The school had fulfilled its part of the bargain, and so had he. The explanation for the apparent discrepancy between what Orwell felt and Blair did is simple and paradoxical: that, for Orwell, to succeed in the way that St Cyprian's defined success was to fail. It was a discovery that Blair himself would make and act upon belatedly, more than a decade after he had said goodbye for the last time to 'Mum'.

Part Two:
Eton

Nineteen seventeen proved to be a year of decisive change not only for Eric but for all the Blairs. The war was in its third year, more pervasive and destructive in its effect than had seemed possible a year or two before, touching them all. That England might be defeated was unthinkable; but victory was still not in sight, and the prospect lengthened gloomily. In these trying circumstances the reaction of the elder Blairs was characteristic: they felt they must do what they could to help. The idea of service to the state was strong in the family, though not at all strident: simply, it was what one did in time of crisis, what one's forebears had done in the past, what one's children would do in the future. This same subdued but unwavering concept of patriotism was ingrained in Orwell himself, no matter how much he might wish to discount it, and it would emerge strongly in 1939.

His father, sixty years old in 1917, might permissibly have cheered from the sidelines as a civilian patriot. Instead, he decided to enlist, and it suggests something about England's circumstances in the third year of the war that he should have been accepted for duty. That September he was commissioned a second lieutenant and so became, according to family tradition, the oldest subaltern in the British army, looking after mules in a camp near Marseilles.* However inglorious his job, the important thing was that Mr Blair in France was helping the war effort; and so, presently, was his wife. Before the end of the year Mrs Blair moved the household from Henley to London, to a flat in Cromwell Crescent, Earl's Court, and she and Marjorie went to work for the duration of the war in the

* Or so Orwell later described his father's military career to Richard Rees, and very likely he drew upon it in *Coming Up For Air* for George Bowling's unheroic wartime duty – to guard a few cans of supplies in the south of England.

Ministry of Pensions, which had set up offices in the Tate Gallery. Avril, aged nine, was placed in a boarding-school in Ealing; Eric by then was already in College at Eton.

Earlier in the year he had spent nine weeks, the Lent Term, at Wellington College, where he was a Scholar of the school and lived in Blücher Dormitory. He had come to Wellington with high expectations, envisaging a freer and more private life than he had known at St Cyprian's – a cubicle of one's own where one could make cocoa at night, as in a Public School novel – but the reality, all austerity and restrictions, had disappointed him. The school, for its part, found Blair something of a disappointment too, for his performance as a Scholar was not of the high calibre that might have been expected. There were thirty-one boys in his Form, Upper IIIA, and he was placed a merely adequate thirteenth.[1] But he had already embarked on a career at school of slacking off, doing as little work as was sufficient to get safely through, but no more: a reaction, Orwell later felt, to the unremitting pressure to which he had been subjected at St Cyprian's.

That winter of 1917, the third winter of the war, was a time when an increasing number of older boys at Eton were leaving to enlist in the army. More places than usual came available in College. In March Blair was informed that he could now join the Election of 1916, if he so wished. He did not hesitate: Eton the unknown was preferable to the Wellington he knew. Nor did his mother hesitate, even though it meant that for the second time within four months Eric would have to be outfitted, money would have to be found, sacrifices made.

Blair, K. S. (King's Scholar) entered College in May 1917, a month before his fourteenth birthday. His outfit included the famous cutaway Eton jacket or 'bumfreezer', prescribed for boys under five feet four inches, and the toga-like short black gown with interior pocket prescribed for Collegers. In appearance he was still very much the schoolboy. George Wansbrough, a member of his Election, speaks of his 'extraordinarily plump cheeks', and Denys King-Farlow, who was also in the Election, of the 'large, rather fat face, with big jowls, a bit like a hamster' and his 'slightly protruding light china-blue eyes'. His adolescent growing period, from which he would emerge conspicuously tall, was a year or so in the future. His voice, just beginning to change, was still uncertain. But there was only certainty in what he said and in his manner of saying it. King-Farlow, who had had an experience similar to Blair's – he too was a late-comer to the Election, entering College in May after two terms at Winchester – asked him at one of their first encounters what he felt about switching to Eton. Blair replied immediately, 'Well, it can't be worse than Wellington. That really was perfectly bloody.' Which was not the way a thirteen-year-old was expected to talk in 1917, and King-Farlow thought it 'not quite right', though he found it tonic as well as slightly unsettling. To be outspoken and cynical became Blair's Etonian style. More than forty years later King-Farlow remembered that 'He'd been the first person I had ever heard running down his own father and mother.'[2] This was not the done thing, either – though it might be what one felt, one did not put it into such blunt words. But Blair continued to say what he pleased, undoubtedly aware of the effect that he was making, and what he had to say was often at odds with the pieties and received opinions of Eton and England in 1917.

The prevailing mood was still deeply patriotic, conformist, and attuned to gallantry. Not jingoistic precisely; still, it did not allow for a dissenting view. The year before, Edward Lyttelton, who had been headmaster of Eton since 1905, was eased out of his position, after saying he thought it monstrous automatically to depict the Germans as beasts. He even went so far as to declare 'that the only ultimate object of sane policy must be to abolish war altogether'. For this he was denounced in the popular press. To spare the school a continuing scandal he offered his resignation to the Governing Body, which rather cravenly accepted it, and in April 1916 he departed. He was not unhappy to go: 'It is a huge relief,' he remarked, 'being quit of that dull nightmare organization, in which I have come to believe less and less.' Under the new regime – of C. A. Alington, who happened to be married to Edward Lyttelton's half-sister – the news of Eton that figured in the press was of a more reassuring and conventional kind. Thus, when the traditional celebrations of the Fourth of June were curtailed in a spirit of saving money for the war effort, *The Times* reported that 'Eton, like other parts of the country, practises economy, if only *pour encourager les autres*.'[3] But on a more serious, and admirable level, tragically so, was the example Eton afforded of patriotism in action, as its young officers went up the line to death.

Since the mid-nineteenth century – that is, since the beginning of the great days of Empire – 'Patriotism and the readiness to sacrifice one's life for one's country had been the quality to which Eton had paid especial – and what to its critics might appear exaggerated – honour.' Christopher Hollis, a contemporary of Blair's in College, from whose history of the school we are quoting, goes on to point out that while the late-Victorian 'code of patriotism' prescribed that 'every English gentleman must at all times be prepared to die for his country, it was not expected that very many of them would in fact have to do so. In the Victorian security no one dreamed of even the possibility of catastrophes such as we have lived through in our days.' Nineteen fourteen changed all that, and as Hollis sums up, 'Eton proved that her boasts of patriotism were not insincere. Five thousand six hundred and eighty-seven Etonians served in the war. Of these, 1,160 were killed and 1,467 were wounded; 13 won the Victoria Cross, 548 won the Distinguished Service Order and 744 won the Military Cross.'[4]

It was against this war-time background that Blair was to spend his first two years at Eton. The patriotic theme was not new to him, of course – he had heard it at home; as an eight-year-old he had worn a sailor suit and been a member of the Navy League; at St Cyprian's the theme had been sounded continuously. But there was a significant difference between being made to care about the death of Kitchener by Mrs Vaughan Wilkes, and being at a school where boys only a few years older than oneself whom one saw every day – heroes of the playing-fields – were suddenly going off to fight for their country and perhaps to die for it. It was as though the fantasies of St Cyprian's were being acted out at Eton. The impressions that these heroic departures and gallant sacrifices made upon the younger boys who were left behind were powerful at the time, perhaps even more so later in retrospect. Long after peace had come, a sense of having avoided but also missed a dangerous yet fulfilling experience would haunt many of those who were at school during the war. They heard the names of the dead read aloud in chapel; new and younger and more familiar names were added to the list each week, and were not forgotten, and left a residue of quite irrational guilt. Years later Orwell said to Richard Rees that 'his generation must be marked forever by the humiliation of not having taken part' in the First World War. Rees comments sensibly, 'He had, of course, been too young to take part. But the fact that several million men, some of them not much older than himself, had been through an ordeal which he had not shared was apparently intolerable to him.'[5] It was not until 1937, by his heroic behaviour during the Spanish Civil War, that Orwell put paid to this humiliation.

The background, then, can be defined by a particular moment in time – England at war. But the foreground, the run of every-day events, was peculiarly timeless – unchanging Eton, with its customs, traditions, and tribal rites, which have been described in so many novels and memoirs. Orwell himself wrote very little about Eton, perhaps because as a subject, unlike St Cyprian's, it could not be made to serve his didactic intention: there is no full-scale, carefully wrought, deeply felt essay comparable to 'Such, Such were the Joys'. Of the little he wrote on the subject, much was critical and depreciatory. But in a piece towards the end of his life, 'Forever Eton', he singles out as the great virtue of the school its 'tolerant and civilized atmosphere which gives each boy a fair chance of developing his individuality'.[6] The truth of this observation would seem confirmed by the noticeable variety among Etonians as they come of age: there is no prescribed or approved mould in which the schoolboy is cast to type. And yet, paradoxically, even as he is becoming an individual, he is also becoming, unmistakably and for the rest of his life, an Etonian. Our intention is to see how the process operated for Eric Blair, who, as Orwell, might justly be described, along with John Maynard Keynes and Harold Macmillan, as one of the three most famous members of College in this century.

College, which he had joined in May, consisted then as now of seventy Scholars – who were on the Foundation, and as such were continuing a tradition that went back to the founding of Eton by Henry VI in the fifteenth century. In 1917, apart from the King's Scholars, there were approximately 900 other boys at the school. These latter were the Oppidans, who paid high fees, and lived in one or another of the several Houses that were owned by the school but that were run, almost as private domains, by the housemasters. Oppidans, especially as they came fresh from prep schools, tended to feel superior to Collegers – or, as they called them, 'Tugs' – whose families might or might not be in straitened circumstances, but almost certainly belonged to a class no lower than middle-middle-middle. It was just as certain that any boy who had had the sort of education that qualified him for a scholarship in College would have attended a prep school. (Truly uncommon would have been a working-class boy from a state school in College – where would he have got sufficient Latin and Greek to win a scholarship?) But Blair's case had its special Blairian aspect. Again, as at St Cyprian's, he felt economically deprived and put upon. Collegers, regardless of financial background, were charged fees of some twenty-five pounds a year. Blair resented this: he told King-Farlow the fees were 'exorbitant'. He knew his family were having to make sacrifices to augment his scholarship. The full cost of a boy in College at the time was about one hundred pounds yearly which was much less than Oppidans would pay; still it was a fair part of Mr Blair's pension. There is little doubt that Eric was not as well off as most (though not all) of his contemporaries in College, that he had less pocket money and fewer luxuries, that he continued to wear trousers long after they were shiny and flapping above his ankles, and that at home money would sometimes be in short supply, literally so. (Once, when he had been home on a visit, Marjorie Blair had to borrow money from Ruth Pitter for Eric's ticket back to Eton from London. That was on a Sunday, and the next day, when the banks were open, the loan was repaid – but by then Eric was gone, and the need to have borrowed so small a sum of money must have left its impression upon a nature abnormally sensitive to such things.)

Looked at objectively, there was nothing in his parents' or his own situation to deprive him of the usual day-to-day life in College, and there is no evidence that he was deprived, especially since the fees the Blairs paid included 'tuition, lodging, board and recreational facilities'.* Subjectively, it might be a different

* Food, from a boy's point of view, tended to be meagre; deliberate 'under-feeding', Orwell later decided, and even more conspicuous at Eton than at St

matter. Collegers had a kind of freemasonry or snobbery of their own as 'intellectuals' – from which eminence they might look down on Oppidans. On the whole, they regarded one another as equals, paying little attention to the question of how much money one's people had. There is no reason to believe they condescended to Blair, nor did he ever say so. But against the pride he might feel in being a Colleger, there appears in his case to have been the shame (as he felt it) of being a 'Tug', and it continued to rankle long after he left Eton. Richard Rees, who had been an Oppidan, tells how 'One day in 1948, when I had known him for eighteen years, I incautiously used the word 'Tug', and although he was too polite to say anything he winced as if I had trodden on his tenderest corn.'[7]

It was a question of temperament. There were boys in College – Cyril Connolly, for example, who came on from St Cyprian's the next year – who had friends among the Oppidans. There were Oppidans every bit as 'intellectual' as Collegers, sometimes more so; the very remarkable literary magazine, *The Eton Candle*, was an entirely Oppidan enterprise. In the 'tolerant and civilized atmosphere' of that ancient Public School much was possible. But venturing among Oppidans was a possibility – remote, indeed – that Blair chose not to explore. He felt safer among the members of his Election, and the story of his life at Eton is virtually the story of his life in College.

His Election, as the youngest, lived in Chamber, a hall in the oldest part of College. Then, as now, wooden stalls, austere enough for a monastery, lined a wide uncarpeted passage. On one side a row of stalls was interrupted for a common room of sorts, open to the passage and furnished with some wooden chairs and a broad table in front of a fireplace; then the row resumed.

Cyprian's. All the Collegers took breakfast and midday dinner together in the College Hall; also supper at eight o'clock, except that for that meal the Sixth Form and Liberty (the form immediately junior) dined apart. The largest, the last solid meal of the day, was at noon. There was a supper of soup or fried fish, or bread and cheese, with water to drink, at eight. In the circumstances tea tended to be the grandest and most idiosyncratic meal. For this the boys would buy, were expected to buy, supplies of their own (eggs, sausages, sardines, buns, biscuits, cakes of varied hues and flavours) to add to the official bread and butter that was doled out to them, and they would often pool their resources.

Each boy was given a stall of his own – to that extent there was the illusion of privacy. But these stalls rose only to the height of a man and were open at the top; voices floated in from anywhere along the row; eyes peeped over the partitions; effectively one lived in public. Stretched out on one's folding bed, or sitting at one's desk – the whole furnishing of a stall – one could see, looking up, the massive carved beams high overhead; closer, one could read in the wood panelling countless initials incised by boys of all those preceding generations of Collegers. It was an historic and uncomfortable setting into which Blair fitted without difficulty; his joining the Election late made no significant difference.

On his first day there was a ceremonial beginning. In accordance with Etonian tradition he presented himself to the Provost to be gowned and, as he knelt, he was adjured to be good, docile, and truthful. This was the ideal. Later that same day he descended to the real: it provided the more vivid memory. Long afterwards he told his friend Mabel Fierz that he had had to bat at cricket, and, as he did badly, he was thrashed, and felt humiliated.

This would not have been an auspicious beginning, for at Eton, as at any other school, to be good at games was an asset, but it did not usher in a season of humiliations such as he had suffered in his first weeks at St Cyprian's. By now he had had a long experience of being away at school, homesickness was not a problem, and he was poised and intelligent enough to hold his own nicely in the maze of Etonian traditions, customs, rules, regulations, codes, and disciplines. Inevitably he would be introduced to the punishments administered by Sixth Form, for pretexts were easily found, and 'the Colleger had to expect to be beaten a number of times during his first two years'.[8] But this was traditional, the common fate of all members of the lowest Election, however rich they might be or whatever handles might attach to their names. If Blair was beaten, he had no reason to feel singled out or victimized. The same held true for 'Chamber Singing', another tradition he was made to participate in soon after his arrival. For this, Collegers assembled in the common room in Chamber to listen to the new boys as one by one they sang solo, standing on the table in front of the fireplace. Blair's choice was an American song of the last century, 'Riding Down to Bangor', and while his performance was not notably melodious, he was spared the indignity of having books thrown at him, which sometimes happened when the audience grew restive.

These details, trivial in themselves, point towards an important conclusion: that Blair, joining the 1916 Election, would now have the experience of belonging to a community. The fourteen boys of the Election were a coherent society of their own, existing within a larger society, College, which in its turn was part of a still larger society, Eton. And beyond Eton was the world, of which Blair in these war-time years knew very little – hardly more than his mother's London flat, and sometimes in holidays the golf club at Parkstone near Bournemouth where his uncle was secretary and with whom he and Avril would be sent to stay. ('There was really nothing to do except go to the local roller skating rink, where we both learnt to roller skate incredibly badly. Neither of us were interested in it in the least,' Avril remembers. 'That was on wet days. On fine days we used to walk over the golf course, which abounded in lizards, and try to catch them. The way of catching a lizard was to put your foot on it, so that the lizard was firmly held under your instep. Then it was possible to pick it up – rather gingerly, because they bit. Our chief nourishment out of doors was picking up pine-cones, of which there were any amount there, and knocking the seeds out and eating them. They tasted horribly of turpentine, but we quite liked them.')[9]

In that world beyond Eton he felt essentially a stranger. For community, for the sense of belonging, he returned to the Election, sharing in its pleasures and difficulties, its grievances and rewards. The hierarchical structure of College – a ladder up which one moved in a group – helped to strengthen the communal bond. On the lowest rung were the boys in Chamber – as we have seen, Blair's Election, at the time he entered College. On the highest rung were Sixth Form, consisting of the top ten boys, and Liberty, the next six. The boys in Chamber had to do fagging, to which they were summoned by long-drawn-out cries of 'Here', rather than 'Boy' as in Oppidan Eton, where fagging was generally more rigorous. (The only excuse for not replying to a summons was that one was not dressed, or was getting dressed. Certain boys, figures of Eton mythology, are said to have kept themselves in a permanent state of semi-dress to avoid fagging.) Throughout one's early years one had the terrors of 'wantings', those fateful moments when a younger boy would be summoned by the Sixth Form, perhaps (if lucky) merely to be given instructions, information or a verbal reprimand; or (if unlucky) to be beaten, sometimes for a specific offence, sometimes for his general good. Of course, as one went up the ladder and one's Election moved towards seniority, roles were reversed: the beaten became the beaters.

In this miniature world there were punishments and rewards; and for some the rewards were so alluring that the world beyond the school could not begin to compare. This latter group comprised the romantics and nostalgics for whom post-Etonian life was a long anti-climax.[10] But Blair was an ironist: his commitment to the community was never to become a passion (least of all in retrospect); he was too cautious, or sensible, for that, and again it was a matter of temperament.

An Eton College Election constitutes, by definition, a kind of junior intellectual élite; and the 1916 Election is recognized to have been outstanding, there and afterwards, as its members dispersed into the world beyond Eton. Orwell apart, the members of the Election went on to distinguish themselves variously as barristers, businessmen, civil servants, teachers, and scholars. Choosing examples only from the latter categories, we discern in Runciman, K.S., Sir Steven Runciman, the historian of Byzantium and the Crusades; in Mynors, K.S., Sir Roger Mynors, the Professor of Latin at Oxford; and in Longden, K.S., the late R. P. Longden, headmaster of Wellington (where Blair had spent a single term) who was killed when a bomb was dropped on the school during the Second World War.

Blair was on amicable terms with his Election as a whole and was more closely associated with its dominating members – he was not one himself – yet he gave the impression of being somewhat apart from them, of going his own way, not quite a heretic but not an enthusiast either. In that promising company he was not one for whom great claims were made or from whom great things were expected. There were boys who were brighter than he, who were better at games, who were better-looking. Inwardly, in that highly competitive world, it may well have rankled. Outwardly he maintained a judicious, sardonic calm, independent of the fads and fashions of the moment, and of those intimate friends that are traditionally a part of schoolboy existence. Indeed, intimacy is precisely the note that will be absent in his relationships – at Eton and afterwards – until his marriage to Eileen O'Shaughnessy in 1936. What is difficult to say, of course, is whether he enjoyed this position, or whether he adopted it as a form of self protection, or both.*

Self protection was linked closely to a dislike or fear of self-disclosure, as well as to a certain pleasure in secretiveness and mystification. Even to his friends he was something of an enigma: this was as true at Eton as later. One member of the 1916 Election writes, 'I knew Eric Blair well at Eton for four and a half years.' Then he adds the familiar, seemingly inevitable reservation: 'I was not a close friend of his; I do not remember that any of us were. That does not mean he was unpopular, or that most of us did not like him; we did, but . . . he soon developed a kind of aloofness which left him on good terms with everyone without being the close friend of any.' The note is sounded repeatedly by his contemporaries at Eton, even though, as one of them remarks, 'We in the Election had the best chance of knowing him, as we were with him every day.' But proximity did not make for intimacy: 'Never an intimate friend or confidant'; 'I knew Blair fairly well'; 'I was never a close friend though I knew him quite well'; 'We were all perfectly friendly and I don't think

* On the 'inward and invisible sense of being physically unattractive which worried Orwell throughout his life', Malcolm Muggeridge, a friend in his later years, makes the following comment: 'In actual fact he was by no means ill-favoured, and possessed of great charm; women, perhaps even more than men, found him appealing, but nothing would cure him of the conviction that his body was ill-proportioned and graceless. The feeling may well have been due to his illness; without any doubt the tuberculosis from which he died was gnawing away at him long before he admitted to himself or others that he was sick. There is also the fact that, at a school like Eton with its strong homosexual climate, a boy who is considered unattractive from that point of view may well become morbidly conscious of lacking physical charm. I once asked Cyril Connolly, who was a contemporary of Orwell at his preparatory school and at Eton, about this, and he agreed that my supposition might be correct. Orwell, he said, was regarded as being decidedly not pretty.'[11]

anyone disliked him. He and I were not close but had perfectly friendly relations.'

George Wansbrough, a member of the Election who became Captain of the School (and, in adult life, a Director of the Bank of England) remembers him as 'obviously a very different type of boy . . . The rest of us came from typical middle-class professional homes with conventional outlooks. Eric was very reticent about his family background. He made no mention of his father, but he talked a lot about his uncle [presumably this was his mother's brother, the manager of the golf club] who seemed to discuss matters with him in a very much more adult manner than the parents of the rest of us would have done.' But, in fact, Blair's background essentially was no different from that of other boys in the Election. His parents came from the same world of civil servants, rectors, barristers and businessmen as did the parents of his schoolmates, though the Blairs' place in that world was admittedly dimmed by lack of notable success and money: they were at the circumference rather than the centre. Blair's reticence, his sardonic enjoyment in keeping things in the dark – it seems extraordinary that he should not have mentioned his father's being in France – encouraged the notion that he was somehow different. At another school this might have made for difficulties; at Eton he got on very well.

An episode in which he figured within a month of his arrival in College extended his reputation beyond his own Election. Christopher Hollis, in the Election two years senior to Blair's, first heard of him as a successful practitioner of voodoo magic. As the 'tale' was reported to Hollis at the time and recounted by him years later in *A Study of George Orwell*,[12] Blair had taken a dislike to a boy in Hollis's Election for being noisy, especially at meals, and decided he must be punished. The boy, whom Hollis calls 'Johnson major', was Leslie Runciman, the son of the Liberal politician and shipping magnate. He had no knowledge of Blair's existence – the 'fags', who comprised the lowest Election, were generally an indistinguishable blur to the older boys. Runciman was not only noisy but also famous for having led a charmed life – during his first two years he had managed to avoid most of the beatings that were the lot of new boys in College. Blair, so Hollis heard, had decided to resort to a counter-charm. Lacking wax, he carved an image of Runciman in soap, which he stuck full of pins and placed under the mirror in his stall. It was only a matter of time before the magic would take effect. On Friday, Runciman's younger brother, Steven, who was also a member of the lowest Election and would become as close a friend as Blair would allow during his years at Eton, told his brother of the existence of the juju, and the curse it had set in motion. On Monday, and again on Tuesday, Runciman major, who had won for himself 'something of a reputation of being magically protected by the gods', was summoned by the Sixth Form and beaten for various infractions. Blair received the news with a 'smile of wry triumph', so Hollis heard, and he concludes the tale, 'That evening just before lights out . . . the soapen image slipped into a basin full of hot water and was dissolved. Blair did not re-erect it on its bracket. It was a symbol, we comforted the damaged elder brother, that the jealous gods were no longer athirst and the curse had been expiated.'

The story as Hollis heard it, and the power it reflects, are somewhat misleading. The truth is not without its Byzantine aspect. For according to Sir Steven Runciman it was he who carved the juju from the soap, with his friend Blair acting as assistant mage, and their chosen victim was not Leslie Runciman – whose fall from grace was a fortuitous coincidence – but another boy to whom they had taken a dislike. The juju was carved, pins were stuck into it, spells were cast. Then the two magicians waited for results, which were not long in coming: the next day the chosen one fell and broke his arm. This proof of their magical power so intimidated them that they decided to conduct no further experiments. But in a veiled (and perhaps threatening) way, the story was related by Steven to his older brother: would his turn be next? And indeed it was: the two successive beatings, coming so promptly, could be made to seem magically induced and apparently were. It was a feat neither magician had counted on, and Steven, as a younger brother, thought it prudent to yield to Blair a major share of the credit. Thereafter he enjoyed a certain *cachet*. As the incident filtered down to Hollis it convinced him that 'Blair must be "an odd fellow" and that it would be amusing to get to know him'. He concludes:

So the next time that we passed each other in the passage I said to him 'Hullo, Blair' – which was an outrageous thing to say to a fag. He replied 'Hullo' and smiled a little feebly.

There are limits to daring, and for the moment I could think of no more to say. So after stopping and staring at one another we both passed on without a further word. It was our first conversation, and it left on me the impression that here was a boy of peculiar humour – a saturnine perhaps and not wholly benevolent humour but above all a humorist. So he certainly was. It is as such that I primarily remember him – as a boy saying and doing funny things.

In spite of this promising beginning, Hollis and Blair never became close friends, partly because of the hierarchic nature of the Election system, partly because Blair was closer in temperament to such members of his own Election as King-Farlow, 'a boisterous sceptic', or Steven Runciman, who Connolly remembers as dividing the world into 'the stupid and the sillies'. Such a world view would particularly appeal to Blair, and his meeting with Runciman was an act of recognition: one sceptic welcoming another into the brotherhood. Connolly himself, the first close friend, came up from St Cyprian's the next year; and, as before, the two went for walks on Sundays, talking of Art and Life and other Subjects – it was now that Blair made his prescient remark that, whoever won the war, England would emerge from it 'a second-class nation'. But the intimacy was not resumed on its old terms. Even without the Election barrier to surmount, they discovered that, as Connolly put it, 'we belonged to two different civilizations. He was immersed in *The Way of All Flesh*; and the atheistic arguments of *Androcles and the Lion*, I in the Celtic Twilight and Lady Gregory's resurrected Gaelic legends.'[13] And there were differences of temperament too that in adolescence make for divergence – which is not to say that the friendship between them ended; rather, it shifted to another, less dominant key.

Blair was fortunate in his Election, and he was fortunate too in being at Eton when he was – a juxtaposition or combination of person, place, and time singularly favourable to him as 'the young cynic', 'the Election atheist', 'a boy of peculiar humour'. The school, like much of the country itself, was curiously ambivalent in mood as the war drew to a close. There was the belief, originating in nostalgia, that everything would go on as it had in the pre-war past: a return to the time-honoured certainties and pieties of English life. And there was the counter-belief, originating in disillusionment, that the aftermath of the war would see a repudiation of the past that had brought it into being, and change and uncertainty for English life in the future. The two contrasting attitudes had a first symbolic expression at Eton on 11 November 1918.

The celebration to mark the war's end was in the best tradition of schoolboy gaiety. One happy young Oppidan in his first year wrote to his mother:

On the Monday of the Armistice at 10.40 a.m. the Headmaster announced that it was to be a half holiday and a *non dies* (that is no work at all) on the morrow. Then a riot commenced, all the school rushed up and down the streets yelling and screaming, one person was beating a bathtub, another a teatray, and you never *heard* such a noise, then for two or three days cheering and singing and fireworks continued and I nearly burnt the house down, then Mr Booker gave a banquet, with fruit salad and chicken and pheasant and cider . . . and then we carried a maid up and down the house and sang songs until nearly 10 o'clock. Japanese lanterns were hung outside the houses, and the place is covered in flags. I have a Union Jack out of my window and a Belgian Flag inside the room. Oh, it was great fun . . .[14]

But also on the day of the Armistice, a large group of Etonians marched upon the Commander of the Officer Training Corps at the school and demanded his resignation now that peace had come.

College in the period immediately after the war gained the reputation of being rather 'Bolshie'. The new atmosphere, anarchic, questioning and anti-authoritarian, was one in which Blair thrived: he became, as Hollis tells us, 'a notable leader'. Changes in what had hitherto seemed an inflexible structure were effected in College, and Blair played at least some part in bringing them about. Granted this was 'revolution' on no more than a schoolboy scale, it seems a not inappropriate scale for schoolboys. To act on behalf of a principle in which one believes, even if it is only the injustice of excessive beatings by the Sixth Form, seems not wholly contemptible. Orwell, however, will have none of this – looking back fifteen years later, he is prepared to credit Blair at Eton chiefly with being an 'odious little snob'. Inevitably so. For Eton is the citadel of privilege, privilege breeds snobbery,

snobbery is the vice of the privileged classes: this was the dogma Orwell the polemicist extracted from the experience of Blair the schoolboy.

Like most dogma it has its own degree of truth. There is no question that Blair was affected by, and profited from that democratic élitism, or élitist egalitarianism, with which a supremely self-confident, privileged institution (such as Eton) is prepared to treat its members, and which is most noticeable at Eton in College. Orwell's complaint of snobbery has little to do with how Blair was regarded by his fellow Etonians, and much to do with how they, he among them, regarded all those others outside the pale. Simply by being there, inside, one was better, no matter how peculiar one's behaviour might be, and more privileged than those outside. As a school at the very top Eton was self-confident enough to tolerate a wide spectrum of non-conformity, even the peculiarities of 'bolshies' and revolutionaries. Yet all the while it went about its appointed task of turning out Etonians, conformists and non-conformists alike, with their hardly being aware of the process, though its mark would be unmistakable and ineradicable.

By the end of the war, having been at the school for a year and a half, Blair already bore the stamp. In the spring of 1918 his mother had moved from Earl's Court to a flat in Mall Chambers, Notting Hill Gate, which would be home for the family for the next three years. Also living in Mall Chambers at that time was the young poet Ruth Pitter, who had been working as a Junior Clerk in the War Office, and become a good friend of the Blairs, especially Marjorie. When Eric was at home on holiday Miss Pitter met him for the first time. He was five years younger than she, most memorable to her then for his pair of perfectly matched light blue eyes, and she thought him unmistakably the young Etonian, in his manner, dress, and way of speaking. (So too people later would claim that Orwell was recognizably an Etonian, though in his writing he would be making a determined effort to disentangle himself from it, and to disavow its effects upon him.)

He was at the school for five years, the greater part of them in the period of anti-*blague*. For Blair it provided a kind of objective correlative: the cynicism and questioning spirit, so characteristic of the time and place, especially when his Election had control of things, corresponded to something already there in his own nature, something that had been there since childhood. But now the outward world, in its disillusionments and rejections, seemed to justify his way of feeling. When he and his fellow Etonians marched on the Commander of the Officer Training Corps on Armistice Day, the episode announced a new tone for a new age: *post-war*.

It is a tone so much written about and experienced in the half-century since it was first heard that it requires no definition or documentation. But at Eton there had been premonitory murmurs even before the war's end. The shift in mood, with its repudiation of the past and espousal of the new, is foreshadowed in a mocking editorial in the *Eton College Chronicle* for 1918: 'This school is not going to be much fun in a little while ... look out for soft collars, they'll be the first sign. That in itself will mean a good many Masters sans starch, sans everything ... Then of course you'll have rational dress by and by; flannel shirts, too, open at the neck; why not sandals? and no hat? Then schoolmistresses.'

A year later the change in mood that had been predicted jokingly was accepted seriously. There was a tradition in College, inaugurated in 1878 by J. K. Stephen and faithfully observed since, that the Captain of the School should write a Retrospect for the College Annals – records of their time there, kept by the Collegers themselves. In his Retrospect for 1919 the Captain of the School felt obliged to write: 'There are some who fear for the present restless state of College, and prophesy a dreadful end for her; but let such remember that, after all, there *has* been a War, and that peace has enabled many to stay on who had expected to serve; and that when unrest is universal, it is only natural that some trace should be found within our walls, and that it is inevitable that the general relief should have resulted in a certain amount of rowdyism.'[15]

Rowdyism, in the circumstances, seems an inappropriate word; the flight from tradition that was a characteristic of those first post-war years was sufficiently strong that *no* Retrospects, of any kind, were written for the College Annals in 1919–20 or 1920–21. And the Retrospect for Summer 1922 tells of the attempts within

College to make it a more liberal institution – this would be the work of Blair's generation, the Election of 1916 arrived at the top. The Captain of the School recorded that they had managed to reduce enmity between Elections, and had eliminated what they thought to be the abuses by College Pop,* chiefly that group's having appropriated to itself exclusive use of the Reading Room which had just been reconstructed as a Memorial to the sixty-seven members of College who had died in the war. The point at issue had to do with assumptions of unjustified privilege rather than with misuse of a Memorial of the War. (*That* had already become a subject for mockery, as is evident from this announcement in *College Days*, the humorous magazine of which King-Farlow and Blair were editor-publishers in 1920 and 1921: 'It has been unanimously decided that the Eton War Memorial shall consist of a nunnery. The site chosen for its erection is the School Field.') Summing up, the Captain of the School (Denis Dannreuther, who was first on the list of the 1916 Election) could include as achievements of his Election that it had reduced the number of beatings to a minimum, and generally had substituted 'a more harmonious system of government for the old methods of repression and spite'.[16]

The Master in College at this period was John Crace, a classicist, who did not take too enthusiastically to the new, reformist ideas put forth by his charges. Still, it was noted in the Annals that 'he has co-operated with every Sixth Form and helped to carry out its ideas for the benefit of College'. This would suggest some degree of tolerance on Crace's part. But Blair was a trial for him – one suspects he would have been too sardonic and irreverent for almost any schoolmaster to cope with especially outside the classroom. Opinions of Crace vary: some remember him as 'a kindly man', others as 'a sex-obsessed prude'; but all are agreed that he was lacking in humour and, as such, easily teased. A story, well known at the time, tells of an encounter between Crace and Blair over an allusion he believed Blair had made to him in a burlesque in *College Days*, though nothing in

* College Pop – a debating society within College that corresponded, but on a much less grand scale, to the Eton Society, or Pop, the most fashionable group in the entire school and predominantly Oppidan, although some of its members were Collegers. College Pop itself went into a decline in these years and did not start to hold debates again until 1923.

the magazine carried a signature. According to the story, whose source appears to have been Blair himself, the Master stormed into his room, waving a copy of the offending publication, and announced, 'Blair, either you or I must go.'

'Well, sir,' Blair replied in what a contemporary describes as his 'Woosterish' drawl, 'Then I think it better be you.'

It fell to Crace also to prepare Blair for confirmation in the Church of England, an unenviable duty since Blair was by then – inevitably, one might say – a confirmed sceptic, with little interest in religious or theological matters. He told his friends that at one of their discussions, when Crace had pointed out the power and helpfulness of the Holy Ghost, he remarked that he, Blair, had personally always considered 'Old Man Ghost' rather a joke. But this sort of showy cynicism did not always go down well, and at least one member of the Election recalls 'an address by the Reverend Neville Talbot in the school library, in the course of which he said something about "the young cynic – and he is a real stinker, isn't he?" which we felt was a cap that fitted Eric.'

He would never pretend to beliefs that he did not have, and his sceptical attitude was not dented when he went up from Crace to Alington, the Headmaster, for further religious instruction. He had been reading with the greatest pleasure Shaw's preface to his recently published *Androcles and the Lion* in which an account of the gospels is set forth, very different in tone from what one would be likely to hear from an Anglican clergyman and one much more to Blair's own taste.* When he in his turn wrote a particularly irreverent, neo-Shavian essay and presented it to the headmaster, Alington, more worldly than Crace and not without humour, declared that while he did not mind impertinence to himself, he would not tolerate it to God, and gave Blair the standard hard punishment – 'Take a *Georgic*' – that is, to write out four to five hundred lines of Latin verse. (It should be

* e.g., '... the story of a prophet who, after expressing several very interesting opinions as to practical conduct, both personal and political, which now are of pressing importance, and instructing his disciples to carry them out in daily life, lost his head, believed himself to be a crude legendary form of god; and under that delusion courted and suffered a cruel execution in the belief that he would rise from the dead and come in glory to reign over a regenerated world. In this form, the political, economic and moral opinions of Jesus, as guides to conduct, are interesting and important: the rest is mere psychopathy and superstition.'

noted that Alington let him off the punishment; nor did Crace ever take disciplinary action against him for his rudeness – which suggests that adults, at least, found Blair more tolerable than Orwell was willing to concede.)

In due time, along with the others of his Election, the young cynic was confirmed by Bishop Gore in the Eton Chapel. But the cricket field rather than the Chapel provides the setting for the most characteristic of the stories having to do with Blair and religion at Eton. Hollis tells how Noel Blakiston, newly arrived in College, was approached on the field by Blair with paper and pencil in hand. The following Shavian dialogue ensued:

BLAIR: I'm collecting the religion of the new boys. Are you Cyrenaic, Sceptic, Epicurean, Cynic, Neoplatonist, Confucian or Zoroastrian?
BLAKISTON: I am a Christian.
BLAIR (gravely): Oh, we haven't had that before.[17]

In College the days began early. There was Early School before breakfast, from 7.30 to 8.20; then, three hours of classes and an hour with one's tutor (in Etonian parlance, 'm'tutor'). Lunch was at two. After it came organized games; then, on three afternoons each week, a further two hours of classes. Three days a week were half-holidays: those afternoons were also largely devoted to games, whose importance was crucial, not only as they related to *corpore sano* but also to one's popularity – to play noticeably hard on the field was to be admired; whereas to work noticeably hard in the classroom was to be a 'sap'.

M'tutor – the so-called classical tutor – was a significant figure, for it was his duty to act as academic and personal supervisor. Blair was particularly fortunate in this regard. He first was in the charge of A. S. F. Gow, then an assistant master and later to gain a distinguished reputation as a classicist at Cambridge. Gow – 'Grannie' Gow, as he was known to the boys among themselves – recognized, under the shyness and surliness of Blair's manner, an authentic intelligence, and unlike Crace he was more amused than offended by his cynicism. For his part, Blair, privately, was fond of Gow, and over the years was to keep in touch with him. In public, however, he took the patronizing tone that would be expected from him – Gow's love of Homer was dismissed as 'sentimentality', and of Italian painting as 'affectation', and he wrote for the titillation of his friends a scabrous rhyming dialogue between Crace and Gow. It was the custom for four or five boys in the Election to gather in Gow's rooms on Sunday evenings, bringing with them to read aloud essays, poems or stories of their own, something apart from the work they wrote for their English master, Hugh Macnaghten. Blair enjoyed writing stories that pointed a moral, and Gow encouraged this – an act of kindness chiefly, one gathers. King-Farlow, a member of the group, found them irritating to listen to, in their self-conscious simplicity and banal point – i.e., 'Honesty is the best policy.' It should be emphasized that his unenthusiastic response to Blair's writing was not exceptional. James Gibson, who was with him in Macnaghten's English class in 1918–19, recalls that his essays were never singled out for praise there, which is suggestive because Macnaghten was 'always very keen to commend any boy who wrote well or commanded telling phrases'. In fact, none of Blair's contemporaries, or teachers, ever thought his writings at Eton remarkable – he was not one of those golden youths upon whose brow the laurel seemed destined to descend. Orwell himself looked back upon what he wrote with a cold, dismissive eye.*

He wrote facilely and plentifully, but without the kind of distinction, those first stirrings of talent however awkward, that one might expect from a future writer. There was nothing in his writing to set him apart. By definition, any boy in College is trained to write a clear, intelligent sentence: it is one of the marks of an Etonian. For his tutors and masters, over his four and a half

---

* Considering his ultimate development as a master of the plain style, it was probably just as well that he was not one of Macnaghten's boys, for Macnaghten was addicted to the 'beautiful'; as an admirer of Pater, he would not have admitted Shaw to the canon. Connolly, in *Enemies of Promise*, writes of him: 'Although a fine teacher, his learning possessed the faults or rather the literary vices of his time. He was an ogre for the purple patch, the jewel five words long, the allusion, the quotation, the moment of ecstasy . . . He told us the most beautiful word in the English language was "little", he liquidated his "r's" in reciting and intoned poetry in a special way . . .

> and hear ver bweeze
> Sobbing in ver little twees.

Jolly good! he would exclaim, and to hear him chant "Ah, poor Faun – ah, poor Faun" was a study in pity which made his severe and even harsh discipline appear the more surprising.'[18]

years, he must have written a vast quantity of essays: all are lost and none are remembered. And he wrote verse and stories for the two periodicals with which he was associated in College.

The first of these was *The Election Times* – Editor, Mr Mynors; Business Manager, Mr Blair; Art Manager, Mr King-Farlow – published from No. 32 Lower Passage. It was entirely the work of the 1916 Election, and it made five appearances, in March and June 1918, in November 1919, and in April and July 1920. There was only one copy of each issue for the periodical was produced literally by hand – each author, under a pseudonym or anonymously, writing out his own contribution, with Mr King-Farlow making the drawings directly on the page – and it was available for reading by other members of the Election at a charge of sixpence each.

Only one issue of *The Election Times* appears to have survived: No. 4, the issue for Monday, 3 June 1918.* Three of its unsigned contributions, a poem 'The Wounded Cricketer', a story 'The Slack Bob', and a parody of Sherlock Holmes, 'The Adventure of the Lost Meat-card', are said to have been written by Blair. The story, the most considerable of these, very likely was one that he had read at Gow's Sunday evenings, and it is given here exactly as it appeared in *The Election Times*:

The Slack Bob

There was once a boy who was a slack bob. He used to walk about and say to his friends 'what fools you are to go worrying about rowing & playing cricket. Look at me.' And they used to look at him & go on their way. Then he went to the other slack bobs, & said to them, 'We are the only sensible people, aren't we?' But they used to pretend that they were not slack bobs, so they laughed & went on their way. So then he decided that he was the only sensible boy in the school. But that year he went to Lords', being unable to avoid it, & there his mother introduced him to his cousins. He had never seen them before, & they were all big fat noisy girls with red hair, seven in number. 'Why aren't you in the eleven?' asked Agatha, who was the eldest. 'I expect he's in the second eleven,' said Tabitha, the next. 'Are you?' said the third, who was called Grace (she turned her toes in & squinted). 'Eer, no. I'm afraid I'm not very fond of cricket,' said the boy. 'Perhaps he's a wetbob,' squeaked Beryl, the fourth. 'Yes,' said the boy, glad of the

* It is the copy belonging to Mr King-Farlow, who very kindly made it available to us.

chance, 'I'm a wetbob.' 'I don't like rowing,' said Mary, the youngest, who was considered the family beauty. 'You're in the Eight, of course?' said all the other six together. 'No, not quite,' said He, 'but,' He went on desperately, 'I'm not far off it; I've got my Lower boats, & I'll get my Upper boats next first of March.' 'That's not bad' said Eliza, the fifth sister. 'I bet I'd be in the Eight if I was a boy,' said Maudie, the sixth. By the end of the day He had told them that He was going to win junior sculling, & probably be in the Eight next year. But this made them so fond of him that he wished he had told them the truth. At last however he escaped, & thought that all was well.

A few weeks afterwards a postcard came saying 'We are all coming to watch you. I hope you win,' & signed by Agatha. 'What's happening today?' he asked a friend. 'Junior sculling,' said the friend. The boy turned pale, but he went & met them. 'If you win I'm going to give you a nice kiss,' said Grace. 'We all will' said Agatha. 'I'm sorry, I can't row,' said he, 'I've hurt my arm.' 'Never mind,' said Tabitha. 'I'm not allowed to, though,' he said. 'Don't mind that,' said Grace. 'But I can't,' said he. 'Coward!' said Mary. 'You're letting us all down,' said Eliza. 'Never mind,' said Agatha, 'we'll all come & have tea in your room now, & next year we'll come & watch you in the Procession of Boats.'

Moral. Honesty is the best policy.

The second of the publications with which Blair was associated was *College Days*, which he and King-Farlow inherited from the previous editor, George Binney, and which they published in 1920 and 1921. It was professionally printed, and, as King-Farlow has suggested, of interest to its editors as a money-making rather than a literary enterprise. And as such it did them very well: a net profit of £86 in 1920, and £128 in 1921. There was a wide circulation among Old Boys who returned for the Eton–Harrow match, when a number, priced at a shilling, was cannily brought out, and it carried several pages of paid advertisements – for Erasmic Shaving Stick ('Does not Dry on the face'), for Pascall Versailles Chocolates, for Aertex Cellular Clothing, and along with Rolls Royce and Sunbeam, for the Chalmers, America's Favourite Six ('Tell the "Pater" about the Chalmers – you'll get him interested from the start. It's no end of a corking car, good to look at, topping to run, and you don't require a science degree to understand its works'). Read from the disadvantage point of fifty years on, its humorous contents (unsigned, as in *Election Times*) aren't noticeably risible, though in its day it was thought to be 'highly entertaining and scurrilous' – in fact, this was the publication that had so aroused the ire of the Master in College. But for the outsider, the drawings, all by King-Farlow, are much the liveliest aspect of it.

Orwell, in his famous essay of 1947, 'Why I Write', tells us that the important writing he was doing at this time (and for several years more) was not on the page but in his head – a continuous fantasy in which he figured as someone to observe, and written, so to speak, in a style that altered as it reflected the writers he was reading and admiring. There is no question that he was a 'late developer' as a writer. His first professional publication was literary journalism for a Paris weekly (on censorship in England) when he was twenty-five, and only hindsight of an exaggerated kind would detect there the future author of 'Shooting an Elephant'. Whereas Connolly's first professional publication, also literary journalism, was a piece on Sterne, written when he was twenty-three, and in its style and poise a logical ancestor to *The Unquiet Grave*. Which is only to say that some writers are more precocious than others, and that a study of the making of a writer must take into consideration a good deal more than his juvenilia – the life as a whole, in which the juvenilia may be only an insignificant part.

There were two terms in 1919 when Blair switched his concentration from Classics to Science. During that period he left Gow and went successively to three tutors: first, George Lyttelton, who took him in Extra Studies in English Literature, and who formed a Literary Society of which Blair was a member; second, John Christie, newly-returned as a master to Eton from the battlefields of France, where he had won the Military Cross;* and third, M. D. Hill. With Hill he did Extra Studies in Biology, which yielded a memorable occasion when they dissected a jackdaw Blair had shot with his catapult. Nonetheless, in 1920 he returned to Classics, and Gow again became 'm'tutor'.

His slow, undistinguished but steady academic progress is recorded in the complexities of the *Eton College Calendar*, which is the basis for the summary that follows.

* Christie was at Eton until 1922. In that year he came into his inheritance, having satisfied the condition that he work for a while. There is no record of his having influenced the musical life of Eton (or Blair) as he was to influence the musical life of England generally by founding the annual festival of opera at his country house, Glyndebourne, in the 1930s.

In 1917 he was a first year specialist in Classics, ranking low in the class. In the first term of 1918 (Lent), he was more or less in the same position. (A typical week's programme at this time would consist of one session of Divinity, seven of Latin, six of Greek, three of French, two of English, three of Mathematics and three of Science.) In the Summer term of 1918 he moved up to the First Remove of the Middle Division of the Fifth Form. But at this point he abandoned the notion, or was advised to abandon the notion, that he was one of those destined for great academic accomplishments, or to win prizes (he never did win any) and changed from a Classical specialist to the less demanding category of Classical General. In Mathematics he was not doing well at all; rather better in French. But in the next term, Michaelmas 1918, he made another change, this time to Science, perhaps in a vain attempt to find himself, academically speaking. He was now in the Third Remove of the Upper Division (B) of the Fifth Form.

Science seems never to have been a passion; in any case, it is hard to say how he could have succeeded in this category, when he was already in the lowest possible Mathematics group for his Form. On the other hand, he was still doing well in French (with Mr Montmorency) and adequately in Classics (with Mr Mc-Dowall). In the Lent term of 1919 he had moved into the Second Remove of the Upper Division of the Fifth Form. He was still doing Science – John Christie had become his tutor. He continued to do Classics (with Mr Kindersley); he still lagged in Mathematics, in the VIIth group out of seven; in French he was in the IId group out of six. But most of his work this term was in Physics. Thanks to the College system of moving an Election upwards as a group, he moved upward, though most of his friends were in higher classes in the same division.

The next term, Summer 1919, he had moved up only one Roman numeral, still doing Science: Chemistry and Physics (Mr Christie); Mathematics (Mr Huson) – he had improved there, and was now in the VIth group out of nine; and French (Mr Larsonnier) in the Ist group.

Then, in the Michaelmas Term of 1919, having given Science a full year's trial and proved that he was not meant to be a scientist, he made another change, and became a so-called General Division specialist. His subjects were Divinity, Geography, Ancient History, French, Shakespeare, and Latin; and he returned to where he had begun, with Mr Gow. There was another move up, and he was now in the third group of the First Hundred of the Fifth Form, the group just below Sixth Form. In the next term, Lent 1920, he continued to pursue the same course; in the Summer term he had advanced to the Second Division. In July, when he did Trials, the end of term examinations, the results were as undistinguished as might have been predicted. Unlike a number of other boys in the 1916 Election – Denis Dannreuther, for example, or Roger Mynors, or Steven Runciman – he was not a brilliantly endowed scholar; he could not be expected to triumph in the exam by sheer bravura; nor had he descended to 'sapdom' and chosen to work hard at his studies. That term the top grade recorded was 83·8. Blair's was 29·7 – which placed him 117th on the list of 140. Only one of his Election had a lower grade.

In Michaelmas term 1920 he did mostly History and Classics in the General course, and he continued, alone of his Election, to pursue the same course in the Lent term of 1921. The next term, Summer 1921, he made a final change, from General Division to Classics. This brought him back with his Election and he took some classes with the Headmaster: Divinity, of course, but also Homer and Lucretius. His last term at Eton, Michaelmas 1921, he was in the Sixth Form, the top of the school, although he had got there largely by seniority; and he continued with Classics, Euripides, Horace, as well as some other subjects. He was receiving the best education that Eton had to offer – and so by general consent the best education an English schoolboy at that time could hope to receive. But it cannot be said he responded to the opportunity with much enthusiasm: from first to last the performance was lack-lustre. Academically, he was a very ordinary schoolboy.

For his distinction at Eton – the degree to which he was *not* ordinary – one must look beyond the classroom. Not, however, to the playing-field, where the heroes of a school come into being. 'He was not good at the ordinary run of our classical studies,' a member of the Election comments, 'his "games" were no better.' And another: 'He was never very much good at games.' And a third: 'Organized games, with the regimentation, exhortation and dragooning which sometimes goes with them, depressed and annoyed him.'

It was not that he was anti-sports. He would take up unorganized games enthusiastically. 'Fives is a pleasant, not too strenuous game,' Maurice Whittome, a member of the Election, recalls, 'of which Blair and I were both very fond. It was played from January to March, and I used to be accosted two or three times each week by Blair asking "Fives after 12?" That was the only time of day at which one could be sure of finding a Fives court free. As at other games, Blair was not very good, but I was only a little better, and it did not matter who won; all one needed was four boys not too different in skill.'

Of all sports he most enjoyed swimming – not competitively, but for its own sake; he was indifferent to 'swimming fast or diving stylishly' – and this was a lifelong taste. At Eton he and his friends from the Election, sometimes joined by Connolly, would come to swim at a sharp bend in the Thames, where the river flows deep and fast, opposite the Windsor race-course. This was 'Athens', which Blair, with his sensitivity to smell, claimed to have 'a subtly delicious exhalation of its own', and King-Farlow, who was an *habitué* of the bathing parties there, catches their special quality: 'Apart from swimming, it was idyllic simply lying about in the sweet hay at Athens, watching the river flow on, conversing about life, memorizing from Theocritus and Gibbon.'

In the jargon of the school, Blair was a 'wet-bob', which meant that in summer his official athletic commitment was to the river rather than to the cricket field. But this did not save him at the time of inter-house competition from being forced to take a place in the Junior house cricket eleven. The experience is reflected in eighteen unsigned lines of free verse for *The Election Times*. Under the title 'The Wounded Cricketer (Not by Walt Whitman)' the poet writes in the first person as a wet-bob who was trying to play cricket, 'Not that I wanted to but because I had to', is hit in the eye by a ball, and then lies face-down in the grass, counting grass blades and meditating – a preferable fate, apparently, to playing the game. He concludes, in a line unmistakably not by Walt Whitman, 'I don't think I shall move. I feel nice and comfortable.'

King-Farlow, given, like Blair himself, to a cynical view, observed that as his friend grew taller and heavier, his attitude towards games began to change. It will be recalled that when Blair first came to College in May 1917 he was not yet five feet four inches; King-Farlow, entering on the same day, was already five feet eight inches, but over the next four and a half years he would grow barely another inch. Blair, however, seemed never to stop. In the summer of 1919 he had reached five feet seven inches, but still felt himself 'undersized and puny'. Two years later, over six feet in height and proportionately heavier, he was playing football enthusiastically, sometimes 'sadistically', but never quite impressively enough to win his colours for it.

He also played in a game that is largely the speciality of College, and perhaps the most arcane of Etonian sports, the celebrated Wall Game. (Collegers celebrate it; outsiders wonder at it; a photograph of the game does little to clarify it.) It appears to be a kind of scrimmage or roughhouse played between two teams interlocked in deep mud alongside a brick wall, 110 yards in length – the actual playing area is 120 yards by five – the object being to secure goals, 'at one end throwing the ball against a garden door, at the other end against a mark on a tree'. Since the rules of sportsmanship do not apply, nor do subtleties of technique, and since almost any defensive means are permissible, to score a goal is no mean feat – between 1945 and 1967, for example, it happened only once in the annual matches between College and the Oppidans.

As one would expect at Eton, the game has its history, going back in its present form to the early eighteenth century when the Wall itself was built, although something like it had been played there long before. Over the years since it has acquired a terminology so esoteric as to be impenetrable: let 'Good Calx' and 'Bad Calx' stand as representative examples. The game, much of which takes place in and under mud that rapidly coats the players from head to foot, is not interesting to watch, but it is said to present the players with problems in the scientific use of force, and certainly it offers them the excitement of competition. (Although the Wall Game is primarily a College game, Oppidans play it too, and by tradition challenge the Collegers on St Andrew's Day, 30 November – for this match, sentiment is at its fiercest, tears of joy and sadness flow among the mud.)

Blair was an active member of the Wall team his last term in College, and a photograph of the team survives at Eton showing him with his arms crossed, cap down over his eyes, looking belligerent and powerful – with his great height and his weight at 170 pounds his value was assured. But the Wall Book, a detailed record of each match kept by the Keeper of the Wall, was not lavish in his praise: 'Erratic and not absolutely reliable, but is a long kick and has done some good things.'

That winter was an arduous one, with two matches in September, seven in October, and two in November, leading to the culminating event, the match on St Andrew's Day against the Oppidans. On 14 October James Gibson, the Keeper of the Wall, recorded that 'Blair made a fine kick more than half the length of the wall'. On 29 October he was made a regular member of the team, and in that match he helped score the famous goal that Hollis has written about in his study of Orwell and that John Lehmann, too, mentions in his autobiography. (A new boy in College, Lehmann wrote a glowing account of the event to his father.) Goals, as we have said, may not be scored for years – in this memorable instance, Hollis, who was playing on the opposing side, recalls that Blair made an extremely difficult throw to Longden, who 'passed it on to the door' and to immortality in the annals of the Wall Game.[19] In the match of 5 November, the Keeper of the Wall felt he deserved special mention. On 27 November he received his colours, and Gibson, who presented them to him, remembers that Blair was 'absolutely delighted' – they were his only athletic honour at Eton.

Finally, but anti-climactically, there was the great match itself on St Andrew's Day. College was defeated, '1 shy to nothing'. The Keeper, recording the score in the Wall Book, felt (not surprisingly) that it had been a disappointing game. But Blair had played well, and distinguished himself in the 10th 'bully', which lasted ten seconds, during which he 'kicked well out', saving the situation, and again in the 23rd 'bully', when he 'kicked soundly out of calx'.

This account of his participation in sports at Eton is not intended, except incidentally, to point towards their possible influence upon him later, in his life and in his writing. (There are a number of sporting images, allusions, and scenes in the books; the attribution to hated characters – e.g., Verrall in *Burmese Days* – of excellence at games; the choice of sports and attitudes towards them as class indices.) Chiefly it is meant to reinforce what has already been suggested: the fullness of Blair's commitment to the Etonian way of life. However sardonic his tone, he was not moved to rebel against it or abstain from it. However aloof in spirit, he was willing enough to take part in what was, after all, a central preoccupation of most of the boys and many of the masters. With no notable gifts as an athlete, he did manage finally to win his colours. No matter that Orwell might later disapprove of Blair the Etonian; while there, he enjoyed himself – or perhaps it would be more accurate, and truer to his temperament, to say that he did not *not* enjoy himself – and conformed readily enough to tribal customs and costumes. So in 1921 we see him at the annual Eton–Harrow cricket match, at Lord's, wearing the approved formal morning clothes – with a certain untidiness, but looking quite grand and impressive, except for those outsize feet.

But sports did not dominate his life, any more than they did the lives of his friends. Collegers were not philistines: this was true certainly of the 1916 Election and, if Blair was not outstanding among them as a scholar, he was legitimately of their company, for he read voraciously, he wrote, he thought, he took positions, passed judgements, held attitudes: it is in the fusion of these aspects of his life – and they are inextricably bound together – that we detect his individuality.

At fourteen, when he was first in College, he stood out as a precocious reader. George Wansbrough remembers that 'he used to quote writers like Bernard Shaw, Chesterton, H. G. Wells and I think Samuel Butler, as if he had read them and absorbed their points of view; I doubt whether any others in our Election had read more than a very little of these authors by the time we arrived at Eton.' There was that element of chance in his reading, so characteristic of the bookish adolescent who falls upon whatever comes his way, unhampered by preconceptions or academic obligations. It was in just this way, for example, that Elizabeth Bowen, who was at *her* school at this same time, happened to come upon a book of E. M. Forster's, *The Celestial Omnibus*, and the shock of recognition was all the greater for not having been introduced to it in the classroom.[20] For Blair there was a comparable revelation when he walked into a master's study, and, not finding him there, picked up a magazine from a table, leafed through it, and came upon a poem by which he was 'completely overwhelmed'. This was D. H. Lawrence's 'Love on the Farm'. Rather strangely, as Orwell later reported the occasion, he failed to notice the name of the author, and so the overwhelming moment did not have the sequel one might expect: that he would try to find more of Lawrence's poems. (Unlike Elizabeth Bowen, who, having read one book by Forster, was 'ready to go any lengths, any expenditure of pocket money to get hold of more from the same pen'.) It was not until five years later, when he was in Burma, that he read work of Lawrence's again – "The Prussian Officer' and others of his stories – and was deeply impressed. But perhaps at sixteen, in the range of his imagination and sympathies, he was not quite ready for Lawrence, for those highly-charged, seismic relationships between men and women, so different, say, from the articulate, witty and iconoclastic interchanges between the characters in Shaw that he then found so much to his taste.

As a reader he had been precocious only in the sense that he came very young to Shaw and Wells and Galsworthy; but these were staple reading for Englishmen of the time who were literate and progressive; and presently they were known in College. (*The Election Times*, No. 4, Mon. 3rd June 1918, contains a lampoon, 'The She-devil', 'by Rita Galsworthy [authoress of "The Mountain of Tears", "Divorce", "The Sin of Laura Paton", etc.]' – the work of Steven Runciman.) In succeeding years, though he continued to read avidly, he did not venture deep into the territory of the 'new'. (Not necessarily a fault, of course, but it must be kept in mind that he was at Eton when D. H. Lawrence and Virginia Woolf and T. S. Eliot and Wyndham Lewis were publishing their work, and were not wholly unknown to other Etonians.)

One writer he *was* ready for was A. E. Housman, a friend of Gow's who came down from Cambridge to lecture to the Literary Society. Housman was then at the zenith of his popularity, at

Eton as elsewhere. So Blair was not unusual in his enthusiasm, only perhaps in the length to which he carried it, for at seventeen he knew by heart most of the sixty-three poems of *A Shropshire Lad*. Two of them – 'With rue my heart is Laden/For golden friends I had', and 'Into my heart an air that kills/From yon far country blows' – he had to put into Latin verse, but even this did not diminish his affection for them. As Connolly acknowledged, in 1936, writing a revaluation of Housman shortly after his death, he is 'a poet who appeals especially to adolescence and adolescence is a period when one's reaction to a writer is dictated by what one is looking for rather than what is there'.[21] Leaving aside the question of what is truly there, and making no attempt to argue for or against Housman as a poet, one sees in Blair's case an immediate response to a cynicism agreeably akin to his own. Further, though *A Shropshire Lad* had been written in the last confident years of the Victorian epoch, it offered a cynicism unexpectedly suited to the immediate post-war mood.

A word which Orwell was to apply to Housman, in *his* revaluation in 1938, and which he uses a number of times in regard to his own years at Eton, is 'antinomian'. In this view Housman comes to represent – how justly is not in question – the repudiation of the official beliefs and conventions of the age. This, in essence, was the attitude of Blair and his friends, who, as 'Antinomians', claimed the right to set standards of their own. 'Antinomian' seems to have been virtually a vogue word of the period, current in everyone's vocabulary. 'College in Eric's time,' a member of the Election writes, 'was going through a rather antinomian phase,' and he adds that Blair was 'a strong supporter of the antinomian faction but could not have been called a leader of it'.

The word is defined as 'the theological doctrine that by faith and God's gift of grace through the gospel, a Christian is freed not only from the Old Testament Law of Moses and all forms of legalism, but also from all law including the generally accepted standards of morality prevailing in any given culture'. In post-war usage, it was, of course, robbed of its religious or doctrinal connection, and any previously accepted code could be substituted for the 'Law of Moses': the discredited wisdom of the Old Men of Whitehall, for example, or the outmoded pieties of the Archbishop of Canterbury, or the tradition-bound disciplinary structure upheld by the Headmaster of Eton College.*

Antinomianism; Scepticism; Disillusionment – they belong to the spirit of the age, and the spirit of the age originates in an historical fact: the cost for England of the war she had won – almost 800,000 dead – a generation of young men decimated. The fact would seem sufficient to explain the 'bad temper', as Orwell puts it, among those under forty. 'The mood of bitterness that emerged from the First World War,' a later scholar writes, 'has no like in any other war that England has fought; no other British army felt itself so betrayed, or so scorned the causes for which it fought. In that mood the post-war generation rejected altogether the world-before-the-war, its propriety, its overstuffed luxury, its conceptions of society and manners, its confidence in England and in Progress.'[22]

It is not surprising that a group of highly intelligent boys, approaching maturity though still at school, should have been affected – admittedly at their own level and on their own terms – by the spirit of the age. Orwell, looking back in 1936, offers an example of the period's 'queer revolutionary feeling': that in an English class at an unidentified Public School (he means Eton) fifteen out of sixteen boys included the name of Lenin on a list of the ten greatest men then alive. But there was an element of prankishness and teasing one's elders in this – as well as *naïveté* – that Orwell, making a polemical point, chose not to remember; and it did not follow from it (however 'bolshie' it might appear to startled Old Boys) that the fifteen would march out of the classroom and enroll in the Communist Party of Great Britain.

A peculiarity of Orwell's analysis of the mood of early post-war England is that it is based almost entirely upon Blair's experience of it at Eton – that was all that he knew at first hand, for from 1922 to 1927 he was out of England – and from that Etonian sampling he extrapolates and generalizes a sweeping view of the adult world that would have gone down nicely at an

* In practice, finally, 'antinomian' proved to be one of those high-flown words that can mean rather less than they are meant to mean. In 1936, reviewing Cyril Connolly's novel *The Rock Pool*, Orwell speaks of 'the kind of sluttish antinomianism – lying in bed till four in the afternoon and drinking pernod – that Mr Connolly seems to admire'. (Which is perhaps more priggish of Orwell than antinomian of Connolly.)

officers' mess in Burma: an England with 'bolshies' in fashion (but surely not in control?) and on every side 'half-baked antinomian opinions', ranging from 'humanitarianism' down to 'free love, divorce-reform, atheism [and] birth-control'. Orwell's implicit criticism has its point: that there was a good deal of revolutionary talk among the *bourgeoisie* and little else – much as a dedicated communist of the 1930s might legitimately complain of 'parlour pinks' who were not prepared to go down into the streets and into the party.

But it is a criticism that is hardly fair, or, looked at with much realism, applicable to Blair and his antinomian friends in College. Political rhetoric is always easier than political action, even for schoolboys, and what is remarkable, one would think, is that they should have done as much as they did – *there*. Orwell, never prepared to be less than harsh to Blair, must of necessity cast a suspicious glance at the revolutionary atmosphere in College. A more generous (and persuasive) view comes from his friend Francis Cruso, two years junior to him in College, who writes: 'Blair was naturally critical and impatient of nonsense, and that undoubtedly was the "ethos" of College too in those days. The First World War was just over, and boys of eighteen were no longer leaving to be shipped out to France and slaughtered. There was an atmosphere of sudden relief and freedom, and a feeling among the young (naïve and absurd, no doubt, but very natural) that we had a real chance to clear away the cant and rubbish of the past and Make All Things New.'

'Make All Things New' was a message that reached the school at many and sometimes unexpected levels. Things were in ferment. There was even a short-lived but intense period of *avant-garde* literary activity (precociously accomplished and the antithesis of Macnaghtanism) which was set off among a remarkable group of Oppidans: Brian Howard, Harold Acton and his brother William, Oliver Messel, Anthony Powell, and Henry Yorke (the novelist Henry Green); on their fringe were such Collegers as Cyril Connolly and Alan Clutton-Brock. They formed a Society of Arts, listening to music, looking at pictures, reading the 'New' (not *Georgian Poetry* but *Wheels*), and to some degree led the life of aesthetic worldlings in the context of a Public School – no mean feat, the more so as they managed not to collapse completely into the dandyism of the 1890s. In March 1922 they published for the first and last time an elegant 'little magazine', *The Eton Candle*, whose pages, bound in pink, offered small blocks of print surrounded by wide margins. Dedicated to an Etonian aesthete of an earlier age, Algernon Charles Swinburne, its fame spread far beyond Eton, and a greater contrast to the boyishness of *The Election Times* and *College Days* can hardly be imagined. There were poems and stories by the editor, Brian Howard (a protégé of Edith Sitwell), Harold Acton, William Acton and Anthony Powell, along with contributions from Max Beerbohm and three recent Old Etonians, Osbert and Sacheverell Sitwell, and Aldous Huxley.* Blair had no connection with this Oppidan group – although twenty years afterwards, in 1941, he and Anthony Powell (who knew him as George Orwell) met and became friends. His sole contribution to aestheticism, it might be said, was to lend a copy of *The Picture of Dorian Gray* to Cyril Connolly. Too late, however – time had moved on, it was the age of Lytton Strachey, and 'I could not swallow it,' Connolly wrote. 'It was not necessary.'

But these literary sorties into the New were marginal activities and had no noticeable effect upon the traditional current of Etonian experience. The central 'engagements', carried on under the banner of the New by the Antinomian or Liberal or Revolutionary faction, were aimed at changing a 'life style' rather than a 'prose style', and they did, visibly if temporarily, deflect the current: for a year or two tradition was subverted.

The centre of the revolutionary movement was the 1916 Election, and the 'moral leaders' of the Election (Connolly's phrase; we are drawing freely upon his account, which is admirably clear and detailed) were the so-called 'Caucus': Denis Dannreuther, Roger Mynors, Robert Longden, James Gibson, and R. M. Cazalet. They were 'five scholar athletes, animated, unlike the rulers of college, by post-war opinions. They hated bullying, beating, fagging, the election system, militarism, and

---

* From 1917 to 1919 Huxley was at Eton as a Temporary Assistant Master in English and French, as a replacement for one of the twenty masters at the Front. He drew upon his Eton experience to comic effect in the opening chapter of *Antic Hay*, but schoolmastering was an ordeal for him. He was ragged by the boys in his classes, who could do so with impunity because of his near-blindness – a cruel exploitation that Blair hated.

all infringements of liberty, and they believed in the ultimate victory of human reason.' Blair, though on friendly terms with the Caucus, stood somewhat 'aloof'. While he shared all their dislikes, he was temperamentally incapable of believing in 'the ultimate victory of human reason'. In Connolly's words, he was 'perpetually sneering at "They" – a Marxist–Shavian concept which included Masters, Old Collegers, the Church and Senior reactionaries'. At the same time, he held the belief, deeply and irretrievably, that in the 'great scrum of life', 'They' would be the winners, and he the loser. But cynicism did not immobilize him; if he could not share the idealism of the Caucus, he did not hesitate to join their battle.

The symbol of militarism at Eton was the O.T.C., the Officers Training Corps. In the Liberal view, 'The Corps was a joke; it had no business to be compulsory and any tendency to increase militarism among a war-weary generation must be exposed and ridiculed.' The O.T.C. was not a hallowed Eton institution – though developed from the earlier Eton Volunteers (or 'dog potters'), it had been established only in 1908 as a part of Haldane's programme of preparedness for the nation. During the war years its reason for being was self-evident, though its effectiveness might have been questioned. But as a post-war phenomenon it represented the outmoded, really detested thinking of the Old Men of Whitehall and their discredited associates, the Generals – the cast of characters of the poems of Siegfried Sassoon, and of the many, yet-to-be-written anti-war novels and memoirs. On the very day of the Armistice, as we have seen, came the first Etonian demonstration against the O.T.C.; and the Peace Celebrations of 1919, organized by the Corps as a kind of military triumph, provoked a riotous demonstration in the School Yard during which the boys invented mocking lyrics for the patriotic songs they had been expected to sing, and in general reduced the seriously-intended proceedings to a level of low comedy. Ridicule thereafter became the accepted weapon to bring out the absurdity of its pretensions, and Blair, as might be expected, was very good at this. Francis Cruso, who for a time was a member of his section of the Corps, recalls 'one sweating summer afternoon when we were on a Field Day somewhere in the Berkshire Downs. Blair sensibly decided that our uniforms were too hot and that we'd had enough of it; so he took us all off behind a distant haystack and we spent a pleasant "shirtsleeved" afternoon listening to him reading *Eric or Little by Little* [a famous, fatuous Public School novel] aloud. I can hear him too one day, as we marched along "In Fours", discussing Corporal Punishment with a friend and declaring, "Of course the whole thing's completely disgusting and barbarous." '

Since elderly bureaucrats are constitutionally unable to hear the voices of young men who do not have the vote, the O.T.C. remained at Eton, but until the approach of the Second World War it was not on the whole taken seriously. Achieving the status of a tolerable nuisance and deprived of whatever military significance it may have aspired to, it continued to lend itself to ridicule:

Signalling was delightful. One sat for hours beside a field telephone while little figures receded into the distance with the wire. 'Can you hear me?' 'No.' 'Can you hear me now?' 'No.' 'Well, try this.' 'This' was the morse-code machine and nimbler fingers than mine would fill the air with a drowsy song. Iddy iddy umpty umpty iddy umpty iddy . . . [23]

Student anti-militarism in the post-war years was an historical-universal as well as an Etonian phenomenon. But anti-Electionism, and the Election system against which it was directed, belong uniquely to the history of Eton College. Discipline in College – as it took physical form, beating, birching, caning, the Corporal Punishment that Blair called 'disgusting and barbarous' – was in the hands of the boys of Sixth Form (*not* the Masters, who were not allowed to cane), and much would depend, then, on their intelligence, humaneness, fairness, and emotional balance.

Of beatings as a mode of discipline there are differing opinions.

Rayner Heppenstall, a friend of Orwell's from the mid-1930s, in his book *Four Absentees*, credits Christopher Hollis with 'a good account of Orwell at Eton' in *A Study of George Orwell*, but complains that 'he expects us all to take a sympathetic interest in the sort of caning that most of us have only read about'. He continues:

Nobody seems to have told him that caning upon the buttocks has long been assumed by some of the male population to be a cause

123

of homosexuality at public schools and among public school men in later life.

What strikes the outsider as particularly shocking, however, is that much of this ritual beating is (or was) done not by the masters but by sixth-form boys. As a reward, so to speak, for sticking it out, Etonians of eighteen were allowed to spend their last year at school bruising the hind parts of younger boys.[24]

A different view is presented by J. D. R. McConnell, a house-master at Eton, in his book, *Eton – How It Works* (1967):

> The fact is that boys occasionally commit indiscretions which have to be sharply corrected. My view is that the alternative to corporal punishment may in the long run be more cruel to the offender. The salacious and picturesque stories of 'savage floggings' related by certain Old Boys to fascinated audiences are quite outside my experiences as a housemaster.
>
> Practically all boys accept beatings as a natural and well-established feature of the give-and-take boy world. It is the adults who surround the question with such sinister implications. Boys who have been wicked generally prefer to suffer a penance which, though painful, is swift and salutary.[25]

In a perfectly detached way it can be said that there is a difference between beating as a form of punishment and beating as a form of bullying. There seems to be general agreement that the Election immediately senior to Blair's were indiscriminate beaters, and along lines closer to Mr Heppenstall's thinking than Mr McConnell's. Painful experience only increased the idealistic fervour of the 1916 Election, some of whom, Blair among them, were still being subjected to mass floggings at the almost unprecedented age of eighteen. They believed that 'Corporal punishment was a relic of barbarism ... as bad for those who administered as for those who received it.' But there was little, in a practical way, that they could do to put their beliefs into effect until, in the hierarchical order, they themselves had arrived at the top, in the autumn of 1921.

Meanwhile, that summer of 1921 'feeling ran so high against the Captain of the School ... and the six other reactionaries in his election that they were cut to a man'. Most of them, as it happened, were members of the Debating Society – College Pop. So too were Dannreuther, Longden, Mynors, King-Farlow, and Gibson, the Liberal faction. So too was Connolly, who felt it was his friendship with the rowing men that had got him in, for if he had been put up by the Liberals, he 'would certainly have been blackballed'. So too was Blair, who was elected on 27 July – it was the one society of which he was to be a member – even though four blackballs were cast against him. Debates had become increasingly acrimonious: one, on the 'election system', and another, on 'corporal punishment', had almost ended in blows. And indeed, during Blair's remaining time in the society, no further debates were held, and in an effort to appease both factions the magazine subscription list was enlarged to include *The Workers' Dreadnought* as well as *Country Life*.

It was the custom to pass votes of thanks on those who were leaving from College Pop, but this year they were mainly the despised reactionaries of the senior Election.

For the first time in history [Connolly writes] these votes of thanks were blackballed. The genial ceremony collapsed: Cliffe the Captain of the School, Lea the Cadet officer of the Corps, Babington-Smith and the boys who beat King-Farlow and Blair and Whittome on trumped-up charges for political reasons faced the unprecedented verdict. Name after name was read out, the vote of thanks proposed and seconded, the ballot box passed, the blackballs counted, and the transaction noted down in the annals . . . The Master in College protested against the breach of tradition, the Old Tugs got to hear of it, the Vile Old Men [certain reactionary Masters] took it up, and there were whispers about Bolshevism which almost reached the news-papers.[26]

It is pleasant to report that when the 1916 Election reached Sixth Form and so were responsible for the discipline of College, they were not corrupted by power. Idealism continued to flourish, hatred of beating, bullying, and the enforced segregation of Elections was as strong as ever, and many of the reforms the revolutionaries had advocated were put into practice.* Denis Dannreuther, in his Retrospect for the College Annals, wrote:

When I was a fag it was considered a poor night for the senior if no one was beaten, and wantings occurred every night, whereas this last

---

* Rayner Heppenstall remarks that neither Connolly nor Hollis 'has told us whether Orwell himself in due course became an assiduous or an expert hand with the cane'. The answer to the question would seem to be No. None of Blair's juniors with whom we have talked, or with whom we have been in correspondence, have any recollection of having been beaten by him.

half it does not happen to have been necessary to use corporal punishment at all, scarcely a dozen to twenty wantings the whole half . . . It is early yet to judge the success of these experiments, and the universal prediction of 'the old men' *may* be verified, but I can at least honestly record that College has been in every way *happier* this year than at any time in the last six years.

Connolly, in his Retrospect for *Enemies of Promise*, sums it up as 'our short-lived and unpopular experiment in happiness',[27] for, as Blair might cynically have predicted, the new order gave way to the old, and the bad old traditions were presently resumed. Blair himself chose not to write anything for the College Annals – there was nothing unusual about this, many others abstained from contributing 'obituaries'. After his name there is a large blank (where his accomplishments and reflections might have been written) and in another hand is inscribed 'College Debating Society'. The Retrospects in the various years in the Annals record the quite precipitous swings back and forth between Elections of the moods of College – but the Election of 1916, in part because it has been memorialized so effectively by Cyril Connolly, will be remembered as one which attempted to move College into the post-war era.

The most famous day in the Eton calendar is the Fourth of June – the birthday of George III – that annual festival or ritual when parents and grandparents and old Etonians (the latter very often being also the former) gather to see offspring and friends, and to feel pleasantly romantic about the old school. As the most recent explicator of Eton has summed it up, it is 'an enormous family party'.

The day is crowded with events, from Chapel in the morning to the Procession of Boats and Fireworks in the evening. But the most serious event is 'Speeches', a series of declamations to a select portion of the assembled multitude by members of Sixth Form. For the Fourth of June celebrations in 1921, Blair was one of the boys chosen to deliver a speech.*

* It is pleasing to learn that the programme of Speeches for a Fourth of June in the 1960s included a selection from *The Lion and the Unicorn* by George Orwell. Among the other authors whose works were declaimed on that occasion were Goethe, Gladstone, Dante, Bertrand Russell, Aristophanes, Vanzetti, Dylan Thomas, and Osbert Lancaster.[28]

His participation – in the full rig of the ritual: knee breeches, silk stockings, buckle shoes, and the rest of court dress – was very effective and made a considerable, perhaps even a surprising impression upon his contemporaries, for he was not the sort of boy who would enjoy putting himself forward in the limelight. He had had slight dramatic experience before this: he had played Prince Charming in the Christmas theatricals at Bellehatch Park in the first year of the war; at Eton, in 1920, when George Rylands was producing *Twelfth Night* (and playing Viola), he had mocked the enterprise but consented to fill the role of a non-speaking officer; and the next year he allowed himself to be cast as a shepherd in *The Winter's Tale*. But Speeches was far more challenging. As it turned out, his flat voice, a liability in the theatre, worked to his advantage in the selection he had chosen.

He had gone to an author he admired, Robert Louis Stevenson, and extracted a passage from 'The Young Man with Cream Tarts', one of the three stories having to do with 'The Suicide Club' in the *New Arabian Nights*. It comes at the point in the story when the members of the Club have assembled to draw the two decisive cards, one to designate the member who will kill, the other his victim; and poor craven old Mr Malthus, who was an honorary member (did Blair appreciate the irony of Malthus in the suicide club? very likely) and had never thought he would draw a fatal card, indeed does so: the card calling for his murder. The episode, delivered in Blair's 'passionless, detached dry tones', proved chillingly effective.

To participate in Speeches on the Fourth of June; to belong to College Pop; to win one's colours at the Wall Game – these are not contemptible items in an Eton dossier. They suggest that Blair was qualified to put himself forward more than he did, might have been more at the centre of things. But he chose not to, fearful perhaps of becoming excessively involved and giving too much of himself. He preferred, no doubt with some private self-mockery, to be an attendant lord, one who would do to swell a progress, as T. S. Eliot had written a few years earlier.

Inevitably one asks Why? To find an answer – tentative, provisional and conjectural though it must be – one starts by admitting that Blair-becoming-Orwell is unique, whereas Blair-being-Blair is not. The child who is solitary by nature or disposition is not uncommon; nor is the solitary child who is given to fantasizing. Such was Blair, when very young and as he grew older. To be solitary has nothing to do with the 'realities' of one's situation: one can be alone in a room crowded with friends. Blair had his friends at Eton, yet it is striking how they are in agreement about his reserve, his aloofness, for all his 'friendliness'. Connolly describes Blair and King-Farlow as 'bosom friends', but against that one must balance King-Farlow's own comment, 'I was never sure that he really liked me.' Orwell tells us that for the first twenty-five years of his life he was writing a story in his mind, in which he himself played a central role; but while he describes the technique of the story, he does not tell us what it was about.

Real life and fantasy life allow equally for imposture. In real life, for example, one can pretend to be brave and act bravely, all the while knowing that one is an impostor – this is to act out a fantasy. Alternatively, one can in a fantasy dare to be a coward – as one would not dare to be in real life – and be punished for it. Bookish children take over characters from books they have read and assign them roles in their fantasies: there, often, they themselves become the characters, as Blair, at six or seven, thought of himself in his 'story' as Robin Hood. Such children (and adults), given to the pleasures and guilts of imposture, are to question the validity of the roles they are playing in 'real' life: to question their own authenticity – am I brave or a coward? am I the child of my boring parents, or am I the illegitimate child of a duke abandoned on their doorstep; or worse yet, am I the legitimate child of a duke, mysteriously exchanged in swaddling clothes with the child of a peasant? There is nothing unusual about this sort of thinking, of course: the whole of Gilbert and Sullivan seems to depend upon imposture. So does much of Verdi. Or the comedies of Oscar Wilde. Or *Der Rosenkavalier*. Or *Twelfth Night*. Or the story of Jacob and Esau. Mark Twain's (or Samuel Clemens's) *The Prince and the Pauper* is a classic example for every well-born or low-born bookish boy to ponder on. Then there are Dr Jekyll and Mr Hyde: which is the more 'real'? Not to speak of Dorian Gray, or the portrait of him hidden away in a room upstairs, becoming progressively more hideous. A boy of Blair's disposition might well be struck by the element of chance, or luck, or fate, as it determined one's life. As an Etonian one was the Prince; but twenty minutes away, on the road to Slough, one might as easily be the Pauper.

It can be argued that of all the books he discovered while at Eton, the one that was most to affect him was Jack London's *The People of the Abyss*. Years later it would have a direct influence upon the writing of the first book he was to publish, *Down and Out in Paris and London*. As an Etonian, Blair read of the 'abyss', and incorporated it into his fantasies and his life. Written in 1903, the book was (and still is) a vivid, powerful, and appalling first-hand account of poverty in the East End of London in the summer of 1902, during what were thought of as 'good times' in England. (It was the beginning of 'the Edwardian garden party'.) Jack London, by his own choice, underwent the ordeal – for how else, he asked, could one know, truly know, what poverty was? Having gone down into the 'under-world' and lived there – not so many miles distant from Notting Hill Gate, but the difference in life was immeasurable – he could write in his Preface with an authority denied to the sociologist, statistician, or clergyman: 'The starvation and lack of shelter I encountered constituted a chronic condition of misery which is never wiped out, even in the periods of greatest prosperity.'[29]

It was an experience of one kind to read in the Preface to *Major Barbara*, 'The greatest of evils and the worst of crimes is poverty,' and to go on from there to the dazzling pleasure of one of Shaw's most provocative and wittiest plays: a masterpiece of imposture, as any work of art must be. It was an experience of a different order to read the piling-up of details – gruesome, sordid, and pitiful all together – in London's account, the more painful for being so unmistakably a transcription. One might be moved to pity and guilt, reading of all that suffering, so remote from one's own life. And yet were these emotions truly authentic? (Questions of this sort were not uncommon during the years of the Edwardian garden party. They occur to the Schlegel sisters, thinking of the 'abyss', in E. M. Forster's novel, *Howards End*. They occur to Major Barbara herself.) Did one alter the current of one's life – go down the road to Slough – because of them? One had the fantasy of being guilty, of doing penance. Yet even guilt, it seemed, could be a form of imposture. To have a true experience of guilt one must first know for oneself the evil that inspires it. Or, to put it another way, one had somehow to get out of fantasy and into the real world.

In the summer of 1920, after the O.T.C. field exercise on Salisbury Plain (where he and King-Farlow had shared a tent), Blair went directly to Cornwall to join his parents on holiday rather than return first to the school.* Wearing his cadet uniform, he boarded the train, along with a number of other Etonians. At Seaton Junction, where the train stopped briefly, he got out of his compartment, carrying all his gear, intending to join a boy in another carriage. But as he was walking along the platform, the train began to move. Burdened down with kitbag and other paraphernalia, he found he was unable to get back on the train, and it pulled out of the station, leaving him behind. He seems not to have been alarmed or regretful; rather, one has the impression that he was enjoying himself – an adventure was about to begin. A thoughtful son, he first sent a telegram to his parents to say he would be late. Then, after waiting for two and a half hours, he boarded the train for Plymouth, where he expected to change to the connecting train for Looe. But when he arrived in Plymouth, he learned that the train for Cornwall had already gone, and there would not be another until the next morning. Now the sense of 'adventure' quickened. The post-office was already closed and so it was impossible to telephone his parents. He was alone: no one he knew, family, friend or housemaster, knew his whereabouts at that moment. Best of all, he had only a limited amount of pocket money: enough for his fare from Plymouth to Looe, and to choose between going without his evening meal or going without a bed – at the local Y.M.C.A. where the charge for a bed for the night was six-pence. He did not hesitate. He bought twelve buns, and spent the night sleeping in a field, under a large tree, in a clump of bushes. It grew very cold; the dogs in the neighbourhood

* The preceding December Mr Blair had been demobilized. Thereafter he was once again a retired gentleman, but less content in London than in Henley, where there had been cronies to talk with and the pleasures of a morning stroll along the river. A friend he had met while serving in France had recommended Southwold, the seaside town in Suffolk, as a place to live: there were no firm ties to hold the Blairs in London, and they moved to Southwold in December 1921.

barked; he slept fitfully. He got back to the station at Plymouth at about 5.20 in the morning, only to discover he had missed the first train, and had to wait until 7.45 a.m. for the next. When finally he arrived at Looe, there was a walk of four miles in the hot sun. All in all, it composed an adventure, as he wrote later to Steven Runciman, of which he was very proud. But, he added, 'I would not repeat it.'

This boyish adventure – so far from the abyss, and one that Orwell himself does not mention – offers a convenient example of the varieties of imposture. For Blair, in fantasy, he was an 'amateur tramp'. Passersby at twilight on the streets of Plymouth thought him a soldier not yet demobilized. In real life, of course, he was a schoolboy at Eton, wearing cadet uniform, who had missed a train. Least productive would be the imposture of a reader who would discern in this adventure an ironic prophecy of things to come – a prefiguration of *Down and Out in Paris and London*. For it is evident that Blair's emphasis in his adventure, quite normally and as one would expect, is centred on 'I, myself' rather than on 'I, feeling as another might feel'. That extraordinary identification with 'the others' that would find expression in the best of his writings was something yet to be learned.

Orwell, dashing off a witty sketch of himself as a seventeen-year-old snob and revolutionary, would have us believe that he divided his time between denunciations of the capitalist system and the rudeness of the working class. But this was no more than his metaphoric way of acknowledging how infinitely little he knew then about either the working class or the capitalist system. Before 1920 the official education of boys of what might be called the instructed class – for our purpose an inclusive category extending from lower-lower-middle up through upper-upper-middle into the high reaches of the aristocracy – was remarkably circumscribed whether at a State or a Public School. Etonian education was the best a boy in England could hope for, and within its self-imposed limits was of exceptional quality. But how much it left out, how much it took for granted could be legitimately left out. Where, for example, would have been an appropriate place in Blair's schedule of instruction (Divinity, Geography, Ancient History, French, Shakespeare, and Latin Construe) for two works of great social importance which had appeared at the turn of the century, Seebohm Rowntree's *Poverty, A Study of Town Life* and Charles Booth's multi-volumed *The Life and Labour of the People of London*? Both, by the time Blair was at school, had already had a positive effect upon the thinking of the leaders of the Liberal Party and so upon the political life of England. To anyone familiar with those books, *The People of the Abyss* was shocking but not surprising: it was one further document that proved the need for political action. This, of course, is as much a part of the mood of pre-war England as 'the Edwardian garden party'; and the war years (though one would never have guessed it at St Cyprian's or Eton) were also years of aggressive social-political change. But of this Blair knew little or nothing; and fifteen years later, Orwell, sketching in the historical background to his time at school, feels the need to name only one political figure, that of the leader of the miners' union, Robert Smillie.* The effect upon him of reading *The People of the Abyss* was prolonged and subterranean and deferred: it would be years before the book would play an overt part in his life. Winston Churchill in 1911 might speak of 'spreading a net over the abyss', thinking in terms of social measures to mitigate poverty – one of those 'problems' for which objective political solutions had to be found. But for Blair it was as though he had heard a voice from the underground, addressed to him alone, to which he could not reply, and which he could not forget.

By the summer of 1921 the time had come for him to make a decision as to his next step after Eton. According to the ladder theory the answer was simple: he should step up and on to university. This was the decision made for themselves by eleven members of the 1916 Election in College, who went on either to Oxford (Balliol and Trinity) or Cambridge (King's, Trinity, and Corpus Christi). Of the remaining three, two went into family businesses (newspaper publishing and banking) and so, in a manner of speaking, did Eric Blair.

Admirers of Orwell in these later years of the century, which

* His statement that the public schoolboys he was meeting in 1936 – how many? – were much more right-wing in their views than he and his friends at Eton had been seems the most questionable sort of Orwellian generalization. The career of John Cornford, a public schoolboy of the 1930s, is instructive in this regard.

have seen the university made as much a part of anyone's education as the nursery school or kindergarten, find it bewildering, even outrageous, that he should have been so deprived – as deprived, for example, as Dickens or Virginia Woolf or Ernest Hemingway – and have pursued a variety of explanations to account for it, helped rather than hindered by an absence of fact.

It can be taken as a general fact that in 1921 the 'ladder theory' was not universally subscribed to at Eton. Many Etonians, who had gone through Fifth or Sixth Forms, felt they had gone far enough, and preferred to go straight into the world. This would be especially true of Oppidans, a considerable number of whom did not go on to university. They had received an excellent education and, from a social point of view, Eton was far more important than Oxford or Cambridge. But Collegers were 'intellectuals', and it was assumed that they would want to continue their education past Eton. Most of them did; but some did not – and what Blair's contemporaries found more surprising than his not going to university was the alternative he chose.

From the foregoing account of his career at Eton, it should be evident that Blair, while he might be called an 'intellectual', was neither a scholar then, nor did he give any signs of becoming one later. True, as Orwell tells us, he had made it a point not to work at his subjects, but then, not many Etonians, 'saps' apart, ostentatiously do. It is possible that a hardworking Blair might have done better in Trials than he did. The fact is that, academically, measured by the highest standard, he was undistinguished. But these are relative matters and, as a King's Scholar in College at Eton, he was qualified to go to a university, always assuming that he wanted to and that he was able to pay the fees.

Both assumptions must be examined; the latter first. Money, certainly, was a complicating factor. Blair, all along, from St Cyprian's through Eton, had been a scholarship student; even so, there had been fees for his parents to pay, which they had done gladly though not without difficulty. If he were to go on to a university without a very considerable scholarship, the fees the Blairs would be required to pay would be far beyond their means: this was one sacrifice more than they were willing, or even in a position to make. Mr Blair was in his mid-sixties; his pension, never munificent, was all that the family could count on in a time when life was growing more expensive (though some years later Mrs Blair would come unexpectedly into a small inheritance). But the circumstances were very different from what they had been when it was a question of Eric's being at St Cyprian's and at Eton. Now he was eighteen; he had been educated at what many considered the best Public School in England; he was old enough and educated enough to make his way in the world. University would have been a luxury, unless he was determined on one of the professions for which it was essential. In fact, none of them had even occurred to him. So it was quite logical for Mr Blair, concerned about his son's future, presently to suggest the Indian Civil Service. But it was offered at first as a suggestion, not an ultimatum, and his parents would do nothing to prevent Eric's going to Oxford or Cambridge if that was what he wanted; however, they made it clear that if he were to go, it would have to be without any sort of financial assistance from them, he must manage it on his own – that is, he would have to be awarded a scholarship.

The crucial fact, the true explanation for the decision he made, lies in his own diffidence. There is nothing in Orwell's writing later, or at the time in Blair's conversation with Etonian friends and members of his family, to suggest that he really wanted a university education or the experience of university life, that he did not all along think of Eton as a terminal point. His friends were not surprised that he had not gone to university for the sufficient reason that he had not given them any indication that he intended or wanted to go. In the light of his secretive nature this may not count as strong evidence; stronger is the fact that he did tell Steven Runciman that he looked forward to being done with Eton, and to going on to something new and different: an education in the world, an experience of life. And he took a rather patronizing view, as one might expect, of those contemporaries, Runciman among them, who had made the unadventurous choice of 'more of the same'. Admittedly there was a good deal of youthful romanticism in this – especially as it led him to choose a vocation for which he was 'comically and tragically unsuited' – but when he spoke of the future to Runciman, there was a clear recognition of his own limitations as a scholar, and his distaste for life at the university as he imagined it to be. That was as early as the summer of 1920, and one has the impression of Blair thereafter doing what is expected of him in the circumstances – consulting with his parents, his tutor – while he had already reached a decision.

It is not uninteresting that it was only *after* the discussion with his parents, which effectively closed the question, that Blair should have broached it to his tutor, Mr Gow. He himself was under no illusions as to his academic performance, and Gow certainly was not. As to his sitting for a scholarship, 'there was not the faintest hope of his getting one', Gow later wrote, and he concluded, 'He had shown so little taste or aptitude for academic subjects that I doubted whether in any case a University would be worth while.'[30] Given Blair's own feelings, this was hardly a blow, and he was free now to do as he pleased.

At the end of the Michaelmas half, in December 1921, he left Eton for good; but Eton, it might be said, did not leave him – its mark was upon him, in a certain authority and assurance of manner, as later in the authority and assurance of his prose. He had made a negative decision – that he would not go on to university; a positive decision, what his next step was to be, had yet to be made. That would be for the coming months in Southwold where he rejoined his family.

It is pointless, with a writer of Orwell's stature, to wish a decision unmade. If Blair had gone on to Oxford or Cambridge, it is quite possible that afterwards, in the approved literary stereotype, he would have climbed aboard the literary express to London, have done his approved stint for the weeklies, have written – who can say? – something or other, the unwritten books of Eric Blair. But it is permissible to suggest that then there would not have been George Orwell. Not going to university was a decisive part in the making of the writer.

N.B. Elegant

Part Three
Burma

In December 1921 the Blairs moved their home again, yet another of the transplantations that were so characteristic of them as a family. In Eric's own lifetime – he was now eighteen and a half – home had been first in India at Motihari and Monghyr. Then, when he was four, had come the return to England, and home thereafter was successively at Nutshell, Western Road, Henley-on-Thames (1907–12); Roselawn, Shiplake (1912–15); 36 St Mark's Road, Henley-on-Thames (1915–17); 23 Cromwell Crescent, Earl's Court, London (1917); 23 Mall Chambers, Notting Hill Gate, London (1918–21); and now, 40 Stradbroke Road, Southwold. It was there – the eighth move for the Blairs in a span of eighteen years – that he joined his family at Christmas, a newly-fledged Old Etonian.

In Southwold for the next several months the resident family would consist of himself, his mother and father, and his younger sister Avril. (Marjorie, his elder sister, had been married to Humphrey Dakin since 1920 – the same Humphrey Dakin who had grudgingly allowed Eric to tag along on a fishing expedition years before in Henley – and they were now living in a flat of their own in Mall Chambers.) Southwold, on the Suffolk coast, was a typical, smallish, lower-upper-middle to middle-middle English seaside resort. If it had none of the pretensions to grandeur of Eastbourne, say, with its mammoth hotels along the front, or the elegance of Brighton with its Regency terraces, neither was it Blackpool with its gaudy pier and jovial fish-and-chips, working-class flavour. 'Resort' may seem too sprightly a word for what Southwold actually was. Still, it had its promenade, its bathing huts, its bandstand for concerts on summer evenings, and souvenir shops where one could buy anything from Staffordshire figures to innocently obscene comic postcards of the kind

Orwell would later write about with fondness in his essay on 'The Art of Donald McGill'. And although the weather even in July and August was often treacherous, with chill winds and wet fogs blowing in from the North Sea, throughout the season stout-hearted Britons would be ranged in canvas chairs along the shingle, taking the sea air.

Crowded and bustling with the illusion of life in summer, quiet and relatively deserted in winter, Southwold was precisely the sort of place where an ageing Anglo-Indian family might choose to retire. As things turned out, it served the elder Blairs very well. Southwold was where they would spend the rest of their lives (though they would move twice again, but within the town), where soon enough, in a way that was characteristic of them, they had acquired a new set of friends to make up for the friends they had left behind them in London – or in Henley, or in the various stations in India – and with whom they would maintain thereafter only a tenuous connection. It was to be Blair's way, too, and easy for him in that his nature did not impel him to deep or passionate friendships. He got on well with the young people whom he met in Southwold – for example, Eleanor Jaques, the daughter of the family next door, and Dennis Collings, the son of the local doctor – just as he had got on well with friends at Eton. But he felt no compulsion or even a mild curiosity to keep up the friendships and acquaintances he had made in College. When he boarded the train for the last time at Windsor Station in December 1921, it was a symbolic as well as a literal departure. He had joined the Old Boys Association before leaving, but Eton was one phase in his life, definite and concluded, and he would never reappear there for celebrations on the Fourth of June. Southwold would be another phase in his life; Burma the next. Throughout his life, in each of its successive phases, there would be friends who belonged to a particular phase, though sometimes earlier friendships, after an interval of years, would be resumed – without embarrassment, explanation or surprise on either side. That was Blair's way. Indeed, until his marriage in 1936, when for the first time in his life he entered into a deep and passionate bond, the only continuous relationship of any significance he maintained was with his mother.

Whatever the virtues of Southwold as a place for retirement, it was not the sort of place where a young man would choose to start a career. And the question of Eric's career was very much in the mind of the Blairs that Christmas. Since Eric himself had by this time decided firmly against sitting for a scholarship at either Oxford or Cambridge, Mr Blair felt free to put forward again his suggestion of the colonial service.* But now it was less a suggestion than paternal advice of a weighty kind – in which Mrs Blair concurred – and the generalized notion of 'colonial service' was narrowed down to the Indian Imperial Police.

Eric and his father had never been close. It had been Mrs Blair alone, even after Mr Blair had been demobilized, who would come to see Eric at Eton and take him and his friends out to tea, much to his satisfaction. Steven Runciman remembers her on such occasions as 'a charming woman, a bit exotic and gypsy-looking with her bright-coloured scarves and gold hoop ear-rings'.[2] And though, when she had gone back to London, Blair would adopt a supercilious tone about her to King-Farlow, deploring her lack of interest in books and serious things, it was evident to Runciman that he was actually deeply attached to her. In contrast, he spoke little of his father, and there were several boys in the 1916 Election who did not know that Mr Blair was an officer in France, or even in the army. That a schoolboy during the fervid war years should have withheld information of this sort seems very odd: the family reticence carried to an extreme degree.

Eric's coming home to live, after being away at school for more than ten years, would make no appreciable difference in the way things went between himself and his father, except as it offered a day-to-day provocation and setting for disagreement.

* Orwell in the 1940s told a good friend of that phase that one of his reasons for not going to university was that he felt he had been too long associating mainly with boys who were much richer than he.[1] But even in the early 1920s, and even at Oxford or Cambridge, it would have been possible to find students of his own economic level if he had wished, and students from the working class were not unknown there. As against this later reinterpretation of the past, there is Blair's contemporary feeling, recorded in the previous chapter, that academic things had ceased to interest him, and that he wanted the experience of something different. Such feelings were not uncommon: as Robert Graves has observed in *Good-bye to All That*, it is possible to become bored with the succession of academic ladders, reaching the top of one and then starting at the bottom of the next, which was one reason Graves welcomed the outbreak of the First World War – it enabled him to enlist, plausibly, in the Fusiliers, rather than, as would have been the ordinary course of events, immediately going up the ladder from Charterhouse to Oxford.

Given the nature of this particular father and son, and given the general proposition that eighteen, notoriously, is an age when sons know much more than their fathers, it may appear surprising that Eric should so readily have accepted his father's advice. But he had no reason to disagree with it, for it fitted in nicely with a wish of his own: that someday he might go out to the East, to India, to Burma.

Thus, with no argument at all, the Blairs and Eric arrived at the same conclusion, although for very different reasons. Mr and Mrs Blair, as one would expect of parents in their situation, put forth a variety of practical and sensible considerations. He was eighteen years old; he had finished his schooling; he had to support himself; he had expressed no interest in any of the learned professions, or in business. (At this time he would not admit, even to himself, that he wanted to become a writer, a denial that Orwell was later to describe as 'outraging my true nature'.[3] But even if he had silently determined on such a career, had he broached it to his parents they would have been as appalled then as they would be later: was this how he proposed to earn his living? The precariousness of it, let alone its slightly Bohemian flavour, would make it unacceptable to them.) The important thing was to choose a career that was respectable and suitable, that would not require a good deal of costly training or other expense at the outset, that would provide a modest but sufficient yearly income, and that, entered upon early, allowed for early retirement – in his case at forty – after which he would receive an assured pension for the remainder of his life. The Indian Imperial Police answered to all these particulars. (This, of course, was how a lower-upper-middle Anglo-Indian family like the Blairs might see it; from the point of view of Eton it would seem an unexpected choice, and it would be the odd Colleger indeed who would choose it.) There were other considerations. It was a career appropriate to family tradition – his grandfather Blair had gone out to India as a young man, his father had served there, his mother's people were teak merchants in Burma, her mother and a sister still lived in Moulmein – and it was suitable.[4] To serve King and Country in an outpost of Empire carried with it a certain distinction: one was placed, and not discreditably.

His parents' considerations, then, were mostly realistic and practical; his own were romantic and deeply coloured by fantasy – a reminder to us that he was, after all, a very young and inexperienced Old Boy. He seems to have had no understanding or premonition of what it meant to become an officer in the Indian Imperial Police, what the job would demand of him. His entire interest was directed to going out, going back, to a dreamscape of India. He had been brought to England when he was four years old, but he had not forgotten his still earlier memories or else they had been incorporated into his fantasies and gathered force there as they were transformed and intensified. He worshipped Kipling; *Kim* was one of the favourite books of his childhood. India, in his conversations with Runciman, stood for the furthest remove from Etonian life, and as such would figure in his fantasies of the future, although what precisely he was to do should he go there (be a journalist, like Kipling?) was never defined. That first, earliest childhood encounter with the hot, flamboyant, red and saffron landscape proved ineradicable: very different in its impact, for example, from Eton, to whose historic architecture and green fields (which have inspired so many other writers) he responded only diffidently. So that there was an almost uncanny congruence between the realistic wishes of his parents and his own romantic notion of going out to India, and it was decided in the early months of that winter of 1922 that he would put in for the examination for the Indian Imperial Police. Neither his parents nor Eric himself thought to ask the crucial question: whether in character and temperament he was suited to such an occupation. As it proved, by becoming a police officer – in the service of Empire – he was truly outraging his nature. And yet, paradoxically, by doing so he was suffering a wound that was essential to his development into the kind of writer he became. Once the decision had been made, realities began to take precedence over romance. It meant, first of all, that he must re-enter the world of schooling and the competitive exam, which, upon leaving Eton, he thought he had left behind him for ever. In January he enrolled in Mr Hope's tutorial establishment in Southwold, which specialized in getting young men ready for the service examinations, and started to cram. The multi-part, comprehensive examination was not to be held until the end of

June, by which time Blair would not only have been crammed, but would also have arrived at the minimum age allowable for a candidate – nineteen. (The maximum age was twenty-two.) The application, sent off to the India Office during the winter, required that Mr Blair should give his consent to his son's applying to join the service, and indicate his willingness to pay for the prescribed uniforms – Full Dress, Mess Dress, and Service Khaki. (Although the Government gave a £30 subsidy for this purpose, it did not begin to cover the total cost, which came to £150. Once more, as at St Cyprian's, at Wellington, and at Eton, the money was found.)

Two testimonials as to Blair's character and scholarly attainments had also to be sent to the India Office. One of these was written by Mr Hope; the other by the long-suffering Crace, the Master in College, who accompanied his with a cool little note which would suggest that the colonial constabulary was not often chosen as a career by Collegers: 'I do not know at all what is required by the authorities for candidates for the India police. I send a formal certificate which is probably all that is necessary. If anything more is required, perhaps you will let me know.'

The examination, identical in its many parts with that given to officer candidates for the army, navy, or air force, was administered over an eight-day period – in this particular instance from 27 June to 4 July 1922.

It began with English. In the first part Blair was asked to 'Write a character sketch of an old gamekeeper, or a retired colonel, or an old farmer'; to 'Write a letter to a relative about a visit to the theatre'; and to write a 250-word précis of a lengthy description of the battle of Sedgemoor. In the second part (one hour) he was to name and describe three members of the Cabinet, write something about mountaineering, and something about Burns, Wordsworth, Scott, or Dickens. With English taken care of he proceeded to the History paper. Here he had to deal with the chronology of historical events; speculate on such topics as 'Who was the greatest Prime Minister since Pitt?' and 'If Nelson had lost Trafalgar'; assess the contributions of three figures from a list including Adam Smith, Rhodes, Faraday, Hastings, Cook, and Burke; answer two out of eight questions in other areas of British history; and indicate on a map the main

College photograph of Eton showing Eric Blair.

Eton. Field Day, Spring 1921.
Eric Blair is third from the left
and Cyril Connolly second from the right.

Eton. Afternoon at 'Athens'.
Blair is on the right.

The Police Training School, Mandalay.
Blair is in the back row, third from the left;
Beadon beside him, fourth from the left.

British possessions in 1763. After History came Mathematics, two two-hour papers; and then, at last, a choice – either a French or German paper. Blair naturally chose the former: two hours of translation – French into English and English into French – and one hour in which he was to write a two-hundred-word story in French based on a series of pictures. For the remaining three papers he was allowed to choose from among German, Latin, Greek, Physics, Chemistry, General Science, Advanced Mathematics, and Freehand Drawing. He decided to exploit his years of having done Classics, and took the Latin and Greek papers; familiar, detested exercises in translation – *into* and *from*. For his final paper, since he was fond of drawing (and would continue to do a little all his life), he chose Freehand Drawing. Here he was asked within a two-hour period to *copy* a picture so that it would be of use to an officer, and *draw from memory* a chair at a certain angle, or a hut, or a bucket.

Blair, fresh from Eton and with the further advantage of having crammed at Mr Hope's establishment, did relatively well in the examination. He was at his best, and for this Eton could take full credit, on the Latin and Greek papers, receiving 1,782 marks out of 2,000 in Latin and 1,702 marks out of 2,000 in Greek. On the other papers – in each of which there was again a 2,000 marks maximum – he received 1,372 marks in English, 1,256 in French, a rather-better-than-might-be-expected 1,158 in Mathematics (his weakest subject at Eton; so credit for this would go to Mr Hope), and a perfectly mediocre 1,019 in History. His drawing was apparently not of the sort that would be helpful – or recognizable – in battle, and he received only 174 marks out of 400.

Passing grade for the Examination was 6,000 marks out of a possible 12,400. This did not mean, however, that all the numerous applicants who had received a passing grade would be accepted as candidates. From this particular group only the top twenty-six were; Blair with a score of 8,463 was seventh on the list. In September, he and the twenty-five other successful candidates were required to take a riding test, for which he prepared himself during the summer at a stable in or near Southwold, and was placed twenty-first on the list of twenty-three who passed.[5]

Once having been accepted as a candidate, it was necessary for him to indicate where in India he wanted to be sent – with no assurance, however, that his request would be granted. He listed his choices in the following order: Burma; United Provinces; Bombay; Madras; Punjab. For the first choice he gave as his reason that he had relatives in Burma; for the second that his father had served in the United Provinces. Since he had done quite well in the examination, he probably could have gone to a more desirable post than Burma, which had the reputation of being the 'Cinderella' province of India; but it was what he had asked for and what he was given. He was now committed to the service for a minimum period of three years, unless he was prepared to pay the expensive passage to and from the East himself (he was not), in which case he would have been allowed to resign earlier, should he so wish.

Out of the list of twenty-six candidates, only three were posted to Burma. One of them, C. W. R. Beadon, had gone out earlier in the month; but on 27 October 1922, Blair and the other, A. J. Jones, sailed First Class on the *S.S. Herefordshire*, from Birkenhead to Rangoon. He was on his voyage out to take up his appointment as a Probationary A.S.P., an Assistant Superintendent of Police on probation, under training in Burma, in the Indian Imperial Police.

'The voyage out' was in no way remarkable. By 1922, as a phrase and an experience, it was already a long-established cliché. Since the early years of the nineteenth century, intelligent, venturesome, educated young Englishmen had been going out to serve in the East, in the outposts of Empire, whether as soldiers, or police officers, or civil servants. Still others went as clergymen, as teachers and missionaries, and some as planters, journalists, and merchants. Fifteen years before Blair, Leonard Woolf, for example, had made his voyage out – to Ceylon – to serve as a magistrate; fifteen years after Blair, Leonard Woolf's nephew, the poet Julian Bell, would make his voyage out, to China – to teach at Wuhan University. The accounts of their respective voyages are much alike; so, save for a few particulars here and there – the odd love affair, the squall at sea, the attack of dysentery – so are they all. But for the individual on the voyage out, it was not a cliché: it was his own, unique experience.

Blair was nineteen, and this was the first time in his life that he was free of the supervision of family or school. The experience for which he was bound was certain to be in the nature of a revelation. He was 'on his own' in a more definitive way than those of his Etonian friends who were now in the transitional period of the university before entering the world of 'telegrams and anger', and with more authority thrust upon him sooner than upon those of his friends who had gone straight into business. He was intelligent, impressionable, and well-educated; yet there was something inchoate about him, ready to be formed; there had not yet been a challenge to put his undoubted abilities to proper use.

Until then he had lived the protected existence deemed appropriate to a boy of his class – not only at St Cyprian's and Eton, but also at home. He moved within the limits of the upper middle class, from lower to upper; of the aristocracy he had only such first-hand knowledge as came from acquaintance with boys at school whose parents or grandparents, or who themselves, had handles to their names; of the working class he knew virtually nothing at all.* As an omnivorous reader, he had acquired a not inconsiderable theoretical knowledge of the complexities of human existence, but it was a theoretical knowledge far removed from experience, and his cynical manner masked an ingenuousness that was less a personal than a class characteristic. Starting on the voyage out, he had a great deal to learn.

The *Herefordshire* was a small ship – very different in scale and style from the great transatlantic liners of the period, the *Mauretanias* and the *Leviathans* – but it was perfectly comfortable,

* As a small boy, it will be remembered, he had played for a very brief period with the children of a working-class family, until his mother had put a stop to it; and his chief impression of the working class, as he grew older, was that they smelt. It was Orwell's claim, later, that he had been *taught* that they smelt, and that this was a lesson ingrained in all boys of his class from an early age on. (He would write some explicit and controversial pages on the subject in *The Road to Wigan Pier*.) But the whole question where Blair is concerned is a vexing one, for there is no doubt that his sense of smell was abnormally keen – and as such inspires epithets and metaphors in Orwell's prose that are worthy of Swift. If it is true (as Orwell claims) that Blair thought the working class smelt, he was equally convinced that as a boy he did too. In fact, none of his friends at Eton have any memory that he smelt; neither did Mrs Vaughan Wilkes, nor Mr Gow, nor his sister Avril; which is not to discount the psychological effect upon himself of thinking he did.

and First Class, in the eyes of a boy accustomed to the austerities of Eton and the economies practised at home by his mother, would seem downright luxurious with its full breakfast, lunch, and dinner, broth and biscuits at eleven, tea and cakes at four, and a bowl of fruit in one's cabin at night. It also recreated at sea that milieu of 'Superiority' of which he had been a part at school; but whereas at Eton the 'others', the 'outsiders', all those who were not Etonians, were far enough out of sight not to be worrisome, on the *Herefordshire* they were constantly, disturbingly in one's range of vision.

Orwell, with his gift for transforming the experiences of his life into moral and political examples, recalls of the voyage that he was 'only twenty years old' (actually, nineteen) and, unlike the hard-working crew members, a parasite – that is, a 'mere passenger'. (Not merely on holiday however; but en route to take up an arduous job of work.) His attention was particularly caught by one of the crew, a muscular fair-haired quartermaster of perhaps forty, who (Orwell tells us) he looked up to as a godlike being, rather as a new boy in College might look up to a Sixth Former. Then, one day after lunch, Blair saw him hurrying along the deck with something furtively concealed in his huge hands: a pie dish with the remains of a pudding (returned from the First Class dining saloon) which had been smuggled to him by a steward. The quartermaster's air seemed guilty as he shot past, and Blair, like an outraged Prefect, felt a 'shock of astonishment'. It is suggestive of his extreme inexperience at this time that he should have been so appalled. For this was not a question of hunger – clearly the muscular quartermaster was not suffering from malnutrition – but of sensual gratification; and life is neither the gentleman's code nor what is done or not done at Eton, which he must already have realized in a theoretical way, but only now was beginning to learn from the particulars of experience encountered face-to-face. Orwell is quick to admit that he did not really understand the incident at the time; however, the moral he eventually drew from it seems questionable. Twenty-five years later he saw it as proving 'the gap between function and reward' in a non-socialist society[6] – i.e., that a skilful quartermaster was so inadequately rewarded that he had to steal left-over food. But this conclusion is hardly confirmed by what Blair actually had seen: a strapping specimen of a man, ready to enjoy a pudding that had been given to him by a friend in the galley, and not at all finicking because someone else's spoon had already been in the dish.

For the most part, though, the voyage was as noticeably lacking in event as such voyages usually are. That, after all, is a part of their charm: days melt into days, an undemanding routine of eating and sleeping, dozing on deck or playing deck games, or taking a brisk turn around the deck in the morning before the sun is too hot or in the evening as the sun is setting, reading in a desultory fashion, engaging in desultory conversation with fellow passengers. The degree that one enjoys this is largely a matter of one's own temperament – Roger Beadon, for example, making the voyage out two weeks before Blair found it 'a month of pleasure and interest and I was almost sorry to see it end'.[7]

But when the *Herefordshire* docked at Colombo, there was another incident that contributed to Blair's education, a first faint foretaste of the lesson he was ultimately to draw from his experience in Burma. Hardly had the ship weighed anchor than coolies swarmed aboard and, under the direction of a white sergeant and some native police, began to take the luggage ashore of those who were ending their voyage in Ceylon.

Blair, going on to Rangoon, and the other remaining First Class passengers, watched the bustling scene from the upper deck. One of the coolies was carrying a long metal case in so clumsy a way that it might have struck people in the head as he passed by, and was loudly cursed. This was enough to catch the attention of the white sergeant. Turning, he gave the coolie a 'terrific kick in the bottom that sent him staggering'. The response of the watching passengers, a number of women among them, was highly approving: that was how someone of *that sort* had to be treated.

Again Blair was shocked into a new awareness – and this time, as had not been the case with the quartermaster and the pie, there was no possibility of misunderstanding or misinterpreting what he had seen – shocked not only by the physical brutality to the coolie, so automatically applied, but by the callous reaction of the white onlookers, in its own way as automatic, even from the women, as though the wretched creature were not even human enough to deserve a murmur of sympathy.[8] (How appalled they would have been if the sergeant had kicked a dog!) For the first time the literary experience of *The People of the Abyss* was being translated into life: that people could be treated as though they were things.

But these unsettling incidents, whatever their momentary impact upon Blair, and though they were all of the voyage out that Orwell made specific literary use of many years later, were no more than that – incidents only, not crises or epiphanies that bring about a change of mind and heart, a change of life. Only the total Burma experience was to do that for him, the cumulative effect of five years in the service of Imperialism. He watched the coolie being kicked, and turned away, and that evening, as the ship set sail again, he ate his dinner as usual in the First Class dining saloon. Not long afterwards, the *Herefordshire* was steaming up the wide, muddy Irrawaddy; Blair was on deck, at the railing, watching the landscape glide by. As they approached Rangoon monuments came into view: first the smokestacks of the Burmah Oil Company, and then the astonishing gold-spired Shwe Dagon pagoda, the ancient Buddhist shrine, which dominates the surrounding countryside. It was the end of November, little more than a month since he had said goodbye to his parents in Southwold, and now he was coming down the gangplank in Rangoon, a coolie carrying his luggage, in Burma at last but not yet quite at his destination: the Burma Provincial Police Training School at Mandalay.

A fortnight earlier, Roger Beadon, the first of the Probationary A.S.P.s to arrive, had spent two days in Rangoon paying 'a hectic round of calls on His Excellency the Governor, the Inspector General of Police, and other officials of importance'. Presumably Blair and Jones also paid the prescribed round of calls; in any event, late in the afternoon of 28 November, they boarded the mail train for Mandalay. It was a sixteen-hour journey to the north; at 8 a.m. the next morning they arrived at the Mandalay station. Roger Beadon and two other young officers had come down to meet them, and Beadon has recorded his impression of the moment: 'From the train stepped two young men. One, fresh-complexioned, of medium height and stocky build; the other, sallow-faced, tall, thin, and gangling, whose clothes, no matter how well cut, seemed to hang on him – Eric A. Blair.' (And he adds, 'George Orwell to be, could I have but foreseen the future!' – the surprised reaction, it must be said, of everyone who knew Blair at St Cyprian's, Eton, and in Burma, and for a long time afterwards.)

The newcomers were taken off to the Police Mess, on the outskirts of the city and close to the school itself, where they were to live during the year of training. The Mess, regarded by its members as the finest among the several Regimental Messes in Mandalay, was approached by a semi-circular drive through a compound blazing with acacia trees and cannas in full blossom. It was a long, low-lying brick building with six bedrooms on the upper floor, three for the Probationary A.S.P.s and three for visiting officers; and on the lower floor the Mess itself, an ante-room, and a billiards room. It was all carried out, as would be familiar to any reader of Kipling, with a certain amplitude of style, though not as amply in the inflationary years of the early 1920s as in 1914, when the Mess servants (paid for by the members) included a butler and second boy, a cook and his mate, a punkah puller, several gardeners, a billiard marker, and a lamp trimmer; and when, on the monthly guest night, the police band was in attendance and Mess silver was on display.

R. G. B. Lawson, who was at the Police School in 1914, and who later, as a District Superintendent of Police, would know Blair briefly, observes that 'All this had to be done on a salary of 300 rupees (£20) a month. It was of course quite impossible and we all left the school heavily in debt. I do not know for certain,' he continues, 'but I believe that in Blair's time . . . the cost of living [had become] so high that the probationers no longer joined the Club and that they lived very frugally. Our pay was increased for the first time in over twenty years about 1924, but too late to have been of any assistance to Blair. Mandalay, to him, must have been a terrible hole to live in.'[9]

But 1914 would inevitably regard 1922 as 'deprived', and 1922, not having known the good old days before the war, would see things differently. For one thing, there was the fascination of being where they were. Mandalay, for Blair, was Kipling country incarnate, a dream realized, and he delighted in exploring the city and countryside. This was a taste he shared with Beadon, with whom otherwise he had little in common. Though the two always got on well together, there was to be no real intimacy between them – the familiar Blair pattern – and at the end of training, after they had been assigned to their respective stations, they said goodbye and would see each other again only on one further occasion.

Mandalay in the early 1920s was still essentially two cities: the British fort and the native quarter. Fort Dufferin had originally been built as a palace-city by the Burmese king Mindon in 1856, and captured by the British in 1885, at which time they dethroned Mindon's successor, Thibaw, and transferred the capital of the country to Rangoon. The Fort was a mile square, enclosed on all four sides by twenty-foot high walls of rosy brick – in each side a great stone gateway guarded by a pair of stone dragons – and surrounding the walls a wide moat, dense with red and white lotus, and shaded by a border of tamarind, acacia, and cinnamon trees. Within the enormous area of the Fort were various Regimental Messes and barracks, the Upper Burma Club – whose members included most of the Europeans living in Mandalay – the sometime royal palace surrounded by an inner moat of its own, bungalows for Regimental officers and senior Government officials, a polo field, a nine-hole golf links, tennis courts, and a chapel.

That was the Fort, an outpost of England. Beyond its rose-coloured walls was the other city, with a pulsing life of its own; the unpaved roads leading out into the dense countryside and native villages; the hundreds of shrines, temples, and pagodas – the Yakaing-paya, with its colossal Buddha coated in gold leaf; the Kuthodaw, a sugarloaf-shaped pagoda, surrounded by more than seven hundred smaller pagodas of identical design. Beadon writes:

I suppose, though, that the great Bazaar was the most interesting part of the city with its colourful stalls – bolts of cloth, lacquer ware, gold, silver, jewelry and ivory jostling side by side with fruit, vegetables, fish, meat and spices – the whole a babel of mixed languages pervaded by flies and the assorted not always pleasant smells of the Silken East . . .
During the hot weather, which was never really unpleasant, everything looked dry and dusty, but in the monsoon and the so-called cold weather that followed it, everything took on a green fresh look, with the flowers and flowering trees and shrubs in full bloom . . . I really

believe that my most unforgettable memory of Burma will be a cold-weather evening in Mandalay, watching the glowing sunset colours, reflected in the moat, slowly fade, the purple-shadowed Maymyo hills merging into the twilight darkness, and the twinkling Mandalay Hill Pagoda lamps light up and vie with the star-studded sky.

If a young man of no literary pretensions whatever could have been moved to this degree by the town and its surrounding country, it is not surprising that Blair, storing up each day new sensuous impressions, would later call upon them for a novel of Burma in which the landscape would play a central role – *Burmese Days* – and which he would describe to Henry Miller in 1936 as the only one of his novels that he was pleased with.*

But the reason for Blair's being there was not to immerse himself in the life of the town but to be trained to take up his duties as an Assistant Superintendent of Police, and the greater part of his time, from early December on, was spent in more humdrum settings: the Police School, the Police Mess, and the parade ground. The school was intended 'primarily for training cadet sub-inspectors – well-educated high school boys, chiefly Burmese but occasionally Indian, Chinese, or from the minor races of Burma – Shans, Karens, and Arakanese. Instructors for these cadets were found from the ranks of serving police officers of the rank of Inspector or Deputy Superintendent.' During the time that Blair was there, there were 120 such cadets in training. The three Probationary A.S.P.s made up an entirely different category. To begin with, they were English; they had also passed the appropriate higher level Examination; they were being trained to become officers in due season the cadets then at the school would be serving under them as their juniors and assistants. With a separate set of instructors, the three were required to take courses in Burmese, colloquial Hindustani, Law, and Police Procedure. The only other requirement was that they attend, on Wednesday and Saturday mornings, a parade in full uniform of the cadets in training. The Wednesday morning parade was taken in turn by Blair, Beadon, and Jones. The Saturday morning parade was regularly taken by the Principal of the School, a senior District Superintendent of Police, who is des-

* In the letter to Miller, he makes no literary claim for the novel other than to say that 'the descriptions of scenery aren't bad'.[10]

cribed by Beadon in an affectionate sentence that fans out to suggest all too vividly why Blair, given the sort of man he was, would not find himself at home in the career he had so romantically chosen. 'This officer,' Beadon writes, 'was a tall, powerfully-built Scotsman with a large moustache, a non-drinker and smoker, but on two glasses of lemonade on a Mess night, a holy terror if it came to a rough and tumble.'

It was, as we have had occasion to remark before, a matter of temperament: Beadon took to the life and enjoyed it; Blair did not. Beadon, for example, revelled in the Christmas season in Mandalay, when (that year) the Governor and his staff came up from Rangoon to Government House, and there were polo and tennis tournaments, dances and dinners, and a continuing round of festivities; Blair, by the time the last holly decorations had been taken down in Government House, had acquired the reputation of not being 'a good mixer'. He had only been in Mandalay a month, but already it was evident that he 'cared little for games, and seemed to be bored with the social and Club life' that, normally, occupied much of off-duty time. He did his work in courses without difficulty, but even in this respect went his own way. While Beadon and Jones were struggling with the difficulties of learning Burmese and Hindustani in successive hours, Blair, to whom the languages came easily, more often than not would not attend classes, preferring to stay in his room and read.

But though Beadon was 'fond of going down to the Club and playing snooker and dancing and what have you' and Blair was not, friendship of a sort – the Blairian sort that asked for a minimum of commitment on either side – developed between them. In order to see more of the country outside the city, Blair decided to buy a motor-cycle, about which he was entirely a novice, and Beadon, who had a New Hudson 2-stroke and was an experienced rider, agreed to teach him how to ride it. The lesson was to take place within the less crowded precincts of Fort Dufferin.

He had an American machine of a make I had never seen before [Beadon writes] and have never seen since. It was very low with 4 cylinders running fore and aft, and the sight of Blair, over six feet tall, astride this midget was ludicrous, as his knees almost came up round his ears, or so it seemed.

All went well until we came to one of the gates which, so we thought, would let us out of the Fort, and we were moving along splendidly when I realized it was not one of the exits, but a gate that was permanently shut. I shouted to Blair to stop but he lost his head apparently and, instead of slowing down, stood up, and the bike went on under his legs and hit the gate. Luckily we were not going fast, and no damage was done, but it was an amusing incident.

Beadon's anecdotes are all of this character, amiable in tone and slight in subject matter, and certainly not revelations; but they are of peculiar interest for they deal with aspects of Blair's Burmese experience that Orwell found no place for when he came to write of it. Of course, his intention then was not to be autobiographical: he selected and shaped his material as it contributed to his chosen themes, and let the rest go. So it is good to be reminded that, whatever his psychological peculiarities and social awkwardnesses, Blair was still a young man capable of sometimes enjoying himself and not always the anguished guilt-ridden protagonist in an anti-imperialist drama.

Another Beadon anecdote, of a would-be tiger shoot in which he and Blair participated, proves to be very different, both in its faintly comic circumstances and in its anti-climactic conclusion, from the successful tiger shoot that figures so decisively in *Burmese Days*:

One night we decided we would go out after tiger, knowing I may say, nothing whatsoever of the method or dangers of so doing! Accordingly, he [Blair] borrowed the Principal's 12-bore shot-gun and ball cartridges and I had a Luger-Parabellum automatic pistol with a wooden stock. Armed with these, we set forth to our destination, the banks of a canal about ten miles east of Mandalay.

There, at a small village, we routed out an elderly villager, somehow explained our intentions, and asked him to get out his bullocks and bullock cart, which he did. Then, for several hours we sat in the back of the cart, guns cocked, eyes alert, waiting for some unsuspecting tiger to cross our path. To say that nothing happened is only the truth, and I imagine the wily old Burman had no intention of going anywhere near where such an animal may have been lurking.

But in spite of these agreeable, shared experiences, Beadon was never deceived that there was any real intimacy between Blair and himself. The next spring (1923), his father, a Consulting Mining Engineer who was working in Burma, came to spend some time in Maymyo, a hill station some 3,000 feet above sea level, forty-two miles east of Mandalay. Beadon was given leave for a week to go and stay with him and he took Blair along. They had a quiet, enjoyable time, playing golf and at the Club in the evenings, in a landscape and atmosphere peculiarly evocative of England – as such, Orwell drew upon it for a point in *Homage to Catalonia* – but Beadon concludes, 'I cannot honestly recall that anything out of the ordinary happened, except that I realized that he and I had very little in common, I presumably being an extrovert, he an introvert, living in a world of his own: a rather shy, retiring intellectual.'

The curriculum at the Police Training School had been established before the First World War and continued without change in 1922, but one has the impression that it was less than adequate, in so far as it was meant to prepare the future A.S.P.s for the duties ahead of them. Although their duties were to be of an extremely practical nature, some were ignored entirely and the rest were presented to them only on a theoretical level: thus, during the year of training in Mandalay, they never set foot in a police station. Again, though they could count on being posted all over Burma, sometimes to stations deep in the jungle, it was not thought necessary that they should be made familiar in advance with either the country, its customs, or the diversity of its people – at least not from first-hand observation. Their training, for Blair, Beadon, and Jones, was a matter of formal classes in Mandalay, except for a period of one month, when they were attached to the British Regiment stationed in Maymyo, the South Staffords. 'I have never discovered what use this was to us,' Beadon writes, 'apart from drill training, but it was a pleasant break in the normal routine and we thoroughly enjoyed it.'*

The most curious omission from the curriculum – perhaps on the theory, demonstrably untrue, that politics and the administration of justice have nothing to do with each other – was any

* Blair apparently enjoyed the experience less; Orwell, putting it to polemical use in *The Road to Wigan Pier*, describes the morning marches in the hot sun, so hot that presently the column of soldiers was steaming with sweat; Blair, bringing up the rear with one of the junior officers, found the smell of their sweating bodies so offensive that it turned his stomach – an instance of class-inspired prejudice. But, whatever its subjective aspects, his month with the South Staffords and his 'service' with the O.T.C. at Eton comprised his military experience up to the time of the Spanish Civil War.

reference at all to the unsettled, changing political situation in Burma. And since Blair's interests at this time were not in 'politics', he did little to repair the omission on his own.

A literary/classical English Public School education, such as he had had, helps to create a keen social observer, aware of the nuances of social distinctions and practices, and so (sometimes) helps to make a novelist. But it is a political education that helps to teach the *significance* of the ways in which people are separated, and so (sometimes) helps to make a moralist. Five years in the service of Empire would contribute to the making of Orwell as a novelist and as a moralist, but his response to Burma was a very convincing demonstration that, for him, personal considerations (the particular experience) were more important than political considerations (the abstract experience) and that he had to move through the former to arrive at the latter. Orwell's single most memorable sentence, 'All animals are equal, but some animals are more equal than others,' may have had its beginnings in social observation – at St Cyprian's, perhaps, as the boys competed for Mum's favour? – but it took final form and gained its international currency as a political statement and a moral judgement.

Blair in Burma, unlike Orwell in Spain, as far as any written record survives, seems to have been singularly uninterested in the interesting political events that were taking place about him, except as they may be inferred in the background of *Burmese Days*, and in the two essays drawn from his police experience, 'Shooting an Elephant' and 'A Hanging'. Yet, in an indirect but important way, the contemporary Burmese political situation had a considerable influence upon the creation of George Orwell. If Blair had arrived in Burma a few years earlier, he would have found a much more orderly, ordinary province, appearing to function in a smooth, untroubled way under a benevolent Imperial administration. It is not inconceivable that the jarring, sometimes quite trivial events that stood out so painfully when he was there, would have been less noticeable, less abrasive, less guilt-producing, if they had not taken place against a background of growing confusion and uncertainty for the once-so-self-confident British rulers in Burma. Paradoxically, it was the very attempts of the British government to liberalize its administration and to allow the Burmese voice to be heard that made Orwell more conscious than he probably would otherwise have been of the Empire as a system in which he could not continue to participate and keep his self-respect.

Although Burma was an administrative part of India it had had a very different history. The Burmese were a gentle people, much less caste conscious than the Indians, and more accepting of their situation, which made them easier to govern. But they were beginning to resent the degree to which they were exploited commercially by the Indians and the Chinese, and by British and other European mercantile interests. Along with this went a growing restiveness at being under British rule.

British influence in Burma had been considerable since the middle of the nineteenth century; however, the country was not officially taken into the Empire until the 1880s. All went smoothly, even placidly, to the end of the First World War, and 1890 to 1920 is generally considered 'the golden period' of Imperial rule. The traditional English attitudes to the people over whom they ruled – benevolent, patronizing, and authoritarian – were evident in Burma, but perhaps in a less conspicuous way than elsewhere. There was a population of thirteen millions, of whom some nine millions were Buddhists. Since they were more 'gentle' than many of the other 'subject peoples', occasions for overt suppression or other extreme forms of discipline were infrequent. They were also 'inefficient', or so it was alleged by the British – not disapprovingly, however, for did it not confirm the need for the British presence in the country to govern it efficiently?

But even during the 'golden period' there had been faint stirrings of unrest. The Y.M.B.A., the Young Men's Buddhist Association, which had been founded in 1906 in a pro-British mood and with peaceful intentions similar to those of the Young Men's Christian Association, by the end of the war had become a centre for the expression of Burmese nationalist sentiment. Such sentiment was fuelled in 1919 when India, but not Burma, was granted, in accord with the Montagu–Chelmsford proposals, the system called Dyarchy, whereby the Indians were offered representation and a voice in the way in which they were governed, although important areas of activity were still reserved to the British administration. But the inevitable resentment of the

Burmese nationalists at being denied the privileges of Dyarchy could not be ignored, and, in 1923, the system was also instituted in most of Burma. Thereafter, all Burmese men and women over the age of eighteen were eligible to participate in the election of three-fourths of the membership of the national legislature. Ministers from the elected group were in charge of local government, education, health, agriculture, excise, and public works. There were also selected Ministers, British appointments, who were in charge of law and order, revenue, and finance. The advance towards self-government was considerable but, as the money that was essential to keep it all going was in the charge of a Minister appointed by the British, it meant (gracious rhetoric aside) that the British still had the ultimate power to decide what action should or should not be taken by the Burmese government.

The thought, or the hope, was that the granting of Dyarchy would satisfy nationalist aspirations, whatever they might be – the idea of 'independence' had not yet been strongly brought forth except by a small militant Burmese minority – it had scarcely entered into the calculations of the British. In any event, the hoped-for result was not achieved. As often happens when an imperial power grants some measure of political freedom to its subjects, the result was only to make it clearer to them that they were not truly and fully governing themselves: they were still a subject people. So there was, on the part of the Burmese, discontent, and a subterranean hostility that was moving closer to the surface: the impassive stare, or the titter, or the *sotto-voce* sarcasm – any of the trivial gestures that in a period of strain can be magnified to major provocations. And on the part of the British government there was a continuing effort at improvement, liberalization, and reform. Indeed, it has been argued that, at the village level, their well-intentioned efforts to improve the traditional 'headman' system were so drastic that in the end the system functioned less well than before. The British were caught in that classic dilemma of a ruling power not native to the country: to what extent should they interfere – where problems ranged from the introduction of Western economic enterprise to the modification of the Burmese passion for gambling?

The ideal of colonial administration found characteristic expression, to give only one example, in *Burma: A Handbook of Practical Information* by J. G. Scott, which was published in a third revised edition in 1921:

> In Burma, as elsewhere in the British Empire, the object of the ruling power has been to maintain the spirit of the native administration and interfere as little as possible with the native executive, legal and land systems, and with the customs and prejudices of the people.[11]

This was the ideal – but of course, the British had notions as to how a country could best be governed, many of them eminently sensible, and it was next to impossible not to interfere and impose them, directly or indirectly, once they were there. The police – native at the bottom but English at the top – would be in the closest daily contact with the Burmese, in the swarming cities and the remotest villages, when it actually came to imposing and administering Western concepts of law and order, based on the straightforward 'Anglo-Saxon' view that there was a right and a wrong way of doing things. Burmese ideas of justice were more flexible, the magistrate less a judge of the right or the wrong than an arbitrator who would attempt to achieve some sort of compromise, a Solomon-like figure presiding over civil disputes or litigation. Presumably there would be less flexibility where crimes were concerned, especially Violent or Important crimes – murder, dacoity* or robbery – but even then, there were radical differences between Burmese and British ways of looking at things, which meant that the high ideal of not interfering with native customs and prejudices was difficult to achieve even when it was attempted. And at the constabulary level, where the British officers went about their daily job, often under adverse conditions and in trying circumstances, it was unlikely that much attention was paid to the ideal.

This was the level where Blair functioned, and it determined not only the peculiar angle of vision from which he looked out at Burma, but also the outer figure he presented to the Burmese. They saw, and he knew himself to be (and later wrote of himself as) a representative of the institution to which he had voluntarily attached himself, the Indian Imperial Police. No matter

* In India and Burma, gang robbery, in which more than four men participate.

how ill-fitting his uniform (in both the literal and metaphoric sense) such was his role, and it was as a policeman, not a journalist, or budding writer, or student of politics, that he had his experience of Burma. One profound lesson that he was later to draw from it was the great distance that exists between institutions and the life they are designed to maintain but more often suppress or confine or destroy; that would be the lesson of Spain also; and the lesson of *1984*. But the immediate effect, in 1924, as he left the Police Training School and at his various postings thereafter, was to prevent him (even should he wish it) from entering into Burmese life except as it related to his institutional role. This in itself is sufficient to account for what he missed of the native experience, so little of which figures in his work; however, by the same token, it ensured him of a full exposure to the colonial experience, which he recorded with an unrelenting distaste in *Burmese Days*. The ferment of nationalist aspiration seems never to have caught his attention, except perhaps as a provocative nuisance, or enlisted his sympathy, or engaged his imagination. It is significant that in his Burmese novel the two principal native characters, the 'good' Dr Veraswami and the 'evil' U Po Kyin are alike in their aspirations: not to reclaim Burma from the English, but to be elected to membership in the English Club. Even the local 'anti-English' riot which dramatically erupts towards the novel's end, and that the English respond to in the pukka sahib tradition, has no real political meaning: it simply has been whipped up by U Po Kyin to further his social ambition.

Of course, one does not turn to Orwell for a 'history' of the country during the period 1922–7. Our interest is in the history of Eric Blair, the experience of a young officer in the police in Burma, in its first version, not its exemplary recapitulation by Orwell, the anti-imperialist. Obviously, his experiences made him the anti-imperialist he became; the 'becoming' extended over the whole of a five-year period during which, from first to last, he was in the service of Imperialism, and outwardly at least exhibiting no qualms about it. That he happened, also, to be a writer-in-embryo adds to the peculiarity of his history.

Early in 1924 [Roger Beadon writes] we sat for and passed our Lower Burmese and other exams and were confirmed in our appointment as A.S.P.s, and so ended our spell at the School. I have always felt, however, that, though from the social angle Mandalay could not have been bettered, from the training point of view the method used at Toungoo, before the school was moved to Mandalay, was far and away more efficient, 'tho undoubtedly more drastic. At Toungoo, training was reduced to teaching the rudiments of languages and law, and then, after only a few months, I believe, trainees were posted to a remote Police Station where possibly only the Police Station Officer spoke English, and told to get on with it or else!

And it worked and worked well, as not only did they have to learn to read, write, and speak Burmese fluently, but also how to deal with the numerous crime and other registers at first hand. I, on the other hand, had never been inside a Police Station the whole time I was under training, which, on looking back, strikes me as most peculiar. Moreover, when I did pass both Lower and Higher Burmese, I took the *laissez-faire* attitude of so many, and expected everyone to speak English. As a result, my Burmese was never very good, though sufficient to get me along. And so, in early 1924, came the parting of the ways, and we were posted to different districts to continue our training under district officers.

Beadon was going to Bassein, Blair to Myaungmya. They shook hands and wished each other luck, knowing that there was little likelihood of their meeting in the future, and with no suggestion that their friendship, such as it had been, ought to be continued by correspondence – though if their paths should cross, as fellow policemen meeting at a district headquarters or Club, fine. In short, it was a parting in the Blair manner. The next year, in circumstances to be described, they did have one further meeting, after which they never saw each other again, though Beadon notes that he 'naturally heard of him from time to time and gathered he was looked upon as somewhat eccentric'.

There was a dramatic, even intimidating contrast between the chiefly theoretical training Blair had received in Mandalay and the responsibilities that awaited him at Myaungmya; and it was reinforced in its impact upon him by the contrast between the two places themselves. The one was a fair-sized city, the capital of Upper Burma, equipped with at least some of the amenities of twentieth-century civilization one took for granted – electric light, for example. The other was a primitive, isolated outpost in the alluvial Irrawaddy delta, where there was no electricity and one read at night (if one was eccentric enough to want to read) by oil lamp under mosquito netting. His colleagues agree that

Blair was not 'lucky' in this starting point for his career: there were other districts to be preferred to the Delta; and his superior officer, they suggested ever so tactfully, may have been a bit difficult. One has the impression from their impressions that his bad luck held through more than the first of his postings. One hears of less than enviable locales, and of other 'difficult' superiors – of one who was a bully and gave him a 'bad time', of another who was a melancholic and eventually a suicide, and of a third who took against Blair as an old Etonian.

In fact, his being an Etonian gave positive offence only to a few bigoted and mean-minded types of the sort he would later pillory in *Burmese Days*. 'What struck most people as unusual,' we are told by a man who was acquainted with him when he was stationed in Hanthawaddy District, 'was that an Etonian should join the police services in Burma.' (And he goes on to express the view generally held, then and perhaps even now, by non-Etonians: 'Eton, as you know, is the school for the sons of aristocrats and plutocrats. Their sons can usually be found some lucrative employment at home and it was rare for them to serve in India except perhaps in the Indian Civil Service.') Although Orwell later may have enjoyed the incongruity of calling himself a 'policeman', with its nicely homely, Gilbert and Sullivan, English overtones – and admittedly, anywhere, 'a policeman's lot is not a happy one' – still, the 'bobby on his beat' conjures up a very different picture from Blair on a tour of duty, going by motor launch or dugout canoe from one village to the next (for there were no roads or railways in the Delta) – not only enforcing law and order, as a policeman would do in the home country, but also playing a role in the administration of government.

Technically, the police officer was subordinate to the Deputy Commissioner, who was in charge of a District, but in many ways he was a parallel, independent authority, as he also took orders directly from his own Inspector General. The Indian Imperial Police had been officially formed in 1861 to cope with the growth of crime; or perhaps, rather, with the extent to which organized crime was interfering with the growth of English influence and power. In 1921, just before Blair arrived in Burma, there was a military garrison there of about 10,000, a military police force of about 15,000, and a civil police force of about 13,000 (mainly Burmese and Indian). It was to the last that Blair was attached. In his postings he would serve either as an assistant district superintendent in one of the thirty-six districts into which Burma was divided for administrative purposes, or as one of the fifty-nine assistant superintendents who were in charge of the more important sub-divisions. Over him was a hierarchy that culminated with the Inspector General and four Deputy Inspectors General, heading an organization independent of any form of popular control, even after the dyarchic reforms of 1923. Although from 1923 on there was a marked liberalization in recruiting, with Indians and Burmese being admitted to the officer ranks, centralization and bureaucratization intensified, which led, inevitably, to a curtailment of imaginative, individual action: the day of the gallant officer, on his own and out of touch with civilization, was virtually at an end. The telegraph, too, made its negative contribution in this regard: it stifled initiative, Orwell later thought, and because of it, thinking and action had been reduced to the 'constipated' attitudes of those who were at their desks in Whitehall, the ultimate source of orders and power.[12] Even so, the sense of adventure, of doing something uncommon, the challenge of responsibility and authority, were still inherent in the life he had chosen; and Blair, whatever his cynicism, evidently responded to them with some excitement. Putting on the uniform of the Indian Imperial Police, with its tight strapped trousers, was not a humiliation to the spirit. Many years later he remarked to his friend Anthony Powell, 'Those straps under the boot give you a feeling like nothing else in life.'[13]

But of course there was a world of difference between taking dress parade on a Wednesday morning in Mandalay, and finding himself Headquarters Assistant to the District Superintendent in Myaungmya. Once again, it might be said, he was a 'new boy', in a situation that reactivated the St Cyprian's syndrome: friendless and inexperienced, not certain of what to expect and fearful of proving to be inadequate, a predictable failure. The post was regarded officially as a continuation of 'training', but it was training of a wholly different order from what he had received at Mandalay. Without preliminaries he was thrust into the demanding responsibilities and, for a 'new boy', highly confusing routines of a District Headquarters. He was expected to run the office; supervise the stores of clothing, equipment, and ammunition; take charge of the training school for locally recruited constables, as well as the headquarters police station with its strength of thirty to fifty men on active patrol duty and a contingent of escorts for hearings and trials in court. He would also check the night patrols in Myaungmya, and when his Superintendent was away, touring the sub-divisional headquarters within the District, he would assume general charge. For a young man not yet twenty-one, and fresh from the classrooms of the Police Training School, it was a daunting assignment, and there is reason to think that Blair did not manage it notably well. For he held the post an unusually short time: only two months – and it seems likely that his Superintendent requested (demanded) that he be moved on elsewhere. Granted that this particular Superintendent was more difficult than most, we are reminded by Lawson, speaking from first-hand knowledge, that no District Superintendent would welcome a junior officer as Headquarters Assistant where 'the duties were highly onerous and calling for experience'. It was part of Blair's bad luck in Burma that this should have been his first assignment.

His luck improved somewhat with his next posting, farther east in the Delta, to Twante, a subdivision of Hanthawaddy District, where he was on duty from mid-May to mid-December 1924. As Sub-Divisional Police Officer he would be responsible to the District Superintendent, but he would not be performing his duties, as at Myaungmya, directly under his observation, and he would have a considerable degree of freedom in carrying them out. In charge of several police stations, he would spend most of his time on tour, inspecting them, checking the investigation of local crimes, holding inquiries into cases of police misconduct, and visiting as many villages as possible with a view to enlisting the co-operation of the village headmen and elders who had minor police powers and duties. He would also see that adequate surveillance was kept over the persistent criminals living in the area. This was the usual routine of his days and nights, but the arrival of a telegram advising him of the occurrence of murder or dacoity meant he must drop whatever he was doing and hasten to the scene of the crime and take charge of the investigation. A demanding life, certainly; perhaps a boring one; very likely a lonely one, for in a small town like Twante there would be no more than two or three Europeans about (though, given Blair's solitary nature, this might have proved less of a hardship for him than for some).

Two possible views of the life he was leading in the Delta – that the same experiences could give rise to very different feelings – are suggested in letters written to the authors by two police officers who were in Burma at the same time as Blair, and who were kind enough to comment on it. One writes:

His work kept him busy on the move around a large area. He lived in his own Government house – a roomy enough bungalow with stabling and quarters for servants. He travelled around his area with houseman, cook, orderly, etc., and put up in a Dak bungalow or any available shelter . . . Every journey from headquarters had its purpose & apart from that, despite some discomforts, yielded great delight & contained some essence of adventure.'[14]

The same writer adds:

He came by accident to a pleasant, warmhearted, tolerant Buddhist country which had no violent class distinction & found the older Europeans already enmeshed in Buddhist benevolence: loving the people of Burma & imposing no real imperialistic sway. Burma gave him time to think, cause to think, and much to think about.

The first sentence may be taken as one point of view (very different of course from Orwell's); the second sentence is undoubtedly true. What is unclear is how much his thinking then had to do with Burma – he himself has left no contemporary record – for the reaction to what he experienced there would be slow in coming, and the revulsion he would ultimately express at having served in the cause of imperialism may well have been part of the greater guilt he came to feel in being a member of the upper-middle classes. Or again, at the plainest, down-to-earth level, it might have been partly a reaction to the unpleasantness of the physical circumstances in which he found himself. That they could be, indeed were, unpleasant is evident in another letter describing the conditions under which he lived in Twante, in the 'usual dismal teak box of a house with no sanitation, electricity, or piped water supply'. As for the Delta itself, it was the most dismal and pestiferous tract in Burma . . . a vast featureless plain of alluvium extending for hundreds of square miles. A few trees exist near the villages and there are stunted nipa palms on the banks of the muddy creeks which intersect the land every few hundred yards. Near the coast there are many miles of mangrove swamps. The insect life, even in the dry season, is a penance to be borne. Mosquitoes both by night and day exist in their millions. In the rain, the greenfly from the paddy fields invades the houses and makes it difficult to eat meals or drink without swallowing quantities of the insect. There is no water to be had other than that collected in small reservoirs. This is so stagnant that it is always opaque with red algae.

It is in this grim locale – of which, oddly, given his sensitivity to the degrading aspects of life, Orwell never wrote – that we catch some direct glimpses of him. R. G. B. Lawson at that time was District Superintendent of Police at Pyapon in the Irrawaddy Delta west of Hanthawaddy. It was there, on one occasion, and on a second occasion at Twante, that he met Blair, accompanying his own District Superintendent, at conferences to discuss matters of common concern – chiefly criminal – 'the activities of robber gangs operating over a considerable area'.

Writing of these two occasions some forty years later, he remembers Blair as being 'tall, good-looking, pleasant to talk to, easy of manner'. Once again we are reminded that 'He did not give the impression of being in any way remarkable; no one at that time would have imagined his later fame.' Lawson found him reserved, but assumed that, 'Naturally, as a very junior officer he would realize that it was better not to intrude his personality. On the other hand, it is possible that his air of reserve might disappear on closer acquaintance.'

To Lawson, then, Blair was not noticeably different from the usual run of young officers, making due allowance for his being an Etonian. But one fact that he allowed to slip through the reticence-barrier did give an impression of eccentricity:

He told me he was in the habit of attending the services in the little village churches of the Karens. The Karens, who inhabit the areas in the south and east of Burma, have been largely converted to Christianity by the American Baptist Mission. The average European official was, in any case, not noticeably religious and the idea of attending a religious service in a tongue – Karen – which he could not understand, was not likely to occur to him.

But Blair, it is clear now, was not 'average', and even then, this particular eccentricity gained him a certain reputation. Beadon heard of it – 'he was known to have spent a lot of time in Hpogyu-Kyaungs talking learnedly with the Hpyongis (priests) and intoning the Mantras' – and he was not surprised, for, as had been evident from the earliest days at the Police Training School, 'the language came so very easily to him'.

Another officer, A. L'estrange Brownlow, who knew Blair first at Twante, found him 'a shy diffident young man ... obviously odd man out with other Police Officers, but longing, I think, to be able to fit in'.[15] The two saw quite a bit of each other for Blair's next post was at Syriam, and Brownlow by then had become Superintendent of River Police, Rangoon, only ten miles distant. But closer acquaintance did not bring them in any significant way closer. Blair asked Brownlow to take him out with him when he went snipe shooting (snipe were the only 'game birds' in the Delta) and there were several such expeditions. But, as Brownlow recalls, 'he had obviously little experience with a gun, and, if my memory serves me right, did not get a single snipe'.

In mid-December 1924 he was posted to Syriam, the headquarters of the Hanthawaddy District. Two days after his arrival there, he received official notification that his probationary status was at an end and he now held the rank of Assistant District Superintendent. His pay was appropriately raised, with various allowances coming to a total of 740 rupees per month;* this was to be his salary until he left Burma.

Since Syriam was the site of the refinery of the Burmah Oil Company, it had a number of European residents and even what passed for a social life, but in its own way it was as desolate and dismal a place as Twante. The surrounding land was a barren waste, all vegetation killed off by the fumes of sulphur

* About £65 per month. By most standards, certainly by Orwell's, it would be an adequate sum in the early 1920s to live a comfortable life. It is worth noting in this connection that, in 1948, when Orwell took part in a symposium on 'The Cost of Letters' in Cyril Connolly's *Horizon*, to the question 'How much do you think a writer needs to live on?', his reply was a minimum of £10 per week after taxes for a married man, and £6 for an unmarried man. The ideal figure he mentioned was a thousand pounds per year.[16] Taking into account inflationary rises, that was virtually what he had been earning in Burma.

dioxide pouring out day and night from the stacks of the refinery. Eventually one got used to the ever-present noxious smell hanging in the air, but at first encounter it was suffocating in its effect, and a continuing irritation to the mucous membranes.

In Syriam Blair's job was a dreary one – looking after the security of the refinery. In the District – which was suffering from a rather high rate of crime, with more than three hundred murder cases each year – his duties were much as before, but now, responsible for a whole district rather than merely a subdivision, he would have to be on tour some twenty days each month. But whether in Syriam itself, making conversation with the Europeans who were associated with the Burmah Oil Company or with his notoriously difficult superior – no easy task for one as shy as Blair, and doubtfully rewarding in any case – or travelling from village to village, alone, isolated, weeks at a time, much of it during the rainy season, it was a life in which loneliness and depression would seem to have been almost inevitable. Lawson, who would end his career as City Commissioner of Rangoon, speaks eloquently to the point:

The system of appointing boys fresh from school to the Indian Police, and then throwing them on their own resources in some foul climate with no one to talk to of their own race and kind, was a most pernicious one. The loneliness was too great and in consequence a number of suicides occurred, and at least two of my colleagues lost their reason. The other Services, the Indian Civil Service, the Forest Service, the Service of Engineers, the Education Service, the Medical Service, all recruited university graduates who began their career in India at the age of twenty-five years. Their maturity made life easier for them.

Blair was a novice police officer, just turned twenty-one. But he had always been remarkably self-contained, and so was better able to cope with the isolation than some of the jolly extroverts who tended to crack, away from the gregarious, ritualized life they enjoyed in the English clubs and compounds. It was a life Orwell would reproduce in *Burmese Days* with an unrelenting irony, an outpouring of resentment long-deferred. That, after all, was years later; in Burma, isolation, whether physical or spiritual, was something to be endured – one has the sense of Blair being as lonely in the crowded Club as in the godforsaken

Dak bungalow with no one save his body servant to talk to. But the 'resource' that got him through the ordeal was one that those who knew him in Burma had no reason to suspect. Although Orwell remembered these years as the time when he was trying to abandon the idea of becoming a writer, he was in fact, consciously or not, already a writer-in-embryo: he could watch, observe, listen, and judge. Experience, his own or another's, was something he put to use: it became part of the non-stop 'story' he was telling to his listening self. (And continued to tell until he was twenty-five, drawing from daily experience, Orwell reminds us, all through the non-writing years.) Even the most painful loneliness, the stupidity and racist cant one heard at the Club, the shame at one's role, the rancour of the natives, became endurable as they were assimilated into the 'story'. If much of *Burmese Days* – and much of its hero or anti-hero, Flory – is subjectively drawn (and so, as those who are familiar with the milieu claim, at times over-drawn), much of it – including a good deal of Flory's personality and history – is simply an objective account of what Blair had known at first hand. (Objective, but not inclusive. The curious thing, as has been suggested earlier, is how much of what he had known in Burma he chose *not* to write about.)

For Blair the chief advantage of being at Syriam – and this would hold true also for his next post, Insein – was its proximity to Rangoon. A cosmopolitan seaport, Rangoon was the largest city in Burma, with a population of 800,000. That it was a mere ten miles' distance from a grim refinery town such as Syriam, or thirty miles from the dispiriting wastes of the Delta, made the difference from them only the more vivid and welcome.

W. Somerset Maugham, a writer whose work Blair greatly admired and whose influence upon Orwell's work is discernible, arriving there as a traveller in the mid-1920s, has caught something of the contrasts in which Rangoon abounded:

... a cordial welcome; a drive in an American car through busy streets of business houses, concrete and iron like the streets, good heavens!, of Honolulu, Shanghai, Singapore or Alexandria, and then a spacious, shady house in a garden; an agreeable life, luncheon at this club or that, drives along trim, wide roads, bridge after dark at that club or this, gin *pahits*, a great many men in white drill or pongee silk, laughter, pleasant conversation; and then back through the night to dress for dinner and out again to dine with this hospitable host or the other, cocktails, a substantial meal, dancing to a gramophone or a game of billiards, and then back once more to the large, cool silent house. It was very attractive, easy, comfortable, and gay; but was this Rangoon? Down by the harbour and along the river were narrow streets, a rabbit warren of intersecting alleys; and here, multitudinous, lived the Chinese, and there the Burmans: I looked with curious eye as I passed in my motor car and wondered what strange things I should discover and what secrets they had to tell me if I could plunge into that enigmatic life and lose myself in it as a cup of water thrown overboard is lost in the Irrawaddy.[17]

Admittedly these are the impressions of a world-famous author – Maugham at his most worldly and Maugham-like – and suggest, at the respectable end of the spectrum at least, a social life unlikely to be experienced by a junior police officer. Blair, not even an apprentice writer, settled for less, 'the occasional festive weekend'. He went into the city as often as he could manage: to browse in a bookshop (Smart & Mookerdum's), going over the new books (Maugham's among them) and periodicals arriving weeks late from England; to eat well-cooked food, imported beefsteak by choice, in a Western-style restaurant, a dramatic change from the ill-prepared chicken and rice served up to him night after night by his houseman in Syriam; to get away from the boring routine of police life and the company of fellow officers among whom he was 'odd man out'. Those were the rewards of Rangoon.

But his weekends had their disagreeable aspect too, for in the city he was brought face to face with the 'new' Burmese – so different from the gentle villagers and their co-operative headmen – the students and Buddhist monks who 'dared to dream of political freedom', whose faces expressed an infuriating contempt, and for whom Blair, as a police officer in uniform, would be imperialism personified. And there was nothing one could do, really – it was not illegal for a Burman to smile mockingly or snigger or brush past one on the railway platform – except to seem to ignore the provocation as best one could (or else to try to understand the 'dream' that inspired it, a possibility that did not occur to him then). Dr Maung Htin Aung, Vice-Chancellor of the University of Rangoon, has told of an episode at the end of 1924 that might have come from the pages of *Burmese Days*, in which a young officer whom he identifies as Blair figured. (Dr Htin Aung at this time was a freshman at University College, Rangoon; Blair would have very recently arrived at Syriam.)

One afternoon, at about 4 p.m., the suburban railway station of Pagoda Road was crowded with schoolboys and undergraduates, and Blair came down the stairs to take the train to the Mission Road Station, where the exclusive Gymkhana Club was situated. One of the boys, fooling about with his friends, accidentally bumped against the tall and gaunt Englishman, who fell heavily down the stairs. Blair was furious and raised the heavy cane that he was carrying, to hit the boy on the head, but checked himself, and struck him on the back instead. The boys protested and some undergraduates, including myself, surrounded the angry Englishman . . . The train drew in and Blair boarded a first-class carriage. But in Burma, unlike India, first-class carriages were never taboo to natives, and some of us had first-class season tickets. The argument between Blair and the undergraduates continued. Fortunately, the train reached Mission Road Station without further incident and Blair left the train.[18]

Whether or not he went to the Gymkhana Club after leaving the train we do not know, though it would have been a logical inference to draw if he were the stereotype he might appear to a Burmese schoolboy, and given to doing what 'one did'. At times, as we will see, he overplayed the part of the imperial policeman; it is doubtful, though, that he 'longed' to be like the others; he took a sardonic pleasure in being 'unlike', and was drawn by temperament as well as by the curiosity of a writer-in-embryo to the 'odd case'. In Mandalay, while at the Training School, he had become acquainted with one such: Captain H. F. Robinson, an Indian Army Officer who had been seconded to the Burma military police and, after a scandal involving his native mistress, had been cashiered. He had chosen to remain on in Mandalay, becoming a Buddhist and an opium addict, and climaxed this phase of his life with a botched attempt at suicide. For a young officer, he would be a classic minatory example of the white man going to pieces in the East (as in a story by Maugham). But for Blair, the future writer, meeting Robinson was a memorable experience,[19] which he later drew upon for a number of biographical details when he was inventing the character of Flory – whose tone is undoubtedly autobiographical, but whose history is not.

In Rangoon he saw quite regularly an old Etonian who had come out to Burma as the representative of a British business firm. The two had first been acquainted in College, where Lawrence (as we will call him here) was in an Election some years senior to Blair's. In London very likely the acquaintance between them would not have been revived, given the ease with which Blair could go unencumbered by past friendships from one phase of his life to the next. But in Rangoon, Lawrence was a welcome 'find', the more so as he was, in his own fashion, also 'odd man out' – in this instance, with the English colony and especially its female members, having committed the unpardonable sin in their eyes of marrying an Indian woman. It was precisely the oddness of his behaviour and the disapproving reaction to it that would have excited Blair's sympathy and interest.[20] Privately, he confided to Christopher Hollis who passed through Rangoon at this time, he thought Lawrence's marrying the woman a mistake. No doubt he found Robinson's arrangement – a native mistress such as he would give to Flory – more sensible as well as more understandable: it fell so easily within the confines of fiction. But where Blair's contemporary attitudes towards marriage, women, and sex are concerned, and certainly when it is a question of his actual experiences, we enter into speculative or hearsay territory. Lawrence recalls him telling him – in what seems a most un-Blair-like burst of candour – that he frequented the waterfront brothels. Perhaps he did. Or perhaps he did not and claimed that he did, out of pride and for effect, to impress a fellow Etonian whose experience in sexual matters was so much greater than his. Against these putative, man-of-the-world descents into the brothels, we must put Roger Beadon's forthright statement: 'As for female company I don't think I ever saw him with one.' It was the sort of thing Beadon would be likely to notice, for, as he says, 'I had an eye for anything that was going.' The next year, when he visited Blair at Insein, he detected no tell-tale hint of a female on the premises, no doll-like Ma Hla May, such as Flory had bought from her parents for three hundred rupees, to come to his bed upon demand.*

* Masculine pride, of which Orwell had his share, accounts for much, and almost certainly for the curious conversation between Orwell and Harold Acton in Paris in 1945 that Acton reports in his *More Memoirs of an Aesthete*:

It was at Lawrence's house that Blair and Hollis had a brief reunion in the summer of 1925. Hollis, Malcolm Macdonald and Christopher Woodruff had been on a world tour as debaters for the Oxford Union, and Woodruff and Hollis had come on to Rangoon from Australia and Indonesia. In the two years since Hollis had last seen Blair, they had not kept in touch. Although he 'vaguely knew that Blair had gone "out East",' he was delighted to learn now that not only was he in Burma but stationed so close to Rangoon that it would be possible for them to meet. They did have two dinners together, and the principal impression that Hollis carried away from their meetings was that Blair, the Etonian rebel and cynic, the friend of the 'revolutionary' Caucus, had been transformed into the very model of a Kiplingesque empire builder, intolerant of any of the natives, the Buddhist monks in particular, who made nuisances of themselves, and so made the work of the police more difficult. Hollis writes:

> In the side of him which he revealed to me . . . there was no trace of liberal opinions. He was at pains to be the imperial policeman, explaining that these theories of no punishment and no beating were all very well at public schools but that they did not work with the Burmese

'. . . I prompted him to reminisce about his life in Burma, and his sad earnest eyes lit up with pleasure when he spoke of the sweetness of Burmese women . . . He was more enthusiastic about the beauties of Morocco, and this cadaverous ascetic whom one scarcely connected with fleshy gratification admitted that he had seldom tasted such bliss as with certain Moroccan girls, whose complete naturalness and grace and candid sensuality he described in language so simple and direct that one could visualize their slender flanks and small pointed breasts and almost sniff the odour of spices that clung to their satiny skins. A description worthy of Gide, I mused, and equally sincere.'

Orwell went to Morocco with his wife Eileen in September 1938, at the advice of his doctor that he spend six months in a warm climate. He had been in a sanatorium suffering from lung disease since March. The Orwells settled in Marrakech, where he began to write his novel *Coming Up for Air*. He worked at it steadily, and finished it in little more than three months, in January 1939. Then he and Eileen went for a week's holiday into the Atlas mountains. They returned to Marrakech on 27 January; soon after, he fell ill and was bed-ridden for a period of three weeks. He and Eileen sailed from Casablanca to London on 26 March. His letters from Morocco, and hers too, suggest that it was a time when they were extremely happy together. There is nothing in Orwell's published or unpublished writing of his having tasted 'bliss . . . with certain Moroccan girls', although, in a letter to his friend Geoffrey Gorer, he speaks of the native women as being 'exquisitely beautiful'. But what was most fascinating about them was that they were 'so dirty . . . their necks almost invisible under dirt'.[21]

. . . If I had never heard or read of Orwell after that evening, I should certainly have dismissed him as an example of that common type which has a phase of liberal opinion at school, when life is as yet untouched by reality, but relapses easily after into conventional reaction.

He was *at pains* to be the imperial policeman.

There was no mention of the loneliness, the boredom, the physical discomfort of life in the Delta, nothing to suggest disillusionment or dissatisfaction. Once more, as with his claim to experience of the brothels, it would seem to have been a matter of putting on a front, essential to his pride. Here was Hollis, who had gone on to university, as he, Blair, might also have done, and who would leave Rangoon in three days and return to London, to Oxford, to the literary-flavoured life he, Blair, had romantically turned down; and here *he* was, committed to the Burma police for another three years. In the circumstances it is hardly surprising that he should have overplayed the role of the tough, no-nonsense imperialist. What one is 'at pains to be', is not necessarily what one is. So the two friends went their separate ways, and they would not be in touch again until 1931.

Blair was at Syriam a little more than nine months; then, in September 1925, he was posted to Insein, ten miles north of Rangoon, as Assistant Superintendent at Headquarters. The advantage of Insein over his previous postings was its more agreeable climate – he had managed to survive two of the May to October rainy seasons, unpleasant in general, particularly so in Lower Burma – and now at last he was out of the Delta. The disadvantage of Insein proved to be his Superintendent who, we are told, was something of a bully and 'may well have played dirty tricks on him'.[22] But a Superintendent's duties kept him on tour through the District much of the time, and he would have been no more than an intermittently annoying presence. For a good part of each month Blair was in charge of Headquarters, caught up in a routine that by now he had pretty well mastered. Socially too he had, to all outward appearance, mastered the routine. Since Insein was a District Headquarters, life centred around the Club, where each night he made his obligatory appearance – there is no reason to think he enjoyed it – just as he had paid the obligatory formal calls and left cards with the married couples at the Station when he first arrived. He had also made his official calls on the senior civil officers – by tradition, these calls were made in full uniform, at noon, the hottest time of the day.

But if in public he conformed to what was expected of him at Headquarters and the Club, in private he could indulge his eccentricities. Beadon, who came out to see him one day when he was living at Insein, found his house a shambles, with 'goats, geese, ducks and all sorts of things floating about downstairs'. Beadon, who prided himself on his own neat house, was 'rather shattered', and suggested to Blair that perhaps he might bear down on his houseman. The suggestion was shrugged aside: he quite liked the house as it was. Beadon changed the subject: was it true, as he had heard, that Blair was attending services in the native churches? Yes, it was true: it had nothing to do with 'religion', of course; he enjoyed conversing with the priests in 'very high-flown Burmese' (Beadon's phrase); he added in his sardonic (or leg-pulling) way that he found their conversation more interesting than that he was forced to listen to at the Club. Whereupon he took Beadon off for a farewell drink – at the Club! – before he set off for Rangoon. It was their final meeting.

Some years later, and after Blair had left Burma, Beadon heard that 'it was the fact of being posted under a bullying D.S.P., who treated him and the men under him very unfairly, and was not the type of whom the Police could have been proud, that turned him against Government service'. Another officer who knew Blair at the time, C. B. Orr, remarks, 'I noticed that he did not seem happy but did not know what the trouble was,' and he too advances the possibility that Blair had suffered from unfair treatment by his superior. But the trouble went deeper than this, and the outcome, it must be said, would have been the same no matter who had been over him or how he had been treated. He was the wrong man in the wrong place: the act of recognition began in Insein.

There was the Headquarters where he worked, and the Club where, in a manner of speaking, he played, and the house where he ate and slept, undisturbed by the fowl and livestock 'floating about downstairs', and where he read and re-read the books he bought in Rangoon, their pages mildewed and their bindings buckling in the sodden air. There was also in Insein the prison, the second largest in Burma, with some two thousand inmates, which became the setting for 'A Hanging', the first of the two Burmese pieces mixing reportage and reflection that Blair was to write after his return to England, drawing specifically and exclusively for their subject matter upon his police experience. (The second is 'Shooting An Elephant' of 1936. *Burmese Days*, the major literary production that grew out of what Orwell described as his 'five boring years' in the Indian Imperial Police, though it contains an interrogation scene in a police station that is obviously based on the real thing, is for the most part centred on the colonial rather than the police experience, observed, heightened and arranged for fiction.)

'A Hanging' by Eric A. Blair was published in the *Adelphi* in August 1931 – some sixteen months before the name of George Orwell would appear for the first time on a title page. (The name itself is said to have made an earlier appearance, however, but would not have been seen by anyone but Blair, in a very early draft of *Burmese Days*. As he later told Richard Rees, he had originally given it to the character who was to become John Flory.) A brief, stylized essay of under three thousand words and one of Orwell's best-known works, 'A Hanging' is as near to a contemporary document as we have from Blair himself for his Burma period. But a document composed five years after the event it describes, recollected in a mood of detachment, is contemporary only by courtesy and in a relative sense: that is, it is closer in time to its subject than are *Burmese Days*, or 'Shooting An Elephant', or the relevant autobiographical pages in *The Road to Wigan Pier*, or the many allusions and references to Burma and India scattered through Orwell's journalism and reviews. But it is very different in character from what a letter written within a few hours after the event would have been, when the pain of confrontation with a particular reality would be at its freshest. Unfortunately, if he ever wrote such a letter, it has not survived; and, for want of it, we will proceed here to treat 'A Hanging' in an extra-literary way, as a document in Blair's life as a police officer.

In a number of respects, one might admit, it is not a satisfactory document. Too much is omitted for that; a complex of things left unsaid – those blotted-out surrounding details that set off in high relief the details that are presented – thus adding to its effectiveness as a work of art but detracting from its biographical utility. The story is very simple: it describes how, on a morning during the rainy season, a condemned man is brought out of his cell, escorted across the jail yard to the gallows, and is there hanged. Who he is, what he has done in the past, what his offence has been that requires this punishment, whether he is innocent or guilty, we are not told. We know that he is a Hindu; that the six warders who are guarding him are Indians; that the head jailer, whose name is Francis (but whether this is his first or last name is uncertain), is a Dravidian. The superintendent of the jail – not to be confused with the bullying District Superintendent of Police – is a gruff army doctor, presumably English (though that is not stated). The narrator is 'I', an eye – logically Eric Blair if this is not a fiction, though about him we are given no information whatever. We do not know why, for example, or in what official capacity he is there. It would have been most unusual, though not impossible, Blair's colleagues in the police agree, for him to have been present at a hanging. As Headquarters A.S.P. his duties would not normally require his presence there; perhaps he was there out of 'curiosity', as a writer-in-embryo gathering 'material' though almost certainly not consciously aware of doing so. On the evidence of the document, this was the first hanging he had attended, and he had been in Burma as a police officer for three years: so that one infers either that hangings were uncommon, or that it was uncommon for an officer such as he to be in attendance at one.

The irony of the situation is beautifully and painfully communicated: the banal character of what is said and done – by everyone present, down to the condemned man himself – is projected in a succession of ordinary but closely, even microscopically, observed details. It is out of one such detail that the crucial meaning of the experience was revealed to Blair. The prisoner, walking towards the gallows, at a certain point steps 'slightly aside to avoid a puddle on the path' – quite as though it mattered to him, as though in another two minutes he will not be dead, swinging at the end of a rope. For Blair, following behind him on the path, the trivial, human gesture had the force of revelation. Five years later, recalling it, he wrote how until then he had never before understood what it meant 'to destroy a healthy, conscious man . . . I saw the mystery, the unspeakable wrongness of cutting a life short when it is in full tide.' But the revelation did not lead to an immediate, decisive action: his life as a police officer continued unchanged.

Long afterwards, when Eric Blair had become George Orwell, he could shrug off his time in Burma as 'five boring years within the sound of bugles'. But that was by no means the whole of the story, for he came back to England with a hatred of the Imperialism he had served, the more intense for his having been in the police, where, as he put it, one saw 'the dirty work of Empire at close quarters'. Orwell, of course, was writing about something that had already happened: a position arrived at with difficulty and thereafter firmly held. Our attempt here is to describe the painful stages by which he arrived at the position.

If one considers first what Blair as Blair wrote on Burma and Imperialism, and then what he wrote on the subject as Orwell, the progression is unmistakable. By the time he left Insein – in September 1926, when he was posted to the Town Subdivision of Moulmein – he had recognized, as indeed he must have done from the day of the hanging, his antipathy to the career he had voluntarily but so misguidedly chosen, his growing reluctance at having to do what his spirit rebelled against and loathed. Thanks to Orwell's later writings, one can read back into 'A Hanging' (though not read on the page) all sorts of anti-imperialist significance. But if Blair had been a police officer in England, witnessing an execution in Wandsworth Prison, he might have produced a similar, equally moving, minute-by-minute account of the event. What was painful to him then was the power of life and death over others that was invested in him by his being an officer in the police, the power to treat people as though they were things. (Ideally, to do one's job properly, one could not afford to see the man who was to be hung as other than a 'thing'; to see him as human was to admit 'the unspeakable wrongness' of taking his life.) Blair's dislike of being a policeman, growing more intense over the five-year period, leads to and reinforces his hatred of Imperialism. Only then, in the fusion of the two deep negative feelings (and with a positive feeling involved also, as we shall see), does he leave Burma. Whereas in fact, he could have resigned and gone back to England, got free of the dirty work, at least a year before he actually did. By September 1926 he would have had enough money saved from his salary to pay for his passage home – as he would have had to do, if he resigned from the police before having served a period of three years. Instead he went on to Moulmein.

Again he was Headquarters A.S.P., but now, for the first time since Mandalay, he was stationed in a city of considerable size with a numerous European population. As a port and trading centre, dominated by the British since early in the nineteenth century, Moulmein offered a community where English customs were understood and practised, and a way of life more agreeable than in such isolated stations as Myaungmya or Twante. More importantly for Blair, it had been the home of his mother's family for generations and it was there that their teak interests, though diminished from what they had been at the turn of the century, were still centred. There were a number of Limouzin connections for him to meet, among them an aunt married to an official in the Forestry Service, and, most impressively, his grandmother. A woman of intelligence and distinction, she made it a point – unlike the conventional Memsahib – to wear the loose-fitting, colourful native costume, arguing sensibly that it was more comfortable and better suited to the hot, damp climate than European dress. In itself it was not an insignificant gesture. And given Blair's distaste for 'Memsahibdom', which would find its ultimate expression in the character of Mrs Lackersteen in *Burmese Days*, his grandmother's determination to do as she pleased would immediately have won his approval.

It is also possible that she won his confidence, for there is some reason to believe that he told her – or else she surmised – something of the anxiety and uncertainty about himself and his future that he was feeling at this time. A fellow officer, seven years older than he, who was to rise to great eminence in the service, has a recollection of meeting Blair at a sports competition when he was accompanied by two ladies, perhaps his aunt and his grandmother. 'What has stuck in my mind,' the officer writes, 'is that

I was asked for advice about Blair by the more elderly of the two ladies. I cannot claim to have given any advice but I did suggest that if Blair was certain that he would not be happy in a career in the Burma police he would be better to get out before he was too old to embark on another profession.'[23]

Whether he did or did not confide in his grandmother is a matter of conjecture – if he did, she respected his confidences and no news of his dissatisfaction was communicated from Moulmein to Southwold. But that he was unhappy in a career in the Burma police is fact, not conjecture. As his own hatred for the role he was forced to play grew, so he felt hatred growing around him and focusing upon him. 'In Moulmein, in Lower Burma, I was hated by large numbers of people . . .' That, of course, is the opening of 'Shooting an Elephant', a masterly essay – one of the masterpieces of the genre in this century – that may well stand as Orwell's finest single achievement in prose. (As with 'A Hanging', however, we will allude to it at this point only as a document, keeping in mind that it was written in England in the summer of 1936 when the incident that provides its subject and title came back to Orwell 'very vividly' almost ten years after it had taken place in Moulmein.)

He hated his job by this time and, as Orwell remembers it, he was also by this time equally convinced of the evils of Imperialism. But though he knew he should, in the circumstances, get out (as his fellow officer had sensibly suggested at the sports competition), apparently he was not yet capable of the decisive act, had still to suffer through more of the (for him) ever more painful experience. Anxiety made him hyper-sensitive. He felt himself a prey to the rising anti-English feeling among the Burmans; singled out, as perhaps he was – subjectively, certainly; objectively, possibly – for insults and provocations everywhere. Orwell's citations are thought to be exaggerated by other English witnesses who were in Burma at the same time as he, but they brilliantly suggest his exacerbated state: European women going alone into the bazaars were said to be spat upon by betel-chewing natives; he himself had been deliberately tripped up on the football field by a Burman and the Burman referee had deliberately ignored the offence, to the glee of the crowd; yellow-skinned faces, passing him on the streets, sneered at him; young Buddhist priests, in Moulmein by the thousands, stood on street corners and jeered at him. His anxiety was compounded by a characteristic ambivalence, for he was, in theory, on the side of the Burmese, the while he hated 'their oppressors, the British'. (That was how Orwell remembered it as being for Blair in 1926; he himself, writing in 1936, knew that the British had not been 'oppressors' in Burma; the evil was in the nature of Imperialism itself, simply their being there, as the ruling power in a country not their own.) But if, in theory, he was on the side of the Burmese, in practice he raged against them for making his job impossibly difficult, and he thought that 'the greatest joy in the world would be to drive a bayonet into a Buddhist priest's guts'. All this should be understood as 'exaggeration for effect', a rhetorical strategy rather than a cool, clinical analysis of what Blair actually felt – this, after all, is the man who only a few months earlier had recognized the 'unspeakable wrongness of cutting a life short when it is in full tide'. And the generalization that Orwell drew from it in 'Shooting an Elephant', that such extremes and divisions of feeling are to be expected from anyone in the service of Imperialism, seems highly questionable. Certainly it is not borne out in the letters of his colleagues describing their individual experiences – let a single example suffice, from the officer of the sports competition: 'I loved Burma and the Burman and have no regrets that I spent the best years of my life in the Burma police.'

Blair's ambivalence grew out of resentment and sympathy, and his anxiety out of the belief that the two were inalterably opposed: sympathy for the oppressed, the underdog, the victim; resentment of the oppressor, the topdog, the victimizer. (From the advantage of ten years' perspective he could see, as he could not in Moulmein, how one might simultaneously resent and sympathize with the oppressed – and even the oppressor.) On the morning of the day described in Orwell's essay, the victim is the elephant, the victimizer is Blair, who feels himself victimized by the Burmese, and all of them together are the victims of Imperialism. The situation of 'Shooting an Elephant', in itself so 'tiny', nevertheless proves large enough to establish the point Orwell wishes to make – he would never make it better elsewhere – the peculiar harm that Imperialism as an institution does to all who enter within its magnetic field, oppressed and oppressors alike. A tame elephant has gone amok, damaging property and killing a man. Blair, at headquarters as the highest police authority in the town – presumably the Superintendent is 'unavailable' – is summoned to the scene by a sub-inspector at one of the local police stations. By the time he arrives the elephant has subsided in his fury and in due course is discovered standing in a field, calmly eating grass, apparently no longer a danger to anyone. It is now that the tyranny of the institution – with its power to impose 'roles' – begins to function. A kind of ritual ceremony is set in motion, which continues until the elephant has been killed and its carcass stripped. One feels that nothing can alter it: their roles have taken over the lives of the people who play them. The Burmese, virtually all the inhabitants of the quarter, will behave as the institution expects them to behave; so, in his fashion, will Blair.

On that morning his resentments are directed as much against the institution that has imposed the sahib role upon him as against the Burmese, in their roles as 'natives', who count on him (challenge him?) to shoot the elephant. No matter that, realistically considered, it is now harmless and itself a valuable property; no matter that he, privately, has no wish to shoot it. That he must do so is the Obligation of the Sahib; to do less, once the ceremony is in train, would be to lose face, to play the role badly, even to be laughed at by the 'natives' and 'that would never do'.

His sympathies are as strong as his resentments, and they are all for the appointed victim of the ceremony, the elephant who must be sacrificed, and whose death Orwell invests with a dignity and pathos that are in painful contrast to the pettiness of the 'natives' who have come to see the show, and of the police officer who is fearful of being laughed at. The death of the elephant, so magnificently and feelingly described, is the pre-ordained conclusion of a ritual that satisfies the 'natives', re-affirms Blair in his role as the servant (the victim) of Imperialism, and adds to the burden of self-hatred and guilt he will take away from Burma.

But there seemed to be no limit to how great the burden must be, how long it must be endured, in how many places. After Moulmein came Katha, a small town north of Mandalay, headquarters of the Katha District in Upper Burma, to which he was posted in April 1927 as Headquarters Assistant Superintendent. This time he could hardly have wanted a more temperate or pleasing climate (free of the extremes of the South, bearable even in the monsoon), or a more luxuriant or visually compelling landscape. (As against the alluvial wastes of the Delta, here was a gorgeous profusion of colour: blood-red of the gold mohur, cream ivory of the frangi-pani, purple of the bougainvillaea, scarlet of the hibiscus, pink of the Chinese rose.) But his stay in Katha was to be as brief as he could arrange it – only three months. Even so, the place in its sensuous aspects made an unforgettable impression upon him: some years later he would reproduce it vividly as Kyauktada, the setting for *Burmese Days*. That was to be in the post-Kathan future: time, and a difficult apprentice-ship, would be required before he could assimilate into fiction something (but not all) of what he had experienced, felt, and observed as a participant in the rite of Imperialism. Yet if *Burmese Days* is a *roman à clef*, the key to its characters is not to be found in Katha, but in all the stations leading up to it, from Myaungmya to Moulmein, where Blair had stopped and suffered and, as it were, made notes en route. Katha, however beauti-ful, was no more than the culminating point of his five years in Burma, and Burma by then had become insupportable to him.

In November he would have completed five years of service, which would automatically entitle him to a long leave. But soon after arriving in Katha he had been ill, and he chose the moment to apply for leave on a medical certificate rather than wait through the six months remaining before his regular leave would begin. At last the point of no return had been reached. In 1940 Orwell would say flatly that his health had been ruined by the climate of Burma. Of course, since early childhood in Henley, he had been susceptible to head colds, coughs and bronchial congestion. He had wheezed through the damp, coastal winters at St Cyprian's, and the damp Thames-side winters at Eton; and though he had passed the medical examination given to candi-dates for the police, the damp, steamy, tropical atmosphere of the Delta had had a debilitating effect upon him. Beadon, visit-ing him in Insein, had been struck by his pallor. And there is reason to believe that he was suffering from some sort of respiratory or chest ailment in the late stages of his time in Burma. In 1938, when he was hospitalized in Kent for several months, he wrote to Cyril Connolly of 'an old T.B. lesion which has partly healed & which I must have had ten years or more'[24] – in other words, since Moulmein or Katha. But this does not necessarily mean that his illness then had been *diagnosed* as incipient tuberculosis – though if it had, it might also account for his being sent, at that particular moment, from Moulmein to the more invigorating altitudes of Upper Burma.

His request for leave was granted promptly: a period of six months to take effect on 1 July 1927. As soon as was feasible thereafter, he sailed from Rangoon. When he arrived in England in August, he appeared to be in good health, and he said nothing to his family of having been ill – but it would have been quite out of character for him to have done so – and nothing to suggest that this was not a usual period of leave, after which he would return to Burma. In fact, his Burmese years were at an end.

The principal story of those years belongs, on the surface where facts accumulate, to Blair the police officer. But there is a 'shadow' story that accompanies it – under the surface and largely speculative – of Blair the writer-in-embryo. Orwell himself paid only perfunctory regard to it. As time went on, he progressively reduced the Burma period to no more than a dismissive sentence or two in the history of his literary development. In 1935, in the Introduction to the French edition of *Down and Out in Paris and London*, he tells of having resigned from the police in Burma in the hope of being able to earn his living by writing – from which one infers that the thought of becoming a writer must have preceded the act of resignation, rather than *vice versa*. The inference would seem confirmed in the autobiographical note he supplied in 1940 to the editors of *Twentieth Century Authors*. There he states that he left Burma because, among other reasons, he 'had the vague idea of writing books'. But in 1946, in 'Why I Write', he tells us that the years between the ages of seventeen and twenty-four were those when he 'tried to abandon' the idea of becoming a writer. And in 1947, in the Introduction to the

Ukrainian edition of *Animal Farm*, he places the decision to become a writer as being arrived at in late 1927, *after* his return to England.

Strictly speaking, it can be argued that a writer becomes a writer at the point when he begins to write: 'On such and such a day in such and such a month and year, X. wrote the first sentence of his first story . . .' But this is to oversimplify an exceedingly complex process: a writer may wake up one morning to find himself famous; but he does not wake up one morning, or sit down at the typewriter one afternoon, and then and there find he has become 'a writer'. There is a period of apprenticeship, whether brief or of several years' duration, itself no guarantee of a satisfying sequel. (The sad fate of how many failed writers is that they got thus far but no farther.) And even before this, there will often have been – consciously, half-consciously, or, in Orwell's word, 'vaguely' – a latent period, before the writer emerges.

Blair's apprenticeship belongs to the years after his return to England: it was then that he began in a practical and considered way to write. But he was a writer-in-embryo in Burma, and his trying to abandon the idea of becoming a writer during the time that he was there is analogous to his being 'at pains to be the imperial policeman'. In each case the psychological need is understandable, and the responsive mechanism evident. As a policeman he had trapped himself in a career for which he was 'totally unsuited' (Orwell's judgement in 1935), but before he could acknowledge this to himself, he had to exaggerate his commitment to it. Again, having tried to abandon the idea of becoming a writer – an ambition or certainty he had entertained since he was five years old – it was natural that he should overreact. He was at pains not to allow himself to 'write' – even his letters home are remembered as being brief and infrequent. He was at pains also to emphasize his separation – as though a final choice had been made – from 'writing' and the London literary life, affecting a philistinism that would have gone down well at the Club in Kyauktada. At least he did so in retrospect, as when in the 1930s he told his friend Richard Rees, who was then an editor and part owner of the *Adelphi*, that he had read the magazine in Burma but thought it a 'scurrilous rag' and used it for target practice.[25] The story is perhaps more revealing than Blair may have meant it to be (and he may have meant it to be a joke – though, as Rees recalled, his manner of telling it was dour and unsmiling). For what he was shooting at from the verandah of his Dak bungalow was a periodical of the sort in which his literary friends from Eton were just beginning to appear as they came down from Oxford and Cambridge, and in which, though he could not consciously admit it, he too would have liked to appear. (Later, the *Adelphi* would be a target at which he would aim for publication; and it is a nice irony that the 'scurrilous rag' should have given him his greatest encouragement in the crucial early stages of his career. In its pages appeared poems, reviews, and essays, first by Eric Blair and afterwards by George Orwell.)

We have alluded earlier to the 'non-writing' years, when Blair was transforming, or incorporating the events of his life as they were happening, into a story he told to himself. But what remains unwritten, no matter how precisely one imagines it to be phrased, is something very different from what is actually written, sentence by sentence, on the page. There is no doubt that Blair's apprenticeship was made appreciably more difficult for him by his not having *written* earlier. The fragments that survive of his earliest apprentice work – all of it unpublished – are proof enough of how far he had to go to arrive at a style. They suggest a writer whose native gift – at the level of language and composition – was remarkably small, considering his later development, or else, simply, remarkably undeveloped. If he had been psychologically prepared to *write* when he was in Burma, if he had allowed himself even to conduct a voluminous correspondence, buzzing with ideas and descriptions of his day-to-day experience – which is to say, if he had been very different from the young man that he was – he might have developed more easily and sooner, and solved some of the quite primitive difficulties that beset him when he made the decision – explicitly – to become a writer. But if he denied himself the chance to practise the rudiments of the craft he was eventually to master, he knew what the craft was. For he was an assiduous reader in Burma, and he read for the art and the craft as well as for the pleasure and escape that reading provided. What he read, though, depended on what was available in the bookshops in Rangoon, Mandalay, and Moulmein: this explains a great deal.

Blair was in the East at the very time when the 'modern movement' was entering its decade of triumph, but its impact (and certainly its productions) seldom got beyond Suez. Joyce, Proust, Virginia Woolf, Aldous Huxley, Gide, Cocteau, Wyndham Lewis, the Sitwells, T. S. Eliot, Ezra Pound – such names did not figure in his reading in Burma, nor were they likely to turn up on the shelves at Smart & Mookerdum's. One is prepared to say 'Just as well', for it saved him from ill-disguised, imitative neo-experimental writing (such as many of his contemporaries were practising under the spell of the great modernist inventors) for which he was suited neither by temperament nor talent. (This is not a speculative judgement: his reading of *Ulysses*, which he discovered after his return to England and greatly admired, prompted him to his one belated *avant-garde* gesture, the Joycean 'night-town' chapter in *A Clergyman's Daughter*; and he is ill at ease in the manner, though the matter is familiar to him and he presented it more convincingly elsewhere, in his own voice.)

He followed no programme or curriculum, but simply read as he pleased: a heterogeneous and, on the whole, an orthodox selection. From nineteenth-century Russia, Tolstoy (but not Chekhov). From nineteenth-century America, Poe and Mark Twain (but not Henry James). There were authors with whom he was already familiar – Thackeray, Kipling, and Conrad – and authors newly encountered – Samuel Butler, D. H. Lawrence (the only 'modern' whom he read in Burma), and W. Somerset Maugham.[26] These latter three were to exert a powerful influence upon him, as much in the embryonic phase as in the years of apprenticeship. Influence, of course, takes many forms: whether in 'the narrowly technical sense' as models of style; or in the broader less easily definable sense, bearing upon subject matter, attitudes, and tone. In the *Note Books* of Samuel Butler, which he carried with him from station to station, he came upon a passage that might have served as a Guide to the Neophyte – if the neophyte was destined to become a writer like Orwell. (And the passage itself reads uncannily like Orwell at his most characteristic, offhand, and assured.)

I never knew a writer yet [Butler declared] who took the smallest pains with his style and was at the same time readable. Plato's having had seventy shies at one sentence is quite enough to explain to me why I dislike him. A man may, and ought to, take a great deal of pains to write clearly, tersely and euphoniously: he will write many a sentence three or four times over – to do much more than this is worse than not rewriting at all: he will be at great pains to see that he does not repeat himself, to arrange his matter in the way that shall best enable the reader to master it, to cut out superfluous words and, even more, to eschew irrelevant matter: but in each case he will be thinking not of his own style but of his reader's convenience ... I should like to put it on record that I never took the smallest pains with my style, have never thought about it, and do not know or want to know whether it is a style at all or whether it is not, as I believe and hope, just common, simple straightforwardness.

Maugham, with his conviction that the best style is the style that calls the least attention to itself, would have agreed that one must write 'clearly, tersely and euphoniously', but he might have cast a sardonic glance at Butler's conclusion – in his own case, at least, he had taken great pains to achieve his undecorated, seemingly casual, highly readable style. So too would Orwell. (Of course if one is meant to write in the transparent style – cf. Orwell's 'Good prose is like a window pane' – once the technique has been mastered, brought to a high degree of ease and confidence, one writes fluently and plentifully thereafter. Some of Orwell's most characteristic examples in the style, where evidently there was no time for 'working over' the prose even if he had wanted, are to be found in 'As I Please', the column of comment on a variety of subjects that he wrote for *Tribune* from 1943 to 1947.) 'I believe the modern writer who has influenced me most,' Orwell acknowledged in 1940, 'is Somerset Maugham, whom I admire immensely for his power of telling a story straightforwardly and without frills.'

To produce writing that was clear, terse, euphonious, straightforward, and without frills – this was an objective to which he could legitimately aspire and ultimately achieve. But there was prose of another order, as he discovered and responded to in the stories of D. H. Lawrence, prose that was written with greater intensity than Butler or Maugham allowed for, expressing a greater intensity of vision and feeling than they were capable of – marvellous phrases and sentences that evoked a landscape, or the physical presence of a character, or the nuances of emotional response, a whole range of possibilities that the storyteller straightforwardly telling his story had not time or inclination for.

Maugham had very shrewdly recognized the limits within which he must work as a writer: since he lacked the vision of the poet, to write 'poetically' would have been to encumber the story with frills. He was above all interested in the behaviour of his characters as they exemplified the ironies in which the human situation abounds. His notebooks are catalogues of such ironies, jotted down against the time he will transform them into stories. When he takes note of 'local colour' it is with a view to the effective touch, the easy reference that lends verisimilitude to the tale: in his stories, no matter how exotic their locale, landscape is literally background against which the important action goes dramatically forward: a tale to be told.

Lawrence's Way led to the deeply felt descriptions of landscape in *Burmese Days*; Maugham's Way to the sardonic observation of the Kyauktada Club in action; Orwell's Way to the anti-imperialism which is a dominant theme of the novel and would find a more telling expression, released from the conventions of 'plot' (for it turned out he was not at his best as a storyteller), in 'Shooting an Elephant'. This is to anticipate, however. The writing of *Burmese Days* belongs to the period of his life when he moved from apprenticeship to authorship. In Burma, as a police officer who was a writer-in-embryo, it was enough for Blair to have found in Maugham and Lawrence authors who revealed possible ways – to which, for all the differences between them, he was instinctively attuned – of imposing some sort of meaning and form upon the experience one lived: otherwise, how pointless it would have been. The determination to begin his career as a writer was the mirror-image of his determination to end his career in the police. Leaving Burma in that summer of 1927, he was at last on his way.

Part Four
Becoming a Writer

I

He returned to England late in August, and went straight down
to Southwold to join his family. There had been changes, of
course. For one thing, the Blairs had made yet another move:
from 4 Stradbroke Road to 3 Queen Street.* But the dramatic
difference was in Eric himself, who had been last seen by the
family as a tall, smooth-faced nineteen-year-old schoolboy,
fresh from Eton, and who returned to them as a weathered veteran
of five years in Burma in the Imperial Police. He had changed
considerably in manner and appearance. Avril thought he now
looked very much like their father, and 'he'd grown a moustache.
His hair had got much darker. I suppose being used to a lot of servants in India he'd become terribly – to our minds – untidy. Whenever he smoked a cigarette he threw the end down on the floor
and the match – and expected other people to sweep them up.'[1]

   He said nothing to his parents of having been ill in Burma,
and nothing to suggest that he would not be returning there
when his leave was over. Lounging about, with nothing in
particular to do that he was yet ready to admit, scattering cigarette
ash through the small rooms in the house in Queen Street, he
soon grew restless and proposed that they all go down to Cornwall
for a holiday as they had used to do. 'We went down for the
whole of September,' Avril recalls, in a laconic sentence that
contains a wealth of drama, 'and it was during that time that he
told my mother that he wasn't going back to Burma; that he'd
resigned his commission.'

   It was as though he had wanted the reassurance of a familiar
and happy childhood setting, as Cornwall had always been for

* They were to move once more, for a last time as it turned out, to Montague
House, a modest house in the High Street in Southwold, which Mrs Blair
bought in 1933 when she came into a small inheritance.

him, and a return to the intimacy with his mother that had its beginnings in childhood, before he felt ready to make his sensational announcement. Sensational undoubtedly it was. In spite of the closeness between mother and son – naturally it would be she whom he would tell first – or perhaps because of it, his mother was 'rather horrified', as Avril puts it, but that was as nothing compared to the reaction of his father, once Mrs Blair communicated the news to him. Very likely it would have been simpler all round if Eric had slightly altered the facts of the case: if he had made much of his illness in Burma (borne out by his being on sick leave) and little or nothing of his wanting 'to write'. If he had told them that he was resigning his commission for reasons of health, his parents, though they would have been concerned, could hardly have complained. But he was careful to establish the reason for what he was doing, or rather, had already done: some time between his arrival in England and mid-September, he had sent in a letter of resignation to the India Office to take effect at the expiration of his period of leave, 1 January 1928. Why? Because, he told his family, he was 'quite determined that what he wanted to do was to write'. So the torrent of parental disapproval descended upon him, particularly from his father, as he must have known it would; perhaps wanted, for it would define the magnitude of the decision he had made. Through the glum remainder of their time in Cornwall, and the few weeks afterwards that he stayed in Southwold, he was not to be swayed by the objections that parents like the Blairs would summon up at such a moment – that he was throwing away a respectable, worthwhile career (very like the one his father had followed) that assured his present and future well-being, for something that almost certainly would prove a will-o'-the-wisp, leading downward to poverty and failure. Then came the sensible, concerned, exasperating questions: how did he know that he could write? what was the evidence to justify his attempting a career as a writer? what had he written? what had he published? There were no convincing answers available to him, not at that time of his life, and what was required instead was an act of faith which *he* had, but which they, understandably, did not.

Life in the house in Queen Street, after the family's return from Cornwall, was not easy for any of them. It was one thing for Eric to be lounging about, doing nothing, scattering cigarette ash, when he was an officer home on leave; quite another when he had resigned his commission and declared his intention of becoming a writer. He had also emphasized that he 'was not going to be any kind of charge on the family' – which is to say that he had saved the greater part of his earnings in Burma, and so had money enough of his own to live on while he began his new career. But when did he mean to begin it? Writers must always appear mysterious in their ways of working to non-writers who imagine, innocently, that writing is the act of pushing pen across paper. A young man pacing from room to room, flicking cigarette ash on the carpets, may actually be working – thinking about what he is to write later, and, for Blair starting out, these would be difficult thoughts – though to an indignant father, or to a well-meaning mother eager to chat 'since you're not busy, dear', he may appear to be simply wasting time. He was twenty-four, with no visible form of occupation, no clear plan of action that his parents could understand or share in; prospectively a ne'er-do-well. His presence in Queen Street was a source of daily concern and irritation. Eric and his father had never been close: now a kind of estrangement grew up between them, the coldness more pronounced, the differences of opinion more abrasive. While his mother quite soon came round to Eric's point of view – though it might be said that she believed in her son as much as she believed in the writer – his father did not, and would not, virtually until the end of his life.*

It is doubtful that Eric had ever thought of staying on in Southwold for an extended period, but the tensions in Queen Street hastened his departure, and early in the autumn of 1927 he moved to London: there he intended his literary career to begin. Before that, however, he had gone up to Cambridge to visit A. S. F. Gow, since 1925 a Fellow of Trinity. No doubt

* There was a reconciliation between father and son before Mr Blair's death in 1939. Orwell told this to Richard Rees 'with great satisfaction, adding that he himself had closed his father's eyes in the traditional way by placing pennies upon the eyelids. He further added,' Rees writes in *Fugitive from the Camp of Victory*, 'that after the funeral he had been embarrassed to know what to do with the pennies. "In the end I walked down to the sea and threw them in. Do you think some people would have put them back in their pocket?" '[2]

it was a traditional thing to do, for an old boy to call upon his old tutor, but it comes somewhat oddly from Blair, who had not written to Gow (or apparently to anyone else he had known at Eton, boy or master) during the five years he was in Burma.

The visit, in its essentials, bears a striking resemblance to that earlier meeting, in the autumn of 1921, when Blair had gone to 'Granny' Gow ostensibly for advice as to his future, but had in fact already decided before seeing him what his future was to be.[3] On that occasion Gow's advice and Blair's intention neatly coincided: perhaps it was the recollection of that which drew him to Cambridge now. Gow was too wise, too kindly (and perhaps too cynical) to try to undo a *fait accompli*. He was prepared to accept that Blair's going out to Burma in the Imperial Police had been a mistake, and the logic, therefore, of his resigning from the service. As to his determination 'to write', Gow was carefully neutral: what could he do but appear to assert in a non-committal way, when it was so evident that a decision had been made. True, he had rather liked the fables the boy had read aloud at those meetings on Sunday evenings in his rooms years before, but there was nothing in them to suggest a literary gift that was destined to prosper. Yet who was to say Not? He did feel called upon to point out the difficulties of the literary life, how little security it offered, and that talent and ambition were in themselves no guarantee of success. Again, though in a different key from the refrain that had already been sounded in Queen Street, the question was raised of how he was to support himself. But this, Blair suggested, would not be a problem: the Burmese savings were referred to. Drawn on frugally, they would give him a year in which to prove himself. A year, presumably, would be sufficient. (It seems clear that in 1927 there was a strong streak of optimism in Blair – strong enough to justify himself to himself in the course he was about to take – that Orwell later forgot: hence his statement in 'Such, Such were the Joys' that until he was thirty he was sure that he was 'bound to fail'.) Whatever Gow's reservations and misgivings at that moment, he kept them to himself, knowing that they would make no difference. Blair sensed them, however – years later he recalled having felt that he and Gow were no longer in the same orbit. Even so, the parting was amicable, and there would be a few exchanges of letters intermittently in the future. But they were not to meet again until twenty-three years later, a few days before Orwell's death, when Gow came to visit him at his bedside in University College Hospital.

From Cambridge Eric returned briefly to Southwold. There he wrote to Ruth Pitter, a friend of the family from the time when they had been neighbours in Mall Chambers, in Notting Hill Gate. In the years since then Miss Pitter had published widely, and was now increasingly recognized as a lyric poet of rare quality. This did not mean, however, that she could live by what she wrote, and she supported herself by working in an arts and crafts studio in Notting Hill Gate. (In 1930, she and her friend, the painter Kathleen O'Hara, opened a studio of their own, not unlike the Omega Workshop though on a very small scale, where they decorated tea trays, tables, chests, chairs, and other small objects with handpainted roses, flowers, birds, and butterflies. From this they earned a small but sufficient income.)

Eric, having begun by asking 'Do you remember me?', rushed on to say that he was back from Burma and wondered if she might be able to help him find an inexpensive room somewhere in London. She replied that of course she remembered him – indeed, her first impression of him in Mall Chambers, a seventeen-year-old Etonian home on a visit, 'a tall youth, with hair the colour of hay and a brown tweed suit standing at a table by the window, cleaning a sporting gun', has stayed with her through her lifetime – and that she had found a room for him in a house at 10 Portobello Road.[4] So the matter was settled, and he announced his departure in Queen Street. Miss Pitter's association with the move would have lent it a reassuring respectability in Mrs Blair's eyes; and though Mr Blair remained stonily silent, the good-byes were managed without drama – he was going to London, but it was only a departure from Southwold, not a break with it.

In London Miss Pitter was surprised to learn that he had resigned from the police; he had not explained this in his letter and she had thought he had wanted a room only while he was on leave. Her next surprise, an even greater one, came when he told her of his ambition to become a writer, that this was why he had left the service. Privately she thought it a great mistake, but her response like Gow's was carefully non-committal. Later when he began to show her the stories and verses he was slaving over in his room in the Portobello Road – so pallid, jejeune and awkward – she couldn't believe his literary ambitions would come to anything. At the least there was a long painful apprenticeship ahead of him; he was starting comparatively late; and though he lived very frugally, what would he do when his savings had run out? But she could not bring herself to say any of this to him: he was so manifestly happy in his new role, even though he was not well, and felt the winter keenly after Burma.

The room in Portobello Road was cheap, small, and austere: a good deal less spacious than his Dak bungalow in Burma, almost as sparsely furnished as his stall in College – bed, wardrobe, chairs, a table on which to write. Still, it sufficed; and the house, in which he was the only lodger, reeked of respectability. His landlady, Mrs Craig, at an earlier point in her life had been the maid to a lady of title – an unforgettable experience which left her, one might say, *plus royaliste que le roi*. From Mrs Craig Blair had an early, absurd lesson in the lengths to which people in England would go to maintain their 'class' position, the more precarious it actually was. For on one occasion when the Craigs (there was indeed a Mr Craig) and Blair were locked out of the house and it became evident that someone would have to climb in through an upper-storey window, Blair suggested that they borrow a ladder from the neighbour next door. Mrs Craig demurred. It would not do. In the fourteen years that they had owned the house in Portobello Road, the Craigs had never spoken to their neighbours, not knowing what *sort* they were (and in Notting Hill Gate one ran the risk that they might not be the *right* sort). To speak to them now, to ask a favour of them, might encourage them to become familiar. It was decided that the only safe thing to do was to borrow a ladder from a relative of the Craigs' who lived almost a mile away; and the three of them trooped off to fetch it and carry it back to Portobello Road. Which they did 'with great labour and discomfort'. (When Orwell recounted the incident some seventeen years later,[5] he ended it at that point, so one will never know whether or not the neighbours came to their windows to watch, peering out over the aspidistras, and if they did, how Mrs Craig bore up under the *humiliation*.)

Alone in London, with a room of his own, his own life to be lived with no regard to the wishes, commands or codes of others, at last he felt himself entirely free of the institutions that in their different ways had controlled him: first the family, then school, then the police. No longer were orders to come down from above. The glory of the writer's life – seen in its ideal, abstract form – is the freedom it allows. In his first few weeks in London Blair gloried in this freedom. Exhilarated by it, he was even prepared to renew Etonian friendships. He got in touch with Maurice Whittome, his old Fives partner. A dinner was arranged; some of the other members of the 1916 Election who were living in or about London joined them. It was a friendly and agreeable occasion but without a sequel, and during the next five years, from the spring of 1928 to 1933, he as effectively withdrew from his fellow Etonians as he had during the five years he was in Burma. The new exhilaration wilted in that reminiscent setting. A gathering of men around a dinner-table inevitably has a clubbish air – perhaps this put him off. Or it may have been merely his being among contemporaries who had followed a road so different from his own, down from Oxford or Cambridge, and who were now beginning their careers as barristers or dons or civil servants or businessmen, with a reasonable certainty that all would go well with them. From Blair's point of view, at this particular stage of his life, what could he say of himself? Disclosure had never been his style: he withdrew into the safety of the Etonian *persona* they all remembered – cynical, faintly aloof, reserved, rather man-of-the-worldly. After all, he had been out in the East, and they had not: if he had wanted he could have told exotic tales of Burma. But that evening the talk was of King-Farlow's experiences in exotic America, where he had been travelling, and studying at what the Eton School Register was pleased to call Princetown University. Yet perhaps the oddest aspect of the occasion was that Blair said so little about himself, in a specific way, that Whittome came away with the impression that he had not even finally decided he would leave the police and, that even if he did so, he had no special idea of what he would do next.

He had his room in the house in Portobello Road, just enough money to live on, and all his time free. He began to write. One can only speak tentatively of what he wrote during this first 'London period' – from the autumn of 1927 to the spring of 1928, when he went to live in Paris. Almost nothing from the period has survived: there are a few undated fragments that may be assigned to it using the test of quality – i.e., the earlier in time, the poorer the writing. Orwell himself, in 1946, when he spoke of his early work in 'Why I Write' was referring to *Burmese Days*, not to these unpublished first attempts.

So far as can be determined, the only person he was willing to show his manuscripts to at this time was Ruth Pitter. They would often meet for dinner over a bottle of cheap red wine, which Blair would insist on paying for, although Miss Pitter, aware of his need to make his money last as long as possible, argued that she should at least be allowed to pay her share. They would go for long walks and talks along the Embankment. And sometimes he would show her what he was writing. Obviously he was more at ease with her than with his Etonian contemporaries; and it is suggestive of his state of mind at this period that he should have not got in touch with Cyril Connolly, who was also starting out on a literary career – but was much further along than Blair, having already published a number of reviews and essays in the literary weeklies. It is suggestive, too, that the friendship with Connolly should have been kept in abeyance until the early 1930s, by which time Blair was already a published author with two books to his credit, while Connolly, though a well-known critic, would not publish his first book (the novel *The Rock Pool*) until 1936. Miss Pitter was older than Blair, an established author; he did not feel in competition with her, and she had a sympathetic interest in what he was doing. She would be the first of the Egeria-like figures who were to play a part in starting him on his way as a writer.

His poems were neatly written, some in rhymed quatrains, some in unrhymed iambic pentameters. Their tone was cynical; their language banal; their ironies predictable. It was as though sub-Maugham subjects had been set to sub-Housman verse. One can sympathize with Miss Pitter: she had no wish to be harsh, but to have pretended that these exercises in verse had a quality they did not possess – the quality of poetry – and so encourage him to continue, would have been a cruel kindness.

She contented herself with pointing out weaknesses in the versi-fication – a misplaced accent here, a line deprived of a foot there. Then, tactfully, she suggested that perhaps prose was a medium in which he would be more at home. It is indicative of their relationship that he did not hesitate to take her advice. In the room in the house in Portobello Road he began to write short stories. Presently he asked her to read them. None of these stories has survived. Apart from remembering how awkward and con-trived they were, how patently made-up, Miss Pitter herself has forgotten them. (She does recall, however, the amusement she felt at discovering that he could not spell the 'rude words' he was fond of using.) The obvious tack to have taken at this point was to suggest in a kindly way that Blair should consider another vocation. But Miss Pitter had been increasingly impressed, not only by his determination but also by a sense of unfocused power stirring within him, a complex of intelligence and feeling that had yet to find a way of expression. So she made one further, simple, and as it turned out, crucial suggestion: that he should try to write about what he knew.

A simple suggestion, however sensible, may be difficult to follow. This was to prove the case now.

There are two main themes that figure in Blair's life during the years between his return from Burma and January 1933: first, the struggle to become a writer; and then, the need to expiate the guilt he felt at having served in the Imperial Police. Eventually the two themes would be fused together, and from their fusion would result the only significant writing to be signed Eric Blair ('A Hanging'), and the earliest significant writing to be signed George Orwell (*Down and Out in Paris and London*).

Orwell wrote virtually nothing about the first theme – his struggle to become a writer was a private matter, without moral or political application – and so it has gradually faded into invisibility. But he wrote very powerfully on the second theme – it belonged to a representative moral/political experience: the rejection of Imperialism – and it has a highly visible place now in his literary history. The result of this disproportionate treatment of the two themes is that the unwary reader, dependent on Orwell's didactive and reductive version, might well decide that he had become a writer in order to describe the expiation of his guilt – or to put it as simplistically as possible: if there had been no guilt, there would have been no writer. In fact, the guilt of which he speaks certainly helped determine the kind of writer he became; it did not determine his becoming a writer.

In the purposefully selective autobiographical section of *The Road to Wigan Pier*, Orwell remarks that by the time he came back from Burma his 'hatred' of the Imperialism he had served was so intense that he doubts (even now, nine years later) that he can make it clear. But in fact, by 1936 he had become so accomplished a writer that he is able to do so brilliantly, in three dramatic, persuasive, and, in the famous 'adulterous couple' episode, even lurid pages.*

In 1927, however, he had neither the technique, nor perhaps even the insight to make it clear. When he came back to England it appears that he said nothing to his mother or father of the 'hatred' he felt – it would be surprising if he had – or to Avril, or to Mr Gow, or to his Etonian contemporaries. He told very little of his experiences in Burma to Ruth Pitter, though they were meeting often and talking about 'everything'. She does remember his once saying how 'horrified' he was to have to watch a man being tried for murder in a language that he (the accused) did not understand, and for a killing, meritorious and perhaps even obligatory by the laws of his own people. But such glimpses into his experience were rare; more often when he talked to her of Burma, it was of its exotic birds and flowers and trees, its temples and gilded buddhas, its haunting landscape. Obviously Burma was what he knew best, and in an inchoate way felt about most deeply, and, if he was to write about what he knew, then

* The episode is one in which Orwell describes an overnight train journey to Mandalay – presumably, judging from biographical evidence, it would have come almost at the end of his career in Burma, when he was being transferred from Moulmein to Katha. He shared a compartment with a stranger, an Englishman who was also in the service of Imperialism, and after a half hour of sounding each other out, they sat up all night, each in his own bunk, drinking beer and damning the Empire. It does them good to pour out their bitterness but, having done so, and having taken the precaution of not exchanging names with each other, they part 'as guiltily as an adulterous couple'. Old Burma hands tend to regard the details of the episode as perhaps 'a bit exaggerated', but it shows an undeniable mastery of the dramatic epithet and detail. What, for example, can be more appropriate to the clandestine, adulterous nature of the meeting, than that even the morning light, when the guilty pair arrive in Mandalay, should be 'haggard'?

that was his subject. Yet he had not had time enough, as it turned out, to clarify, to define, to understand the experience. He would need months, years even, before he would be able to say what it was that he truly felt. If he was to make it clear to others (the writer's task), then he must first make it clear to himself.

Orwell has said of *Burmese Days* that it was written when he was thirty, but projected many years earlier. Conceivably its inception goes as far back as the first 'London period'. An undated manuscript fragment, surviving from early drafts of *Burmese Days*, 'My Epitaph by John Flory', has been posthumously published. It is conceivable that it was written in 1927-8; there has even been the suggestion that it was written when Blair was still in Burma. Our own view is that it belongs to a slightly later time – early in 1930 perhaps – after Blair's return from Paris, where his literary apprenticeship had really got under way. The fluency in the writing suggests a considerable gain in technique. If his early attempts at putting to use his Burmese experience had been written in the house in the Portobello Road, it is hard to believe that he would not have shown them to Ruth Pitter, and she has no recollection of his having done so. We will be referring to them again; at this point we would emphasize only that they give no indication of that hatred of Imperialism that Orwell himself would later so eloquently describe.

London was a time of discovery. He had much to learn – in life as in art – beginning with the rudiments of the craft to which he meant to devote himself. As a would-be author, he found it was easier to write in lilting verse of a Burmese whore than to write a truthful, exact account of watching a man be hanged; more difficult still to describe as truthfully as possible one's own response to such an event; most difficult of all to describe the event in such a way that one's response to it would be implicit in the description. Obviously he was not yet ready, whether in terms of craft, self-knowledge or a meaningful over-view, to write of his experience in Burma: it was still too fresh, too raw, too much in need of sorting out. But this did not invalidate the advice Ruth Pitter had given him. If he could not write of the past he had known, perhaps he could write of the present he knew, or rather – to describe the process as it took place – certain aspects of the present that he set out to know and found himself able to write about almost contemporaneously.

In the winter months of 1928, after the cynical light verses and the cynical contrived short stories had come to nothing, he made his first approach to the abyss: he ventured into the East End of London, on the first of the occasional sorties he would make to discover for himself the world of abject poverty and the down-and-outers who inhabit it. Like Jack London earlier, he put on their rags and wandered among them, and suffered with them and for them, and reported back to the world above the abyss how it was down there. He had found a subject.

These sorties, explorations, expeditions, tours, samplings, or immersions were made intermittently over a period of five years. Some were only of a single night's duration, others extended to three or four weeks. They culminate with the publication of *Down and Out in Paris and London*, whereupon they cease.

How a writer comes to a subject and recognizes it, consciously or instinctively, as peculiarly suited to his art, must always be something of an enigma. And it will be so even to the writer himself, though he may write a persuasive-sounding explanation afterwards, when the subject is no longer alive for him – that is, when the subject is no longer material. All experiences are useful but some are more useful than others. It is the latter that provide a writer with his material: what he writes about best. Thus, the experience of Eton was of no use to Orwell as material; Burma was; so was poverty, degradation, going down and out.

He would not begin to convert the experience into material – a subject to write about – until after he had arrived in Paris; and we will postpone until then a consideration of the literary result. But what of the experience itself – at first, and as it continued? When, and How, and Why?

Chronologically, it divides into three uneven segments. First, in London, a brief exploratory venture. Then Paris, where for a time circumstances make him one of the poor himself, a victim rather than an observer. Then London again, where the range widens – out of the East End, on to the road, and into the hop fields of Kent – and a new depth is brought to the experience, thanks to his ordeal in Paris. During the first London period, the only people he will tell of the experience are Ruth Pitter and Kathleen O'Hara. In Paris, so far as one can determine, there are no confidants at all. But in the second London period, their number has dramatically increased: Miss Pitter and Miss O'Hara again, Richard Rees, Jack Common, Brenda Salkeld, Dennis Collings, Eleanor Jaques, Mabel Fierz – an audience of friends who know of the experience when it has already become material and is undergoing a literary transformation. Towards the end of the five-year span there will be still another audience, any author's audience, that knows the material only as it has been transformed and is presented by the author: in Blair's case, the readers of the *Adelphi* and the *New Statesman and Nation*.

The question of 'How' – the method he followed to obtain the experience – is easily answered: he was yet another recruit to a tradition that goes back at least to the *Arabian Nights*, when Caliph Haroun al Raschid put on the rags of a beggar and wandered freely and unrecognized among the lowliest of his subjects. Quite apart from the literary use of the tradition by many of the later Victorian and Edwardian storytellers whom Blair had admired since his schooldays – Robert Louis Stevenson, Oscar Wilde, Conan Doyle – it was not unknown for serious-minded students of the ills of society to disguise themselves as tramps for the purposes of investigation. R. C. K. Ensor, a Fabian and historian, had done so; so had Lionel Curtis, a Conservative political philosopher. But it is plain that Blair's principal guide to the underworld of the poor was *The People of the Abyss*. There are too many similarities of procedure in his account and Jack London's to shrug them off as mere coincidence – step by step, for example, when each writes of spending a night as an indigent in a casual ward, London in the chapter of his book he calls 'The Spike' and Blair in his essay 'The Spike' which later becomes two chapters in *Down and Out*. In 1928 the passage of years had not turned *The People of the Abyss* into an outmoded curiosity: it remained a useful and regrettably up-to-date guide. In spite of the political furore it had stirred up (as one of a spate of books and reports on poverty) when it was published in 1902, and in spite of the not inconsiderable advance in public welfare that had been made since then, the squalor and wretchedness that London had uncovered in his explorations had not disappeared. They were there, in the same streets and tenements, for Blair to see.

But why should he have wanted to see them?

Why in the winter of 1928 should Eric Blair have chosen to go down into the abyss? Why should he have wished to expose himself to the taste, touch, feel, look, sound, and smell of poverty – to experience, as though it were his own, the ordeal of others?

Here Jack London provides a contrast, not a precedent, and the contrast emphasizes the strangeness of what Blair did.

Jack London, in 1902, was already a world-famous author. He had come to London from America during the Boer War as a foreign correspondent, intending to interview the British leaders. But his journalistic assignment was abruptly cancelled, and I. O. Evans tells us, in his Introduction to a recent edition of *The People of the Abyss*, it was 'a serious blow; he had spent his travelling allowance and was almost penniless and workless in a strange country. To Jack London [adventurous by temperament, and a convinced if idiosyncratic Socialist] this was a challenge and an opportunity he was not slow to seize . . . His sociological studies had told him that the East End of London was one of the most appalling of the western world's slum areas, and he could not forgo the opportunity of investigating its conditions for himself.'[6]

London, in his Preface from Piedmont, California, explains:

The experience related in this volume fell to me in the summer of 1902. I went down into the under-world of London with an attitude of mind which I may best liken to an explorer. I was open to be convinced by the evidence of my eyes, rather than by the teachings of those who had not seen, or by the words of those who had seen and gone before. Further, I took with me certain simple criteria with which to measure the life of the under-world. That which made for more life, for physical and spiritual health, was good; that which made for less life, which hurt, and dwarfed, and distorted life, was bad.

After three months, his explorations – mostly in the East End, but also briefly in the hop fields of Kent – were concluded. As an experienced professional writer, who knew what he wanted to say about what he knew, he set briskly to work. Before the end of the year the result was in hand, a vivid, highly readable document whose value – to quote from Evans once more:

lies partly in its factual basis of first-hand observation, supplemented by an exhaustive study of the relevant literature, partly in its objective outlook. Only in a few places does Jack London give vent to his indignation that human beings should receive such treatment. For the most part he was content to record the facts and let them speak for themselves . . . Nor does he suggest any remedy for the ills which he describes: he was writing not Socialism but reportage, and any suggestion of propaganda would have ruined the effect at which he aimed.

Here, then, is the example of an established author, 'with firmly held political and humanitarian positions', who takes advantage of an opportunity to explore at first hand a subject in which he has long been interested, and which is congenial to him as a man and as a writer; who spends a summer on his researches (or explorations) at the end of which time he has enough material to begin writing; who, when he does, knows in advance that his reputation is so great that he need not explain who or what he is to the reader, and simply prefaces his book with a brief, explicit statement of his intentions and expectations. The summer of 1902 and *The People of the Abyss* comprise a sympathetic episode in the history of Jack London, but if the episode had never happened, it would not significantly change one's view of his life and work.

With Blair it is altogether otherwise.

He is twenty-four years old, a would-be author, unknown, untried, and unpublished, who at this time has written virtually nothing and is in no position to judge what is or is not, will or will not be, a congenial 'subject'. He has no politics; his humanitarian instinct is still dormant. By temperament he is fastidious 'to the point of squeamishness': offended by the sight of hairy bodies and the touch of unclean hands; by certain basic bodily functions (sweating, excreting); by the smell of decay, rancid food, soiled beds, grease in stale air – an obsessive catalogue of the foul and distasteful. So that the mere act of entering the abyss, where all that he is most repelled by is in the air one breathes, becomes a physical as well as a psychological ordeal.

Yet he subjects himself to it, voluntarily, again and again, intermittently over a period of years. Between times he is leading a different life, out of disguise, going on with his struggle to become a writer. When at the end of five years he publishes his first book, which is the culmination and termination of his experience of the abyss, there is no preface, no explanation of how the book came to be written or of what his intentions might have been, and he signs it with an invented name.

Nor does he give any clue as to why he should have chosen to go down and out in 'The Spike' or in 'Common Lodging Houses', the two most considerable pieces having to do with poverty that Blair published under his own name. Both are forms of reportage. 'Common Lodging Houses' is a straightforward impersonal third-person account, a more generalized and factual rendering of much the same material that was presented as personal history in 'The Spike'. But although the experience of 'The Spike' is told in the first person singular, it is rigorously uninformative about 'I'. We know only that he is a 'gentleman' down on his luck; and this single bit of biographical information is conveyed in an oddly oblique little recognition scene. The tramps, among whom is 'I' the narrator, are ordered to strip and be searched in the disgusting bathroom of the Spike. As 'I' goes in, he is approached by the man in charge, the so-called Tramp Major, who, after a hard look, recognizes that under his rags 'I' is a gentleman. Asked if it is so, he reluctantly concedes that it is.*

Nor was Blair much more communicative about the subject with his friends. Some of them knew of his explorations, and that he was writing or planning to write about them. But in the past he had never confided his deepest feelings to anyone; it was unlikely that he would do so now. He explained, if pressed, that he wanted to find out what it was like to be a tramp, or a hop-picker, or as he told Brenda Salkeld, 'what it was like not to have anything'.[7] His manner was friendly but reserved, his tone offhand, diffident, Etonian; it comes as no surprise to find him writing to a friend in Southwold in the summer of 1931, just as he is about to go to pick hops in Kent, that he hadn't much of interest yet to report about 'the Lower Classes', and reporting instead, in careful detail, his having seen a ghost in Walberswick churchyard.

In October 1934, Orwell wrote a brief preface for the forthcoming French edition of *Down and Out in Paris and London*. (It was published in Paris in May 1935 as *La Vache enragée*.[8]) His

* When 'The Spike', in altered form, was incorporated into *Down and Out in Paris and London*, this 'recognition scene' was omitted.

manner there was friendly but reserved, his tone offhand and diffident, as he provided a bare minimum of biographical background: first, the year of his birth; then a long blank until his arrival in Burma; a short sentence to dispose of his job as a policeman ('totally unsuited'); then 1928, resignation, the struggle to begin a career as a writer; and so to Paris, where in due course, finding himself almost penniless, he is ready to take whatever job he can get. At that point – not before – the experience of poverty, which is the declared subject of the book, begins.

If one were to judge only by what Blair told his friends and Orwell his French readers, one might reasonably conclude that his going down and out was the result of economic necessity on the one hand (being penniless in Paris) and literary curiosity (wanting to know what it was like) on the other. At the level of the reasonable, such explanations are entirely convincing. But there are deeper levels than the merely reasonable, where much of human behaviour in both its creative and destructive forms has its beginnings; levels that Blair was not willing to talk about, perhaps was not even wholly conscious of at the time. It was left to Orwell to approach them, eight years after his first descent into the abyss of East London, in *The Road to Wigan Pier*. The result was a vivid, highly selective, close-up account – so vivid that it has almost obliterated the more drab and inclusive reality – of his experience as he had come to interpret it in the summer of 1936, and as he could put it to exemplary use in the history of his political development from Imperialist to Socialist.

The difficulty with the Orwell version, it should be said at the outset, is that Orwell's genius is for the *reasonable* – one is made to hear in his prose the voice of a man who is eminently sensible, intelligent, and humane. It meant that when he came to write of the 'irrational', inevitably he would have to explain it in a reasonable way; which, just as inevitably, meant that something had to be left out. One's own irrational acts can be made to seem rational, or understandable in a logical sequence, by tilting the mirror ever so slightly. And something like this does happen in the famous ninth chapter of *The Road to Wigan Pier*, in which Orwell looks into the mirror of the past to re-create the ordeal of Eric Blair.

More clearly and more dramatically than Blair, or the friends who knew him in those early years, Orwell sees himself in 1927, coming back from Burma with a hatred of the Imperialism he had served, and determined to break with it. This he does (as we know) by the simple expedient of sending in his resignation. But to resign from the police is not sufficient to relieve him of a 'bad conscience'; he must also be punished (and who better able to punish him than himself?) for having been one of the oppressors. 'I was conscious of an immense weight of guilt that I had to expiate.'

Elucidated in 1936, a kind of primitive political dialectic sets him in motion in 1928: the world is composed of the oppressors and the oppressed; in Burma, the oppressed were the Burmese, and the English their oppressors; in England it is the poor who are the oppressed; it is logical to transfer one's guilt from one group of the oppressed to another. If he were to go down among 'the lowest of the low' in England, be accepted by them as one of themselves, be forgiven, so to speak, for his sins as an imperialist, then he would be cleansed of his guilt. Therefore, the descent into the abyss. In the Orwell version, what follows is a drama of expiation: the first act of a political pilgrim's progress. But 'guilt' and 'expiation' are theological (or psychoanalytical) rather than political concepts, and it can be argued that the deeper levels of human behaviour are better approached through religion or psychoanalysis than through politics.

In 1936, writing an exemplary chronicle, Orwell passed over without a word – as though it had never been – his struggle to become a writer. The mirror reflected back only his struggle to cleanse himself of guilt. But in 1928, to judge from what he did – and the use he made of his experience – becoming a writer was his immediate and unremitting concern.

Early in that spring, like so many aspiring young writers before him, he went to Paris to live.

2

It was late in the day – historically speaking – for him to come to Paris. The halcyon time of the expatriate invasion was approaching an end that the poets, painters, novelists, and dilettantes who comprised it could not have foreseen: the great depression that began with the collapse of the stock market in October 1929. Thereafter, the retreat was under way, and at the end of the year Blair returned to London. During the little more than eighteen months that he spent in Paris, however, he conformed not at all to the stereotype of the expatriate who turns up in the standard period memoir, talking of the books he will never write at a café table where the saucers are piled higher through the long lazy hours. Nor was it consistent with his character (or his extremely limited funds) to give way to a sluttish antinomianism, lying in bed till four in the afternoon drinking Pernod. In fact, he was an extremely hard-working as well as aspiring young writer, and the sheer amount of work he produced during this period testifies to the seriousness with which he dedicated himself to his career.

The official reason given for the move to Paris was that there he could live cheaply while going on with his writing. But he was paying very little for his room at the Craigs' in the Portobello Road, and it is hard to believe that there was much difference at that level between the cost of living in London and in Paris. Evidently the six months in London had been a disappointment: he seemed at the end of them as far from his goal of becoming a writer as when he had started out, and meanwhile six months of his savings had been used up. He had written a few stories, a few poems, none of them publishable nor even of any discernible merit. Burma was still an unwieldy subject: how was he to get at it? And while he had had the fascinating and disturbing first experience of the abyss, which he intended to write about, he had not yet been able to put it down on paper.

And so he crossed the Channel to Paris 'to write', that traditional gesture of liberation since the days of George du Maurier, which meant traditionally 'to live the Bohemian life and *then* to write'. At first he went to stay with his Aunt Nellie and her husband. Nellie Limouzin Adam was his mother's favourite sister, a warm, vivacious woman whose experience of life had taken her some distance beyond the Portobello Road, where she had lived at the same time that the Blairs were living in Mall Chambers. From Notting Hill Gate she had gone on to the vaudeville stage, and from there to Paris where she had married a Frenchman who was a teacher of Esperanto. There was no question of Eric's not being welcome *chez* Adam – between aunt and nephew there was a genuine fondness – but to settle down in a French version of Queen Street was not why he had come to Paris, and he soon took up residence at 6 Rue du Pot de Fer, on the Left Bank, in the fifth *arrondissement*.

Rue du Pot de Fer was (and is) a narrow, shabby little street not far from the Ecole Normale Supérieure, and indistinguishable from numberless other little streets like it in the heart of Paris, lined with five- and six-storey tenement-like hotels, the ground-floors given over to shabby little bistros, garages, and the occasional frowsty shop or market. Nondescript and slummy, but unmistakably Parisian and local in flavour – you would never think you were in London, and Orwell's 'leprous' when he came to describe it as the Rue du Coq d'Or seems too harsh, though Orwellian enough. It sheltered a heterogeneous population drawn from the working class, students, drifters, fringe types (from the middle class on the way down), White Russian exiles, the aged living on inadequate pensions, and the inevitable eccentrics and 'crazies' – a not unpromising street for a young writer whose material came from the life about him; for Blair in the end it proved to be exactly the subject he needed. It also had the virtue of being within walking distance of the Deux Magots, and naturally he would stroll there under the trees of Boulevard St Germain – especially beautiful to him because their bark kept its natural colour and had not been blackened by grime as in London – and on one occasion he was rewarded when he arrived by the sight of someone he took to be (and who may well have been) James Joyce.

There is little reason to doubt that Blair enjoyed the greater part of his time in Paris. Though Orwell himself said so only in a few oblique references – the pleasure he remembered in going to the Jardin des Plantes; his conviction that Paris was at its best for him when he was in his twenties and that on subsequent visits it had seemed ghostly – one might safely make the deduction on the principle that enjoyable experience never ignited Orwell's moral or creative imagination. Of the eighteen months that he spent in Paris, he got usable material only from the weeks in February 1929 when he was hospitalized in a charity ward (the basis of his appalling essay 'How the Poor Die', published in 1946) and from the last three months of 1929 when his money ran out and he underwent the ordeal he converted into the first part of *Down and Out in Paris and London*.

Most of the time he was writing – stories, novels, poems, articles, he was willing to try anything and he wrote as though driven, not by what he had to put down in words but by the determination to prove that he was a writer. Time was precious, his savings were dwindling, the words came easily, and he wrote and wrote and wrote. During those fifteen months before he found himself almost penniless and had to take an exhausting, time-consuming job (which put a stop to writing), he produced a vast amount of work.

We know from his own account that he wrote two novels while in Paris and sent them off to publishers from whom in due course they came back, in the summer of 1929 (and which he later destroyed). But as to what the novels themselves were, their subject matter, characters, settings, themes, and style (poetic-Lawrence or plain-Maugham?), even their titles, we do not know. Still, if the minimum length of each was no more than 50,000 words, they represented a formidable accomplishment in a short period. And they were only a part of what he was writing.

He also wrote several short stories, none of which were taken (and which, like the novels, he later destroyed). Some of them he submitted to the McClure Newspaper Syndicate in Fleet Street, who in the person of a Mr Bailey sent them back with the comment that 'The Sea God' had too much sex and 'The Petition Crown' too little action, and with the general observation that if he wrote stories that were a little less worldly, they would have a greater appeal.[9] In spite of the advice of Ruth Pitter, he was still manufacturing fiction that had more to do with what he had read – one of these Paris stories bears the worldly title, 'The Man with Kid Gloves' – than with what he knew, and even more with what he hoped would sell. The excuse, of course, was that he needed money.

But novels and stories were not the end of his literary activity. He also wrote articles, and here his luck and his instinct were better. He was able to sell a number of them; he had the satisfaction of seeing his name in print; and, although hardly a financial success, he had reason to hope that before too long he might be able to live by what he wrote, and so vindicate himself in Southwold.

These articles make no claim to be more than journeyman journalism, written for the moment (and the small cheque) and with no thought of outlasting it. The notion had occurred to him that he might report, as a freelance, on Things French to the London weeklies, and on Things English to their Paris counterparts. The latter prove the more receptive. His first professional publication since the poem on the death of Kitchener in the *Henley and South Oxfordshire Standard* in 1916 was '*La Censure en Angleterre*', which appeared in *Monde* on 6 October 1928. It was something of a *coup*, and he would have more than ordinary reasons to be pleased, for *Monde* was a very highly regarded political/literary journal edited by Henri Barbusse and numbered some of the most famous contemporary European writers among its contributors. But the article itself – signed E. A. Blair and 'translated from the English by H. J. Salemson' – seems a bit pallid for its rather grand setting: it is the sort of piece on censorship in England that could be readily worked up by any competent journalist with a passing familiarity with the subject and neither the time nor inclination to go into it deeply. But the piece is undeniably competent, and that is what needs to be emphasized, for nothing he appears to have done in London would prepare one for it. There is a distinction made between the censorship of plays (*before* production; and he cites the obligatory examples, *Ghosts, Mrs Warren's Profession, Damaged Goods*) and the censorship of novels (*after* publication; *Ulysses, The Well of Loneliness*). Then there is a brisk run through the puritanization of the British literary tradition – from Chaucer to Fielding to Dickens, with the Victorians substituting death for sex (a pornography of its own) – and in conclusion, a disdainful, comic last judgement: that if censorship in England were ever to be abolished, in retrospect it would come to seem as fantastic as the marital customs of Central Africa.

Encouraged by his first success, he made time between the novels and stories that were his principal occupation for more reportage, and at the end of the year his articles were appearing on both sides of the Channel, in London in *G.K.'s Weekly* for 29 December 1928, and on the same date in Paris in *Progrès Civique*. The piece in *G.K.'s Weekly* – a paper edited by Chesterton – was 'A Farthing Newspaper', [10] and it is the only one of his articles published while he was living in Paris that did not suffer a sea-change of translation. Perhaps because all of these articles were dashed off rather than worked over – it was the novels and stories that got the richly wrought prose, the similes and metaphors and purple patches that Orwell later deplored – one has a sense, at least in 'A Farthing Newspaper', of a voice. That it is the voice of Eric Blair, rather as it had been heard by his Etonian contemporaries at dinner in London the year before, amused, detached, ironic and sceptical, should come as no surprise. He is reporting on the recent establishment and rapid rise in popularity of a newspaper in Paris, the *Ami du Peuple*, which is sold at a remarkably low price and purports to be published in the interest of 'the people'. Actually, it is the creation of M. Coty, the millionaire industrialist, and it is being published to 'sell' to the people the virtues of paternalistic capitalism. But the question that matters, Blair continues, is the effect that a low-priced paper such as this will have upon freedom of the press, since its success will crowd out some of its less affluent competitors and so cut down dissenting political opinion. But what can one do? In an appropriately ironic coda, it is suggested that English press lords might follow the example of *Ami du Peuple*: if their papers were priced at no more than a farthing, the public would at last be getting their money's worth.

We have referred to the sea-change of translation. There are signs of it in Blair's piece in *Progrès Civique* that was appearing at the same moment as 'A Farthing Newspaper'. In London he began with a simple declarative sentence; in Paris, with a burst of rhetoric that might have been declaimed in the Chamber of Deputies: 'England! Unemployment! One is not able to speak of the one without evoking the spectre of the other!' But after this initial concession to Parisian fervour – or perhaps it is not Blair's voice but that of his translator, Raoul Nicole – the prose cools down, and the rest is straightforward exposition.

The piece itself is one of three that appeared in successive weeks in *Progrès Civique*, having to do with the miserable plight of the British worker.[11] The first takes as its central topic unemployment, a continuing problem in Britain since shortly after the war – as Blair suggests, ironically, it was the government's reward to its returning soldiers; the second, a day in the life of a tramp; and the third, the beggars of London. Though he begins with the basic problem of unemployment, the ordeal of those who want work but cannot find it, and the dole, which is the government's attempt to cope with the result but not the cause, he is reporting mainly on life at the bottom (as he had glimpsed it in the winter of 1928), of the common lodging houses with thirty to forty beds crowded together in an airless dormitory, of the squalor, hunger, and interminable hardship, the life that is less than life of the lumpenproletariat.

Taken together the three articles foreshadow in a rudimentary and sketchy way many of Orwell's deepest concerns in the 1930s, particularly the question of poverty. In one or another of its destructive forms, poverty was to become his obsessive subject – at the heart of almost everything he wrote until *Homage to Catalonia*. His dealing with it expressed a genuine concern for others; it expressed too a way of coping with his own profound sense of financial inadequacy – to bring it down to its proper scale – for whatever inferiority he may have felt at St Cyprian's or Eton for having less money than the others, it became a form of self-indulgence when his lot was compared to that of the truly destitute: the respectable working-class worker out of work, and far below, out of sight, the down-and-out who are the outcasts and unemployables of a capitalist society.

By mid-January 1929 he was able, for the first time, legitimately to call himself a writer: in the space of less than a month four articles by E. A. Blair had appeared in professional publications. He had even been paid for them – the rate of pay from *Progrès Civique* was seventy-five francs per page. But his prospects, bright at one moment, darkened at the next: there was no glowing sequel to his promising start. For the remainder of his time in Paris – another eleven months – he would sell only two more pieces, and his total earnings for almost two years of literary effort came to twenty pounds.

Meanwhile in February he had undergone a traumatic experience of illness and hospitalization whose effect upon him was to be decisive. It was a grim ordeal, so grim that Orwell could not bring himself to write about it until seventeen years later in 'How the Poor Die'; and compared to the stark pages of that brief essay, with their even-voiced piling up of true and agonizing details, the horrific fantasies of *1984* seem suitable reading for schoolboys. In his unheated room in the Rue du Pot de Fer, in the Paris winter weather, he fell ill with pneumonia. After several days of high fever, he was taken to the Hôpital Cochin, a free hospital maintained for the teaching of medical students, providing them with an endless supply of the living and the dying to practise upon, and for the care and treatment of the poor. He had, of course, no idea of what to expect. What he discovered was a version of hell, beginning with twenty minutes of questioning at the admission desk, continuing with a compulsory bath in five inches of warm water; then, in bathrobe and nightshirt but without slippers, being made to walk in the cold night two hundred yards across an open courtyard to the ward to which he had been assigned; searching for his own bed in the dim, sweetish, foul-smelling room, jammed with three ranks of beds, each virtually head to foot; then, having found it, after a few moments of rest being hoisted up by a doctor and student and forcibly cupped, which was only a beginning. For after the cupping (a succession of small glasses applied to the skin to draw out spoonfuls of blood) two slatternly nurses buckled him into a mustard poultice, the painfulness of which was unimaginable. It was the climax to a night of horror during which he slept not one minute.

There is no need to continue detail by detail with what Orwell has so ruthlessly engraved, like a modern Goya, for us to read. The significant point of these weeks in the Hôpital Cochin is that now he was among the poor, not as a visitor in tramp's clothing who after a night of self-abasement could return to his neat, austere digs and undergo the agony of writing his day's quota of words – not as a visitor but as one of them, one who suffered as they did, experienced the indignities, callousness, and stupidity which they endured as their lot. He watched, because he could not do otherwise, how the poor lived. He was the prisoner of his sick body and the victim of the temporary social position enforced upon him: for the time that he was in the Hôpital Cochin, he was one of the poor.

After several weeks, when he had regained his strength and could recover his clothes, but without waiting for a medical discharge, he fled back to the familiar world. He knew what he meant to write, and for the first time began to perceive how it might be done.

It was a year since he had made his first explorations in the East End, and he had drawn upon them in writing his pieces for *Progrès Civique*, but thus far the reality of the experience had eluded him. He had wanted to know what it was like. Now, thanks to his experience in the Hôpital Cochin, he understood that there was a point of knowing that took one beyond *what it was like* to *what it was*. Reporting on poverty from the outside, no matter how skilfully, accurately, and sympathetically, you could not do more than describe what it was like. But to write about what it was, you could not be outside. The material he had accumulated until now had to be re-invented if he was to use it truthfully – which meant not a surface honesty but to get under the surface (any honest reporter could take care of the surface), to get down to the essence of it. He began to write in the first person, without intervention: simply, I was there.

But the 'I' who was there was not Eric Blair, the St Cyprianite, the Etonian, the man who had served five years in the Indian Imperial Police. 'I' in the beginning had no biography at all. No previous history intervened. He was 'I', one of a group. To be precise, and 'I' was as precise about details as he could possibly be, he was one of a group of forty-eight men and one woman waiting on a patch of lawn for a door to open. It was the door of a Spike, a public workhouse, and when the door opened, they would be allowed in for a free meal and a free night's sleep.

He had known what it was like; now he knew what it was, and he began to write 'The Spike'. To be able to do so, he had to re-invent (or re-create) the experience, he had to invent a style, very different from the style of the novels he was writing at the time, and, as the style took form, he began to become the person to whom the style belonged. The time was not far off when 'I' would discover himself to be George Orwell.

'The Spike' was the first experiment in the new style. The plainness and directness that are its outstanding characteristics were not easily arrived at. His taste was still for the purple patch, the metaphor, and the decorative phrase, all those encrustations that got between the experience and its literary reincarnation. Almost two years intervened between the writing of the early sketches of 'The Spike', and its first appearance in print. What must have made the experiment of creating a new style more difficult for him was that he was still writing his novels and stories in the old style, and still making brief excursions into literary and political journalism. But in early August, he thought (mistakenly) that 'The Spike' was in its final form, and he sent it off to London to the *Adelphi* – the same 'highbrow' *Adelphi* he had used as a target for pistol practice in Burma. A month later, much too soon, he was writing to the Editor the traditional letter of anxious and inexperienced authors, asking if a decision had been reached (it was his only copy, etc.). Soon afterwards the manuscript was back in his hands, presumably with a note of rejection that left the door open to submitting it again, for it was in the *Adelphi* that 'The Spike' would ultimately appear.

But that was for the indefinite future. In the immediate present, September 1929, his situation was discouraging. Since he had come out of the hospital, things had been going from bad to worse for him. In March there had been a disconcerting experience with *Monde*. He had sold them a piece on John Galsworthy, and on the front page of the number for 23 March 1929 it was prominently listed. But inside the magazine, on the page where 'John Galsworthy' by E. A. Blair was supposed to be, there was

'*J'execute les citoyens*', translated from the Russian of Ph. Paneroff (and unlisted in the table of contents); while Blair's piece was nowhere to be found in the magazine, nor would it make a belated appearance in some future number. The episode began to take on the quality of an omen. During the summer his two novels were turned down; he had not been able to sell his stories; even his journalism, his one source of income from writing, petered out. In May he had published another piece in *Progrès Civique*, but they had taken nothing since. And the money he had saved to finance the first stage of his career was almost gone. A simple law of schoolboy banking had been in operation during the twenty-one months since he had left Southwold: if one takes out more than one puts in, the amount of money available to be taken out will diminish until there is none at all.

Orwell in the autobiographical statements he wrote in 1934, 1940, and 1944 makes it clear that this is what happened. The day came when he was almost penniless. In *Down and Out in Paris and London*, the literary re-invention of his last four or five months in Paris, 'I' tells us that the process had been hastened along when his and eleven other rooms in the hotel were robbed by a young Italian with side whiskers. All his money had been stolen except for forty-seven francs that had been overlooked in a pair of trousers.

A romantic variant of this circumstantial account (more circumstantial than anything in Orwell's three statements) came to light only in 1971. It was given by Blair to his friend Mabel Fierz in the early 1930s after his return to England. In Mrs Fierz's re-telling of the story, first heard on B.B.C. television and then reprinted in *The Listener*,[12] Blair told her of

a little trollop he picked up in a café in Paris. She was beautiful, and had a figure like a boy, an Eton crop, and was in every way desirable. Anyway, he had a relationship with this girl for some time. One day he came back to his room, and this paragon had decamped with everything he possessed. All his luggage and his money and everything.

As Mrs Fierz recalled, she went on to ask when Blair had told her the tale, ' "You would never have married this girl, would you?" And he said: "Oh yes I would".'

Whatever his explanation for his predicament – robbery by a young Italian with side whiskers, or robbery by a little trollop with an Eton crop, or the commonplace functioning of a law of economics – the fact was, that by the middle of September 1929, after twenty-one months in which he had published five articles that brought him a total of twenty pounds, he was almost penniless and his career was at a standstill. The scepticism and foreboding that had been expressed in Southwold when he declared his intention of becoming a writer, now appeared to be justified; the darkest fantasies of the St Cyprian period – that one would end up 'poor' – seemed on the verge of coming true.

Yet looked at objectively, there was really nothing unusual about where he found himself: the struggling young writer is the rule not the exception; being penniless, he would have to do what most struggling young writers do: he would have to find a job. It was a quite ordinary predicament, and the ordinary solution would have been to return to London, to look for a job in publishing or teaching, tutoring or translating, on a paper or magazine, something suitable. The extraordinary thing – what makes him Orwell – is the solution he chose.

Nothing would have been simpler than to have borrowed money from his Aunt Nellie and gone home to England and Southwold. But there was to be no thought of borrowing, or going home in defeat. He would stay in Paris and look for work. His explanation in 1934 was that he had not wanted to go back to an England where there were already two and a half million unemployed and jobs were scarce. But it is hard to believe that after September 1929 there would be more jobs in Paris, especially for an inexperienced freelance journalist. Why he stayed is that he wanted the experience he had been taught since childhood to fear most. He had already repudiated the privilege of his class; now, with his money gone, there was nothing to protect him from it: the time had come to know life at the bottom, to be at ease there, home at last.

He adopted the same strategy while he was there as he would use afterwards, writing about it. Having *chosen* the experience, he had to go on as though it had chosen him. It meant that he had to stop being Eric Blair, for Eric Blair, penniless, was by definition in a different case from the man of the working class or below it without a *sou* in his pocket. He had to blot from his consciousness the invented or synthetic character of the experience: that he could terminate it at will, by the simple expedient of making a telephone call to his Aunt Nellie. Looking for a job, he had to close his mind to the suitable possibilities that might have been open and certainly would have occurred to Eric Blair, the Etonian beginning a career as a writer. At the bottom, where 'I' had chosen to be, one took the bottom jobs.

The choice was made, the strategy adopted – and he held to it with an admirable courage and single-mindedness. On the surface, at least, he obliterated Eric Blair. Not one document concerning him is known to survive from the autumn of 1929. There are no diaries or journals; no notes made on the spot to be worked up later; there are no letters by him, to him, or about him; there is no contemporary testimony at all. The document that one uses as a guide to Blair, autumn 1929, is *Down and Out in Paris and London*, a literary re-invention, selected, rearranged, and written during 1930 and 1931, and published in an expanded and reworked version in January 1933. It is as though Blair had disappeared for three months and returned later in the guise of 'I' to tell where he had been.

The composition and publication of *Down and Out* make a later chapter in his development: the conclusion to Blair's struggle to become a writer. Our intention here is very briefly to transmute the material back to its raw state, out of which the book grew. Doing so, one recognizes that much of it antedates autumn 1929. The life of the quarter, the local colour, the raffish and picturesque types were all at hand from the first day he came to live in the Rue du Pot de Fer, and there is reason to believe he began writing about them, or writing them up, early. Some of the types as he portrays them, especially in their Frenchified speech, are so typical as to be fictitious – Charlie, for example, the worn-out twenty-two-year-old amorist, whose tale of a night in a blood-red *bordel* might have been one of those lost, early stories for which Blair found no takers.

The crucial contemporary experience begins when his money runs out. He did then what a man of the newly-poor would do who wanted to go on eating: he pawned all his clothes except for what he was wearing, and used the token payment he got for them to live on while he looked for a job. Even at the bottom it was not easy to find one, and he reduced his chances drastically by looking for work only in the kitchens of restaurants and hotels – this on the advice of an unemployed waiter friend, Boris, whom he had got to know as a fellow patient in the Hôpital Cochin. Three weeks went by, used up in fruitless, picaresque misadventures and listening to Boris's colourful tirades against the Jews. Before the end of the third week he was penniless again, and with nothing left to pawn. For several days he had to live on hard bread; the last two days he starved. Then, at the moment of extreme desperation, tipped off by Boris, he went round to one of the luxury hotels off the Rue de Rivoli and had the good luck to be taken on as a *plongeur*, a dishwasher. (What would have happened if his luck had not fallen out this way? – would Blair have emerged from behind the mask and telephoned his Aunt Nellie, as he was ultimately to do?)

The hours were long (from seven in the morning till nine at night with three hours off in the afternoon, six days a week); the work arduous and stupefying; the conditions dreadful, hellishly hot, underground, in filthy cellars and sub-cellars; the pay, miserable. Still, it was an end to starving; and if he was a scullion, a drudge, a beast of burden, there was a certain brute satisfaction in proving that he could survive, and in the rock-bottom, drunk-on-Saturday-night quality of the life itself. There was a certain justice, too, in this degrading role he had willingly taken upon himself – for if he had been at the top and was served by those at the bottom in Burma, now it was he who served. the sahib had become the victim.

The worked proved more varied than his first grim experience of it promised. Presently he was sent up one day each week to act as assistant to a floor waiter. High above the infernal regions where he ordinarily sweated and slaved, he polished silver and crystal in a small pantry, helped prepare trays to be delivered to the elegantly fitted rooms, listened to stories of highlife told by the cheerful, snobbish waiter, who at twenty-four looked eighteen, and had the fresh face of an Eton boy. ('I' himself proved capable of a bit of snobbery: he was appalled that the guests at the hotel should know so little about good food – but, of course, most of them were Americans.)

He was at the hotel, as a *plongeur* in the *cafeterie* – in status as low as one could get – for about six weeks, and left it to work for a fortnight as a kitchen *plongeur* at a newly-opened restaurant where his friend Boris had been hired as a headwaiter. In all he spent some two months as a dishwasher. Gradually, as he settled into the life, much as a soldier settles into the army, he grew used to it; for the time being he enjoyed the sensation of it, which he no longer even thought of as poverty. And so, although it was very different from his original intention, he had an experience of hotel and restaurant catering behind the scenes: harried and squalid in its operation; disgusting in the details concealed from customers (the cook spitting in the soup; the waiter, at one moment running his fingers through his brilliantined hair, at the next dipping them in the gravy); and fascinating in its social gradations and nuances.

From St Cyprian's on he would always be acutely sensitive to the hierarchical structure of the organizations and institutions in which he found himself – as formal as government or as amorphous as the London 'literary establishment' – and he soon recognized the pattern of rank, from top to bottom, at the hotel: *patron*, manager, assistant manager, chief cook, assistant cooks, headwaiter, waiters, and down at last (the list here is curtailed for convenience) to the *plongeurs*. Yet even they, at the bottom of the hierarchy, turned out to have a curious pride: an eagerness to be recognized as a '*débrouillard*', a man who could do the impossible.

Was 'I' himself a *débrouillard*, though he was too diffident in writing the account of his experience to say so? Diffidence, we know, was a characteristic of Blair's – he was no more likely at the hotel than at Eton to put himself forward. But there was also something characteristic, obsessive even, in the way he identified with life at the bottom, his need to abase himself as low as possible, to be the *plongeur* of *plongeurs*, so to speak. Merely by being what he appeared to be – one of them – was he not doing the almost impossible? And if every *plongeur*, as he tells us, wants to be a '*débrouillard*', would he not, carrying the role to its logical conclusion, have wanted it also?

Among the *plongeurs* there was one, a German, whom Orwell singles out to exemplify the *débrouillard*. An English lord staying at the hotel had ordered a fresh peach to be sent up to his suite. The staff was in despair, for there were no peaches at all to be found in the larder. At this point the German *plongeur* stepped forward: *he* would take care of it. As though determined to prove that nothing was impossible for him (a proletarian equivalent of the 'Public School' spirit at its best) he set out into the streets, and before long returned in triumph. He had stolen four peaches from a nearby restaurant.

There is another version of this story which appeared in print twenty-eight years later in an unexpected, not to say wildly unlikely, source: the memoirs of Loelia, Duchess of Westminster. But English life, especially in the higher reaches where everyone eventually knows everybody, seems to abound in just such coincidences as the Duchess here describes:

We often stopped for a day or two in Paris – a town Benny [her husband, the Duke] much preferred to London. Looking back I think that Benny must have had a permanent suite in the Hotel Lotti, as we always had the same rooms. The staff bowed before him and hastened to gratify his slightest wish.

Years later, at a party, I met a frail-looking man who said, 'You won't remember me, but I have a very vivid recollection of you and your husband.' He then told me that he had once worked at the Hotel Lotti. Late one night Benny had rung the bell for the floor waiter and asked for a peach. It turned out that there was not a peach in the hotel so my friend, who was an apprentice waiter, was sent out into the streets and, under threat of instant dismissal, told not to return without at least one peach. Of course all the shops were shut, so he wandered forlornly about (I tell the story as he told it to me) until he saw a small green-grocer's with a bucket of peaches in the window. Desperately he rattled the door, pounded on it, but all in vain. He dared not go back empty-handed so, as the street was quite deserted, he picked up a cobble-stone from a heap where the road was being mended, smashed the window, seized a peach and dashed back to the Lotti, happy to think that he had kept his job. However, soon after that he gave up trying to be a waiter and became a writer. His name? George Orwell.[13]

One has no wish to worry a charming coincidence into the ground by attaching too much importance to it; by saying, as one might, that it offers a neat example of the difference between life and art, and going on to speculate, in this case which is which? The significant point, anyway, is not in the discrepancies between Blair's version of the story when he wrote it and Orwell's when he told it to the Duchess – though if the latter version is the more 'accurate', it suggests how ingrained the diffidence was: that Blair could not bring himself to admit that he had been a '*débrouillard*' but gave the honour to someone else.

What stands out, surely, is the 'false element' in the story no matter how it was told: that Blair at the Hotel Lotti was acting a part in violation of his own nature and gifts – he was meant to become a writer, not a waiter. And as the Orwell version of the story suggests, he recognized this himself. To go on living at the bottom any longer would have been an absurdity, of no use to himself or to the submerged life he had chosen to know and now had to re-invent, to bring to life again on the page. The time had come to rise up to the level at which he could be the writer he wanted to be.

3

There is the raw material, and there is the work of art that is made of it – as in *Down and Out in Paris and London* – and it is a convenient biographical fallacy when other evidence is lacking to assume that the two are identical. Especially this is so with the work of art that pretends *not* to be artful, where the strategy of the artist is to write as though he were giving us the material raw. It is a mark of Orwell's success in maintaining the strategy throughout the first of his books (and in much else that he was later to write) that over the years since its publication in 1933 the distinction has been so blurred that the 'raw material' and the 'work of art' have been treated as interchangeable and essentially the same. As to the occasional inconsistencies and obscurities that turn up in its lucid pages, there is a built-in rebuttal: since life is so often inconsistent and obscure, does this not add to the lifelikeness of the story? – and so the strategy of 'truth before art' has the further advantage of seeming to convert flaws into virtues.

To restore the difference neither reduces Orwell's literary stature nor impugns his honesty as an artist. It is simply to emphasize – as one must in a study of Eric Blair becoming the writer George Orwell – that a man's art and life are not indivisibly fused, though for a certain kind of writer (the quasi-autobiographer, drawing and enlarging upon his own experience) they may appear to be so. The story of Blair, in Paris and coming back to Southwold, and the story of 'I', as he wrote it in *Down and Out* during the two years after his return, are not indistinguishable, though they have grown so in legend. Our aim here is to consider them separately and in turn: life first, then art.

Early in 1930 he was back in Southwold – damp, wintry, out-of-season – in his parents' house in Queen Street, and whatever his or their initial expectations may have been upon his return, he continued to live there off and on until the spring of 1932. It was more than a year and a half since he had come down to say good-bye before leaving for Paris, but nothing of any significance had changed in Southwold. The Blairs had been at home in the small, seaside town as long as anywhere before in the years of their marriage; they had put down roots, and were absorbed in a daily round that they thoroughly enjoyed. Mrs Blair was an enthusiastic bridge-player and golfer; Mr Blair, out for a stroll in the High Street, armoured against the English weather in one of the extra-thick tweed suits he had his tailor make up for him, was sure of meeting one or another of his cronies; and through Avril they had become acquainted with younger people in the town.

Satisfying though this was, it hardly made for enlivening conversation; by the third cup of tea the last morsel of gossip would have been extracted. Whereas Eric had been in Paris, and presumably had tales to tell of his life there: these would make up for the uninformative letters he had sporadically thought to send home. In theory, of course, there was a great deal he might have told: the sum of eighteen months' experience. In fact, he told them very little: as little as he had disclosed in the past of his experience in Burma (no swapping anecdotes with his father) or at Eton or St Cyprian's. The habit of reticence was by now second nature, and would never be overcome to the end of his life. Besides, it was not as though this particular homecoming was cause for celebration.

He had left Southwold for London in the autumn of 1927 intending to become a writer; he returned to Southwold from Paris in the winter of 1930 only imperceptibly closer to his goal and financially worse off than when he had started. At twenty-six he was the author of six or seven magazine pieces which altogether had earned him some twenty pounds. It was not an achievement his parents would find reassuring, and, while it did not need to be said that he was to stay in Queen Street as long as he wanted, still, they could not help wondering among themselves, what would Eric do? how did he intend to support himself? As to the first question, the answer was evident in what he did almost from the day he came home: he intended to go on writing. Undeterred by his lack of success thus far – the two novels rejected and the stories that no editor wanted – he had made a total commitment to becoming a writer. It was the dominating passion of his life, which may account for the apparent thinness of his 'personal relationships' in this period, no grand love affairs, no intense time-consuming friendships, nothing to distract him from the chosen vocation. As to how he would support himself, the evidence was speculative and unsatisfactory: by whatever he might earn from his writing (and perhaps by the occasional odd job). In private Mr Blair grumbled, and Mrs Blair, also in private, gave Eric a little money – this, added to what he had got from his Aunt Nellie before leaving Paris (his passage and something over) and what she sent him on occasion thereafter, meant that he had enough to tide him along; not enough, however, for him to set up on his own.

One thing he did not intend to do, and gave no sign of doing, was to look for a 'safe' respectable job, working on a regular schedule (for a regular salary) that would dominate his life, with such time as was left over to be given, if he had energy enough, to his writing. Immediately upon his return to England he had been in touch with the *Adelphi* to ask if there was anything he might do for them, and Max Plowman had sent him a book to review: Lewis Mumford's biography of Herman Melville. The review, signed E. A. Blair, appeared in the March–May number. Generally favourable, and written with quite as much assurance as though the reviewer had just come down from Oxbridge rather than back from the lower depths of Paris, it included in the next-to-last paragraph the observation that, though Melville's had been a 'wretched life . . . at least he had an improvident youth behind him' when he had lived adventurously, ungenteelly, irresponsibly. The observation was not likely to be well received in Queen Street, where Mr Blair over the months would interpret Eric's refusal to take a job, even to look for one, as proof of irresponsibility. Whereas he himself felt his responsibility to be a matter of literary obligation: to write, to make himself a writer. It is this sense of vocation that explains what must otherwise seem inexplicable: his willingness to stay on and on in his family's house (with interruptions, however) until the spring of 1932, to allow himself to become what he had vowed he would never be, a charge upon the family, while he wrote the successive versions of *Down and Out in Paris and London*.

During these two and a half years that make up 'the Southwold period', the need to be writing outweighed all other considerations and appeared to domesticate him. But going down and out still had its adventurous, disrespectable appeal, as well as its sociological interest and its usefulness to him as a writer gathering material. Starting in the autumn of 1930, from time to time in the next two years, overnight or over a period of weeks, he would take off from Southwold, when the pressure had built up and the need for the ungenteel experience was at its strongest, to go down and out.

His history in these years is marked by dualities and contrasts. There is Blair leading a respectable, outwardly eventless life at his parents' house in Southwold, writing (which of course is the crucial event); or in Bramley, outside Leeds, where he went to stay for extended periods with his sister Marjorie and her husband Humphrey Dakin, and went on writing; then, in contrast, there is Blair as Burton (the name he used in his down-and-out episodes) in search of experience in the kips and spikes, in the East End, on the road, and in the hop fields of Kent, at a punishing cost to his health and sensibilities. Contrasts as extreme as these are also to be found in his writings, his friendships, indeed in most aspects of his life between 1930 and 1933, so that 'Blair/Orwell' seems only the final formulation of a division that had existed long before the mask was chosen and given a name.

Pleased with Blair's treatment of the Mumford *Melville*, Max Plowman sent him further books to review, the inevitable 'mixed bag' that falls to the writer who can turn out a deft, authoritative-sounding thousand words or so on any book whatever. So in his first year of reviewing for the *Adelphi*, he is equally at home in the eighteenth century with Edith Sitwell's *Alexander Pope* and *The Course of English Classicism* by Sherard Vines; in the nineteenth century with the marriage of the Carlyles; in the twentieth century with contemporary fiction (J. B. Priestley's *Angel Pavement*); and he completed his first year's assignments with some brisk observations on French penological methods on Devil's Island. Blair proved surprisingly adept: he seems to have mastered from the start the technique of elegant reviewman-ship as practised in England. The prose flows along smoothly, aphoristically and allusively; the manner is discriminating, un-ruffled and faintly superior – but even as a schoolboy he had been at ease with the authoritative tone ('Of course you realize, Connolly, that whoever wins this war, we shall emerge a second-rate nation.') If there were only these *Adelphi* reviews to go on, one might have predicted the eventual emergence of Eric Blair as yet another useful, middle-range gentleman of letters, a kind of Desmond MacCarthy *manqué*. But the Blair who was writing about books for the *Adelphi* was very different from the Blair who was simultaneously writing about life for himself. The division between the two, at this stage, seems irreconcilable: in style, in subject matter, even (perhaps especially) in the contrast-ing *persona* each self adopted while writing: the one a 'literary gent', the other a 'down-and-outer'.

When he was in Paris he had tried on the 'down-and-outer' for the first time, writing his account of the night he had spent in a London spike in the winter of 1928. That piece had been rejected by the same *Adelphi* that now, in the winter of 1930, was accepting the productions of his gentlemanly other self. Nonetheless, it was the anti-Blair *persona* he assumed once again when the time came to deal with his Paris experience. The choice, here, was of the greatest significance in the emergence of George Orwell. For if he had been content to go on as a 'literary gent', writing of Paris in the prose and pose of his first year's contri-butions to the *Adelphi*, we would have had, almost certainly, a variation on a familiar theme – the artist as a sensitive young man – as the first book by Eric Blair. But once he had decided on the 'down-and-outer' *persona*, it meant that the greater part of his life in Paris was inconsistent with it and therefore not usable material: he had embarked upon a book whose subject matter would be far removed from the conventional unconventional Left-Bank blend of Pernod and poetry.

In Southwold, early in the winter of 1930, he made his first attempts at writing a book about Paris. By March, when he went to stay with Marjorie and Humphrey Dakin in Bramley, he was already engrossed in it.[14] The Dakins' house, standing between an elementary school and the local Liberal Club, had once been a vicarage. It was now in a sadly run-down state, but in those first hard years of the depression, with Humphrey just beginning a new job as a civil servant, there wasn't money to spare to refurbish it. This would not bother Eric: shabbiness would always appeal to him as a natural setting. Besides, there was the pleasure of his sister's company. Marjorie was in her early thirties, much warmer and more tolerant than Eric, as clever as he, but not astringently so, and a good listener. Her husband has described her as 'the sort of human being who instinctively invites confidences'. While Eric never confided to her what precisely it was that he was writing, he made it clear that writing was to be his life; and like her mother, she was sympathetic, and set about being helpful in a practical way. Money she could not give him, but she could provide a room of his own, a good place to work, for as long as he wanted. There he settled in for the next three months.

He wrote as though driven. The tap tap tap of the typewriter was heard all day and half the night. Long afterwards Dakin told Orwell's friend T. R. Fyvel:

I remember the impression he made on Marjorie and myself – that he was determined to be a writer, come what may. I must confess that I thought the chance of making a living from writing was hopeless . . . In common with most philistines I used to tell him: 'For heaven's sake, get an income. Don't accept help from your mother or your aunt. You can always write in your spare time. Don't pursue an unprofitable career but get a job.'

But in Bramley, as in Southwold, Eric was not to be deflected from his chosen task: 'All the time his typewriter would go tap tap tap in the upstairs room.'

Dakin had always thought his brother-in-law something of a prig, dating back to their boyhood days in Henley, and nothing in his behaviour now caused him to change his mind:

I tried hard to get Eric to come to our pub round the corner in Bramley, the 'Cardigan Arms'. It was only a Yorkshire working-class local, but even in those years in the slump it was always bright, cosy, and warm, with a big fire going and quite a merry crowd in the evenings. From time to time I managed to persuade Eric to come along . . . but I could never make him join in any game or conversation. He used to sit in a corner by himself, looking like death, until it was with some relief that we'd hear him say: 'I must go home.' Through the window we'd see him walk past on the pavement, wearing a long muffler over a threadbare overcoat and no hat. The landlord used to say to me, 'That bloody brother-in-law of yours gives me the willies!' I think he gave everybody there the willies. And half the night I'd hear his typewriter go tap tap tap.

In June he returned to Southwold, a much livelier place now with the coming of summer and holiday visitors than when he had left it, and there are some attractive, unexpectedly cheerful glimpses of him at this time. An Anglo-Indian family in the town, friends of the Blairs, were looking for a tutor-companion for their three schoolboy sons (Richard Peters, the eldest, was ten) who would be at home during the holidays – actually, what was wanted was a friendly and companionable young man who would keep the boys occupied and out of the way of the grownups for a few hours each day. Mrs Blair suggested Eric for the job, Mrs Peters welcomed the idea, and Eric himself, perhaps remembering his brother-in-law's strictures, or perhaps simply to please his mother (and knowing that he would still have most of his time free for writing), agreed to give it a try.

'Friendly' and 'companionable' may not seem quite in keeping with the dour figure Blair cut at the Cardigan Arms; but as he is remembered by the Professor of the Philosophy of Education in the University of London, Richard Peters, this 'rather strange but very nice' young man proved to be an ideal holiday tutor. (The arrangement was so satisfactory to all concerned that it was resumed again the next summer.) From the first he was at ease with the three small boys, and they with him, perhaps because he never thought to treat them as 'children', never condescended or preached to them. And no doubt talked over their heads sometimes: when he held forth on the wickedness of politicians in his dry, analytical way, they had 'a vague impression . . . that making money entered into it rather a lot'. He would come round to the Peters's house on weekday mornings to collect the boys and off they would go: through the town, across the estuary to Walberswick, following the sea, or into the country, Blair leading the way, 'swinging along with loose, effortless strides and a knobbly stick made of Scandinavian wood'. And as he walked he talked entertainingly and informatively of anything that came to mind or into view. The conversation wound its random way from birds and animals – of the habits of the heron, of the red-shanks and their nests, of the behaviour of stoats – to the heroes of boys' magazines and the scientific fantasies of H. G. Wells. Chiefly one has the impression of a Blair who was natural and free with his small companions, as he was unable to be with his contemporaries and elders. He had no role to play or to live up to. Simply by being himself he won their admiration. Of course there was the glamour of his having been in Burma, he had seen the tiger and the elephant in their natural habitat. And they thought him very brave, very daring: once, going to Walberswick, he strode along the girder, about eighteen inches wide, from which the old disused railway bridge over the estuary was sus-pended, while they walked beneath him on the bridge itself. He took them bird's-nesting. He taught them how to make bombs – the same energy and detached interest went to making and firing a bomb as to looking for a redshank's nest – and the boys, whose nickname for him was 'Blairy-boy', took up the war cry of 'Blairy-boy for Bolshie-bombs'. In the millpond south of Walberswick he showed them how to catch roach with tiny hooks and pellets of bread. He talked about history: once he remarked that he would have sided with the Cavaliers, against the Round-heads, because the Roundheads were 'such depressing people'. He brought the boys home with him to Queen Street for lunch, and impressed them by helping his mother to clean up afterwards – not for nothing had he been a *plongeur*. In the sand dunes out-side the town he played war games with them, and they would stalk each other armed with small sandbags. 'I suppose the nerve and quiet confidence with which he played . . . was the quality in him which we admired most,' Professor Peters remarks, adding, 'Perhaps he was really at home only with animals and children.'[15]

The writing of the book about Paris went on at full speed through-out the summer. The pages of the manuscript were piling up, written with an exhilaration, vivacity, and naturalness that have their counterpart in his behaviour with the Peters' boys, and which explain better than its 'sociological content', its continuing life into the present: why there are admirers of Orwell's work who have a special affection for it, and even some – Henry Miller, for example – who consider it his best book.

Admittedly the material of *Down and Out* is sordid, but it is deployed with rare high spirits. The tone throughout is curiously boyish – not a defect, of course; so is the tone of *Huckleberry Finn* – and it is made more noticeable by the exclusion from the narrative of even one female character of any consequence to 'I' who tells the story and is at the centre of the action. Seldom can a book set in the lower depths of Paris have had so little to do with sexuality. Given its autobiographical nature, however, and given Blair's limited experience of women, it could hardly be otherwise. Before 1932 his closest relationships with women seem to have been with his mother and sisters, or with mother- and sister-surrogates. Possibly, as he had told Lawrence in Rangoon, he had frequented the brothels there; and possibly, as he was to tell Mabel Fierz, he had had a passionate *affaire du coeur* in Paris. But in each case the story was told to a single listener and to no one else, and in each case it is possible that he created the story, either to please or deceive the person to whom he confided it, with the end result that he would seem more experienced in such matters than he actually was.

It is enlightening to compare the Paris episodes of hunger, squalor, and bistro life among the lumpenproletariat in this earliest of his books with the account of his hospitalization written thirteen years later, the one so exhilarating to read, the other so truly painful, drawing upon material he was unable to use in *Down and Out*, though it might logically have fitted in. (There is only a glancing reference there to the narrator's having met his friend Boris when they were fellow patients in the hospital.) And it must be said that the description of starvation and squalor in the earlier work has none of the power and conviction, the terrible strength of the description of physical suffering and indignity in the later. It is as much a question of tone as of mastery: *Down and Out* is a young writer's book, the book of a young man who was in many respects still unformed and inexperienced.

Blair finished the book in October, and upon the advice of Mabel Fierz, whom he had met earlier in the summer and who was knowledgeable in such matters, he sent the manuscript to the publishing house of Jonathan Cape. Mrs Fierz, it should be said, had not been allowed to read the manuscript – nor had anyone else – but she did not allow this to stand in the way of her enthusiasm. She was convinced that he was a 'true talent' and that the book would be splendid: that was how she was.

Mabel Fierz and her husband Francis, a London businessman, had been coming to Southwold in the summer for a number of years now, and were on friendly terms with the Blairs. Mrs Fierz was a lively and enthusiastic woman in her late thirties; she kept up with the new books and plays and music and psychology and politics (Socialist); she was artistic, and even wrote a little herself; she was always ready to sympathize, to draw one out, to listen to stories of difficulties, to give advice. It was natural, then, that she should have heard of the Blairs' brilliant son Eric, such a disappointment to them, who had been in College at Eton, and then had thrown up a promising career in the Indian Imperial Police to go off to Paris and write. In her eyes nothing could have been more splendid than to go off to Paris and live in a garret and have thrilling love affairs and write marvellous novels that nobody would publish. On the other hand, she certainly could understand and sympathize with dear old Mr Blair, such a charming man, who had had such high hopes for his son – but such bourgeois notions of what would be sensible for him. And she did her best, especially after meeting Eric, to mediate between father and son, though with no conspicuous result.

Even so, Mrs Fierz was to play an important role in the history of George Orwell.[16] For along with her enthusiasm, she had her practical side, and it was on the practical side, between 1930 and 1933, that she proved extremely helpful to him. At first she had only his reviews in the *Adelphi* to be enthusiastic about, but she was unstinting in her praise, and by a happy coincidence it turned out that she knew the *Adelphi* people. John Middleton Murry, who had founded the magazine in 1923 and continued as its editor until 1930, was an acquaintance. So too was Richard Rees, an associate of Murry's on the magazine who in September 1930 became co-owner, restoring it to its status as a monthly (it had been coming out as a quarterly since 1927) and editing it jointly with Max Plowman. Most important, Plowman and his wife were particular friends of hers. Of course Eric must get in touch with Max – she would arrange it in the autumn when she was back in London. It would make a difference, for 'knowing people' helped, she told him, and that was her practical side. Meanwhile they had long, interesting conversations over tea, first in Southwold and later at the Fierzes' house in Golders Green. She was quick to sympathize with his literary ambitions, about which he spoke candidly, and curious as to what else he was writing, about which he was inexplicit; but she felt that he was confiding in her. Perhaps he was; or perhaps he was allowing her to have the impression that he was. Certainly he appears to have told her things he told no one else – from a literary point of view, the most sensational confidence was that his essay 'A Hanging', which came out in the *Adelphi* the next winter, was not, as it purported to be, an eye-witness account but a work of the imagination, for (she remembers him telling her) he had never been present at a hanging.

There is not a great deal that can be said with absolute certainty about the first version of the book that in its second version became *Down and Out in Paris and London*. The manuscript, which Blair submitted to Jonathan Cape in the autumn of 1930 and which Cape in due course sent back to him, has not survived; neither has the reader's report on the manuscript, nor the letter from Cape to Blair turning it down. We know that this first version ran to about 35,000 words (the length of the Paris chapters in the published book) and that it was written in the first person in the form of a diary. Cape's letter, as Blair summarized it a year and a half later to the literary agent that Mabel Fierz had persuaded to represent him, was not an out-and-out rejection. It appears to have been a variant of the standard letter declining a manuscript – 'We find this very (interesting) (remarkable) (unusual) and we wish that we could . . . BUT (insert reason) and so we cannot —' that publishers send to promising young writers with whom they would like to keep in touch but not so strongly as to make any kind of formal commitment. ('A publisher will make mistakes. He will say no when he should say yes, and yes when he should say no . . . The common error is to say yes too often; no publisher ever went bankrupt because of MSS rejected.' These cautionary thoughts appeared in Cape's house-journal, *Now and Then*, in 1930.[17]) According to Blair,

Cape had liked the manuscript and wanted to publish it . . . BUT (it was too short and fragmented) and so. However, if he were to make it longer, 'they might be disposed to take it'. No hint of a contract, no suggestion that he come along to discuss the manuscript: in fact, it was a version of the formula. But there was no reason why an ingenuous and inexperienced young writer, as Blair evidently was, should know that it was a formula, nor any reason why he should not pore over the handful of sentences, reading into them subtleties and shadings that very likely were never intended, putting the brightest, most positive construction, as Blair evidently did, upon the formularized phrases of encouragement.

And while it is true that the letter did not contain an offer of immediate publication nor even an assurance of later publication contingent upon his making such-and-such changes and additions, still, from Blair's point of view it represented a progression upward. For what the letter from Cape said, or seemed to say, as he read it, was very different from the outright, terminal rejections he had suffered with his two novels in Paris.

Encouraged by this optimistic reading – and reinforced by it in his conviction that soon he would achieve the goal he had set for himself, and so was justified in staying on in Queen Street until he had – he began the revision. It was an arduous process that asked for more of him than literary expertise. Later, in his diffident fashion, he would minimize it as only a question of his making the book longer by putting in 'some things' he had omitted, and then sending it back to Cape. Actually, it was another year before he was ready to submit the manuscript again. No longer in the form of a diary, it had been recast as a continuous narrative: it began with the adventures of 'I' as a down-and-outer in Paris (Chapters I to XXIII) and concluded with a major addition, his adventures as a down-and-outer in London (Chapters XXIV to XXXVIII). Since it is impossible to compare the texts of the first and second versions, one must depend on circumstantial evidence: but that is sufficiently strong to justify the assumption that the London adventures were the things he put into the second version, and which he could not include in the first because many of them had not yet happened to him.

It will be recalled that he had made his first explorations of the abyss in the winter of 1928 before leaving for Paris; and in the summer of 1929 he had written the account of his stay in a casual ward which he offered unsuccessfully to the *Adelphi*. Early in the winter of 1930 he came back to Southwold. There he began to write the first version of *Down and Out*. He spent the spring in Bramley with the Dakins and continued to write. In the summer he was back in Southwold, tutoring the Peters' boys and writing. The first version was finished and sent off to Cape early in October. Until that time, there is no evidence that he resumed the explorations of down-and-out life in England that he had begun almost four years before. It is hard to see how, writing as steadily as he did, he would have been able to fit them in.

In April 1931, his essay 'The Spike', signed Eric Blair, was belatedly published in the *Adelphi*. Told in the first person, it is a graphically detailed account of his stay in an unidentified casual ward from the moment its gates swing open at six in the evening to allow him into its reek and torpor until the moment two days later when the gates open again and let him out into the bright, sweet, windy air. Presently 'The Spike' was to be canni-balized in the second version of *Down and Out*. There, rather curiously, the experience which had served for the original essay, is apportioned out into two distinct chapters, one devoted to the spike in Romton, the other to the spike in Lower Binfield, with 'I' out on the road for several days between them. That Blair should have dealt so thriftily with the materials already available to him suggests the extent of the problem he faced once he had committed himself to bringing 'I' from Paris to London (rather than simply adding some things to the Paris chapters) and des-cribing his life in London as a down-and-outer. This new plan for the book seemed to offer an attractive symmetry in structure, along with an opportunity to contrast French and English life at the sub-poverty level. But it required not only obvious literary additions – some pretext would have to be invented to get 'I' from Paris to London – but also additions of experience. The first literary result of his explorations in 1928 was 'The Spike', and it had taken him as far as he could go: he still did not know enough about what he wanted to write about. At this point, from the autumn of 1930, an extraordinary, fluctuating pattern of down-and-out writing and living was inaugurated: comfortable Southwold for the manuscript, poverty-stricken London for the experience, the two interacting and alternating until the book had been lived and written. That would bring him to September 1931.

There were no schedules, no fixed periods decided upon in advance – so much time allotted for Southwold, so much for London – and he was more often and longer in Queen Street, writing, than he was in London going down-and-out. But when he wanted to go down-and-out, he did. The procedures for these episodes were simple. He would come up to London, stop off at Ruth Pitter's flat (or at the Fierzes' or at Richard Rees's) and put on his tramp outfit – he kept a suitcase of ancient clothes at Ruth Pitter's for the purpose – and disappear into the streets. A day or two later (sometimes longer) with a minimum of explanation as to where he had been and what he had seen and done, he would reappear, bathe, change clothes, become Eric Blair again. As Blair he would spend a bit more time in London, going out to dinner with Miss Pitter, dropping in for a cup of tea over the gas fire at the *Adelphi* office in Bloomsbury Street, staying overnight with the Fierzes, before returning to Southwold and continuing with his book.

Miss Pitter was struck by the change in his manner and appearance, and in his writing, since he had been in Paris. He was much more formidable looking (wearing a broad-brimmed hat he'd brought back from the Left Bank), much more assured – his reviews in the *Adelphi*, surprisingly professional compared to the stories and verses he had shown to her in 1928, gave some substance to his literary ambitions. Even in the ragged clothes he put on to go down-and-out, his height and bearing made for an un-tramp-like impression. One might apply to him the remark that Robert Graves made of himself in *Good-bye to All That*: that he feared that under the shabbiest of clothes he would always be recognized as an English gentleman. As Miss Pitter has said in an observation confirmed by others of his friends in the period, 'He didn't look in the least like a poor man. God knows he was poor but the formidable look didn't go with the rags.'

Still, the rags were a kind of passport to the lower depths, and essential to the enterprise. If the poor wore rags and suffered in them, then he must too; hence, even in winter he would go into the streets without overcoat, hat, gloves, or muffler. Miss Pitter was concerned about the effect on his health which she knew was not good; as she later put it, 'I felt he wouldn't make old bones.' One day, 'a perfectly horrible winter day with melting snow on the ground and icy wind', she ventured to protest. He listened politely but was not to be dissuaded: out he went. 'I felt quite sure he was in what is called the pre-tubercular condition. And here he was, exposing himself in such weather in totally inadequate clothing. It wasn't just poverty. It was suicidal perversity.' It was also a kind of heroism: a willingness to undergo whatever the experience of the abyss required from him. While he was down there, however briefly – the longest continuous time was the month when he went to pick hops in Kent – he wanted to be unconditionally there, not as a tourist or social worker.

He waited until 1936, in *The Road to Wigan Pier*, to describe the earliest of his experiences, but by then, as we have suggested, Orwell was interested in the exemplary, political character of what he had done, laying bare his secret motives and guilts as a 'casebook' member of his class, and he made no reference at all to the quest for material that at the time and on the surface had been an animating force. At a friend's house he prepared his clothes, dirtied them, made them authentic-seeming (it is all a little too artful and self-conscious, and so differs radically from the involuntary first experiences that are thrust upon 'I' when he arrives in London in *Down and Out*). Then, in his careful disguise, he wandered through the East End, and came at last to a common lodging-house in Limehouse. He was afraid to go inside, fearful of the working-class denizens of the place, so brutal and threatening as they must seem in the fantasies of any member of his class: what if they should recognize the Etonian under the rags and do violence to him? The image that occurs to him as he stands outside is of entering 'a sewer full of rats'. But eventually he screwed up his courage and went through the doorway and down the dark passage to the communal kitchen. There a drunken young stevedore was reeling about. He lurched towards Blair, who stiffened in his rags, readying himself for the violence he expected to come next. But instead, the stevedore

241

offered him a cup of tea and called him 'chum'. He felt it was a baptism.

'Nearly all' – the words are Orwell's – nearly all of *Down and Out in Paris and London* is true: that is, nearly all of it is composed of incidents that Blair actually witnessed or participated in or heard about between the winter of 1928 and the summer of 1931. These incidents have been chosen and rearranged to take their place in the simple picaresque structure of the book which covers a period of four consecutive months, the first three in Paris, the fourth in London. Blair was writing in a troublesome, suspect genre: the factual account, lightly (or not so lightly) fictionalized – which is something very different from the work of fiction based lightly (or not so lightly) upon fact. Such an account, as *Down and Out* purports to be, succeeds to the degree that it persuades us that it is reporting things that actually happened. Whatever the author invents must blend invisibly with the rest. The best pages in *Down and Out* are those that have the most truthful sound: believing what we hear, we go with 'I' from the Rue du Coq d'Or to the Hotel X to the Auberge de Jehan Cottard. The invented pages, by contrast, lack conviction: we hear the voice of 'I', and under it, unmistakably, the machinery creaking. Most of the inventions are devices tailored to suit the plan of the story. Thus, in the second version, Blair has to introduce 'I' to down-and-out experience not once but twice, first in Paris, then in London. (Of course, if he had reversed the order, as in his own life, it would have been simpler; it would also have been autobiography, which *Down and Out* is not.) In Paris, it will be remembered, the precipitating cause is the theft of his money. He finds himself with barely a *sou* – explanation enough, in the context, for the events that follow: his introduction to and progressive intimacy with life at the bottom. In his third month down there, a moment comes when 'I' cannot go on any longer as a *plongeur* at the Auberge de Jehan Cottard, and being in a special case (one senses this from the first despite the deliberate absence of biographical information), unlike the ordinary *plongeur* who has nowhere to turn, he writes to his hitherto unmentioned friend 'B.' in London, asking him to find a job for him, any job that will not require him to work seventeen hours a day. 'B.' replies promptly, like the *deus ex machina* or plot-device that he so transparently is. He has found him a job, as a kind of companion or attendant to a congenital idiot, and he also encloses a five pound note, enough for him to reclaim his clothes from the pawn-shop and for third-class passage to England.

In London, 'I' goes to 'B.''s office, where his friend tells him – the creaking of the machinery is very noticeable here – that the idiot's family has taken him abroad for a month, and the job will not begin until they return. He is so flabbergasted at the news that it is not until he is in the street that he realizes he had not even thought to borrow money from 'B.'. To do so now would not be 'decent', he feels – the creaking is louder still – and the situation on which the remainder of the book depends is that he is in London and in desperate straits. So it is down-and-out, as in Paris, all over again, a way of surviving for the month until his idiot returns – the thought that he might look for a temporary job never occurs to him.

Obviously, the exigencies of plot made it impossible for Blair to reproduce his own first experience of going down-and-out in London. If 'I' were to go to the house of a friend and change into tramp clothes before venturing into the East End, it would have been necessary to explain at least something about him, to provide him with a few tags of biography and a motive for what he was doing, as well as an authentic-seeming costume. The plot required only the latter: he goes into a rag shop in Lambeth to trade the suit he is wearing (his second-best suit; his best one has been left with his luggage in the station cloakroom) for a tramp's coat, dungaree trousers, scarf, and cloth cap, all superlatively filthy. He puts them on in a back room of the shop, then goes out into the street and into a new world.

Here invention ceases: the parallels with Blair's own experience are unmistakable. Like Jack London before him, he discovers that changing his clothes has changed everything.

No sooner was I out on the streets than I was impressed by the difference in status effected by my clothes. All servility vanished from the demeanour of the common people with whom I came in contact . . . I had become one of them. My frayed and out-at-elbows jacket was the badge and advertisement of my class, which was their class. It made me of like kind, and in place of the fawning and too respectful attention I had hitherto received, I now shared with them a comradeship. The man in corduroy and dirty neckerchief no longer addressed me as 'sir' or 'governor'. It was 'mate' now – and a fine and hearty word, with a tingle to it, and a warmth and a gladness, which the other term does not possess.[18]

So London wrote in *The People of the Abyss*, and Blair, in his turn, on his own first afternoon in the streets was to hear that 'fine and hearty word' addressed to him. A hawker had upset a barrow, and when he went to help him pick it up, the man grinned and said 'Thanks, mate'. It was the first time: 'No one had called me mate before in my life . . .' Moments such as this were of signal importance for Blair – the stevedore in the communal kitchen saying ' 'Ave a cup of tea, chum'; the hawker saying 'Thanks, mate' – moments of comradeship and acceptance such as he had never felt at St Cyprian's, or Eton, or Burma, which happened to him not as Eric Blair but as the man with an assumed name (Edward or P. S. Burton) who went down-and-out, and that culminate unforgettably in the Lenin Barracks in Barcelona during the Civil War in Orwell's brief exchange and handclasp with an Italian militia man whom he was never to see again.

These epiphany-like moments were the psychological rewards of the down-and-out experience, making up for the physical discomfort and degradation inherent in it (though later he came to think of the bugs and squalor as a kind of reward also: an expiation). The literary reward would be in the book he was writing. Yet the experience itself, the role that he chose to play in the experience, had its evasive, inauthentic aspect: that he had the option to be free of it whenever he pleased. No matter how sincerely he participated in the experience at the time, or how convincingly he later presented it on the page, his friends and acquaintances in this period could not help noticing the element of pretence it entailed, the more so as they saw him only before or after the experience, and he was incapable of taking them into his confidence as to the details of what it had been.

The longer one had known Blair, or the more one knew of the actual circumstances of his comfortable lower-upper-middle life in Southwold, the more puzzling it became. An instance of this was in his relationship with Brenda Salkeld. They had met in the autumn of 1928 in Southwold, where she was the gym mistress at St Felix School, and the friendship was resumed when he came back from Paris. They went for long walks, bird-watching, and talking of writers Eric admired and felt she should read – Joyce, E. M. Forster, Swift – they went fishing and riding together, they dug in a Roman barrow which yielded up only a bronze button. Although he would not show her what he was writing, he talked of his literary ambitions and disappointments, so much written and so little published, the meagreness of the rewards. With a certain grim pleasure he told her that since coming back from Burma he had earned one hundred pounds by his writing, whereas in Burma, doing a job he loathed, he had earned two thousand pounds: obviously he had only to find a job he hated more than being a policeman and he would end up rich.

On the whole, judging from Miss Salkeld's recollections and those portions of Blair's letters to her she has allowed to be published, it was an agreeable companionship for them both, in Southwold and away from it. Once, for example, he took her to Eton for the day to show her his old school. On another occasion they had tea in London with an acquaintance of hers, the author of several books, the political theorist C. Delisle Burns, and the conversation was not about politics, in which Eric had no interest, but about the practical details of authorship – how to deal with agents, editors, and publishers – which were of absorbing concern to him.

Yet although he and Miss Salkeld got on well together, there were undercurrents of tension, perhaps because they were close in age to each other: it is evident in these years that Blair still was more comfortable with women who were older than he, with whom he fell easily into a kind of filial or fraternal or, as Richard Rees has suggested, a Candida–Marchbanks relationship. But Miss Salkeld was a forthright, intelligent, and independent-minded young woman. She was prepared to let Eric play a pedagogical role in literary matters, about which she agreed he knew much more than she; but she was not willing to yield her right to question and contradict the generalizations he was so fond of making (as he had been ever since he was at St Cyprian's) upon a minimum of evidence or none at all. She came to the conclusion that he really did not understand people, women in particular, that he could not give himself. And while no doubt some of this grew out of their immediate circumstances, there clearly was a quality of 'apartness' and abstraction about him that many had noticed before – a short-circuiting of the emotions, a failure to connect. And then, there were these prejudices of his: he had not yet solved the problem of how to live with them. 'He didn't really like women,' was Miss Salkeld's verdict.[19] 'I used to bring up the women who I thought were good writers, and he would very occasionally praise their writing, but he used to say that it stuck in his throat to have to do it.' Nor was he any more favourably disposed to people who liked music, whatever their sex: music and concerts were a waste of time (Miss Salkeld was very fond of them), and when she reasonably pointed out that his being tone-deaf might disqualify him as a judge in the matter, he swept her objections aside. So it was not surprising that she should have regarded his tramping experience with considerable scepticism.

One morning he turned up at her house in Bedford, still in tramp's clothing, having spent the night in the local workhouse. After he had bathed, and before he set out on the road, aiming for the spike further along the way where he meant to sleep that night, they argued about what he was doing. He told her that he 'was getting to know what it was like to be a tramp'. But she was quite certain that 'if you've put on tramp's clothes and walked, well, that didn't make you a tramp. It was the attitude of mind that was much more important; and how could you claim to have the attitude of a tramp, or know it and understand it, if you knew that you could always go back home.' Of course, she had no way of knowing what it was that he felt since he could not tell her. But the only effective way the argument could have been resolved would have been for him to show her what he was writing about his down-and-out experience, and this he chose not to do.

It is understandable that Miss Salkeld and others who were familiar with his Southwoldian life should have found it difficult to reconcile the would-be writer and the would-be tramp. But even the new acquaintances and friends in London, to whom Southwold was unknown territory and his life there unimaginable, had some sense of the anomalies of his situation, though he told as little in a specific way as possible, and his disclosures were carefully selected. Jack Common, a young working-class writer from Newcastle who had joined the staff of the *Adelphi* in 1930 when Rees and Plowman took over from Murry, has recorded the disappointment he felt at his first meeting with Blair.[20] He had 'heard of this interesting man who had been a tramp and who at the same time was capable of writing extremely good reviews for the magazine'. But when Blair came into the office it was obvious that he was 'a public school man, perfect manners, and had not known the desperation that makes the real tramp'. It was a disappointing beginning – for here, it seemed, was just another struggling young writer, in that respect not so dissimilar from Common himself, and when it came to life among the proletariat (the Marxist term, like Marxism itself, was coming into vogue, even in the *Adelphi*) he felt he knew much more about it, having lived it, than Blair did. But they met again: 'We had a cup of tea over the gas fire.' So begins an anecdote by Common that catches the quixotic nature of Blair's enterprises at this time as they would appear from the outside:

It was just before Christmas . . . probably 1930. He outlined his plans for Christmas; he intended to spend the holiday in jail. His idea was to light a sort of bonfire in Trafalgar Square, and get run in. I counselled him against this. I always firmly held that if you were going to jail you might as well have something for it. My advice was 'Take to theft. A bonfire simply suggests something undergraduate-like.' He'd probably be let off. But Blair didn't take my advice . . . There was no jail. I don't know how he spent Christmas.

As time passed Common grew 'very friendly' with him. There was no doubt that Blair was having 'a hard time' – even though Common did not accept his being a tramp out of necessity – and it was a mark in his favour that 'he had to some extent dissociated himself from his class'. Still, there were those embarrassing class signals that proved as ineradicable as a birthmark: the voice, the manner. Once on a summer afternoon Blair turned up at Max Plowman's house. Common was already there – he had been listening to Beethoven's music on gramophone records – and now they went out into the garden to play badminton. 'This put Orwell to shame. He had to remove his jacket.' When he did so, he was discovered to be wearing braces, an invincibly upper-class thing to be doing, and it stayed in Common's memory.

The closest and most enduring of the friendships that Blair formed at this time was with Richard Rees. Theirs was a relationship that strengthened as it continued, and it continued to the day of Blair's death in 1950. But when they met in the winter of 1931, either a little before or after 'The Spike' came out in the *Adelphi*, the prognosis could hardly have been favourable. Blair had his prejudices, and Rees, accordingly, had his liabilities. For one thing, he had, as Mrs Vaughan Wilkes would have noticed with pleasure, a handle to his name, Sir Richard. (True he did not use the title, but it was *there*.) For another thing, he had money. (Not a great deal, but enough to subsidize a 'literary mag' and to have a flat in Cheyne Walk, to buy books and pictures.) Then, at their first meeting – they were having tea in a shop in New Oxford Street not far from the *Adelphi* – Rees recalls 'It came out that we had been at the same school, Eton, though the difference in our ages had prevented our knowing one another.'[21] But Blair had been in College, and Rees had been an Oppidan, a difference to which, Rees felt, Blair attached excessive and unjustified importance. 'I do not remember if it also came out that he had been there on a scholarship, but if it did, he must certainly have been embarrassed, and I equally certainly was unaware of his embarrassment.' Eighteen years later came that strange embarrassing moment, earlier referred to, when Rees 'incautiously used the word "Tug"' and Blair 'winced as though [Rees] had trodden on his tenderest corn'. To which Rees appends the observation: 'That a famous middle-aged writer should have retained such a deep trace of boyhood sensitiveness and suffering seems remarkable.'

But in spite of all these potential obstacles to their ever being more than editor and writer in an amiable, quasi-professional acquaintance, the friendship between them took hold. Rees was so diffident about his 'advantages' – the title and the assured income – as to neutralize their power to give offence; in his attitudes he was at once reticent and sympathetic, a combination nicely attuned to Blair's suspicious temperament. His expectations upon meeting Blair – and 'expectations' is too high-pitched a word for the low-keyed curiosity he felt – were the reverse of Common's: he had published reviews by this interesting young writer who was also, for one reason or another, capable of living the life of a tramp – so that when Blair came into the *Adelphi* office, and they went nearby to the tea shop to talk, Rees was neither disappointed nor surprised: it would not have occurred to him that a tramp might have written those reviews. In the account he published of their first meeting, one sentence stands out: 'He made a pleasant impression and I did not guess that he was having a struggle to live, though he struck me as rather lacking in vitality.' But this was a first impression, and he soon recognized the intensity of Blair's commitment to writing, to which everything else was subordinate. He had a cynical disinterest in politics, and Rees, a socialist committed to social change, found it extraordinary that Blair should make no connection between the plight of the men he met on the road or in the spikes and the sickness of the society that could find no function for them. This, of course, was in 1931, when Blair, if pressed, would describe himself as a Tory Anarchist. Years later Rees said of him, 'He was the most "literary" man I've ever known – absorbed, obsessed with wanting to be a writer.'

The book about his down-and-out experiences was only a part of his voluminous literary activity in the first eight months of 1931: the tap tap tap of the typewriter must have been incessant. In the March number of the *Adelphi* he had reviews of *The Two Carlyles* by Osbert Burdett and *The Horrors of Cayenne* by Karl Bartz; in the April number, his essay 'The Spike', along with 'Poverty – Plain and Coloured', a joint review of two novels, *Hunger and Love* by Lionel Britton and *Albert Grope* by F. O. Mann; in June, a review of Pearl Buck's novel of China, *The Good Earth* ('. . . can be added at once to the very small list of first-rate books about the East'). During this time too he had begun to write about Burma, his first serious attempt to deal in fiction with his experiences there, which took shape over the next three years as *Burmese Days*. But the immediate result was the essay 'A Hanging' which was published in the *Adelphi* in August.

Literary activity, obsessive and unceasing, had the paramount place in his life. The extraordinary thing is that he found time and vitality also to go on with down-and-out explorations. How many they were, and the duration of each, cannot be precisely established. To judge by the relatively small number of incidents that make up the London chapters of *Down and Out*, they need not have been very many to provide him with material enough for a manuscript of publishable length. But the search for material was only one of his motives; and that he should have continued his explorations, even after he had finished the second version of the book, suggests the extent of his involvement with them. Also his dissatisfaction with what he had made of them thus far. Arriving at the final page of the manuscript, he felt that he had not yet got beyond the 'fringe of poverty' – someday he hoped to explore more deeply in the world of the down-and-out, to know its people 'not from casual encounters, but intimately'. That, however, would not happen. His class, his education, the complexity of his nature, the development of his still dormant political intelligence, his literary ambitions – all militated against it. These various strains would make themselves felt in *The Road to Wigan Pier*, which vividly and sympathetically describes life in the depressed areas of the North in the winter of 1936. Yet the book is reportage, told by an outsider, that makes no claim to intimacy except perhaps in the second half, an account of Orwell's political progress to socialism, where he writes of himself with unshielded candour, as though in an intimate relationship with the reader.

He had been sustained since the previous autumn by the conviction that Cape would want to publish his book once he had suitably lengthened it. Now, in the summer of 1931, he grew impatient to be done. In July he was in Southwold, tutoring the Peters' boys again, meeting with Brenda Salkeld and other friends. A month of agreeable diversions, but it meant that the amount of time free for writing was drastically reduced, and in August, when the Fierzes went back to London from their holiday in Southwold, he went with them. In their house in Oakwood Road, Golders Green, with Mrs Fierz seeing to it that he should have ideal conditions for working, he wrote steadily, and before the end of the month had written the last sentence, typed a title page, *Days in London and Paris* by Eric Blair, and sent off the manuscript to Jonathan Cape. It was all managed with such speed that there was not even the opportunity for Mrs Fierz, who would have welcomed it, to read what he had written.

The haste and impatience of these weeks, the determination to have the book out of his hands no matter what, very likely account for a certain slackening, a haphazardness in the final portions. True, the plot, like an afterthought, enters once again at the very end: 'I' will soon become caretaker for the wealthy idiot (rounding off the London month); and there is a reference to the Auberge de Jehan Cottard and to the word '*plongeurs*' to remind us of the episodes in Paris. But despite these rudimentary formalist devices, the effect is that of a book that simply stops (or runs down) rather than ends. Blair himself was aware of this: he does his best to disarm criticism by claiming to have written no more than a 'fairly trivial story'. Later, he would disown the book in a quite literal way, giving it to a pseudonymous author, saying he was ashamed of it. Nonetheless, he sent it out, to be published or turned down. There is a time when an author can do no more with a manuscript than he has already done, even as he admits its flaws: that time had come for him now. A few days later, as though to prove he had not merely turned a phrase when he wrote that he wanted to explore the lower depths 'more thoroughly', he went down and out again.

This was to be the most prolonged of his explorations, extending from 25 August to 8 October, and it is also the best-documented for he kept a diary covering the entire experience: three nights in London (one of which he spent sleeping out in Trafalgar Square), four days on the road, seventeen days picking hops on a farm in Kent; then back to London for two weeks in a common lodging-house. The diary, fascinating as a record and admirably alive in the writing, was published for the first time, twenty-nine years after it was written, under the title 'Hop Picking', in *The Collected Essays, Journalism and Letters of George Orwell*. Reading it, one can only wish that Blair had not been quite so eager to have *Down and Out* off his hands – that he could have tolerated it for another two or three months – for the diary then might logically have been made an impressive part of the book, augmenting or supplanting the re-cast portion of 'The Spike' which is the last of the down-and-out experiences that 'I' chooses to describe. Four years later Orwell would draw upon the material of the diary for the hop-picking episodes and the 'night scene in Trafalgar Square' in his novel *A Clergyman's Daughter*.

251

And when he came to London from Kent, during the two weeks that he and his 'mate' Ginger were living in Bermondsey in a common lodging-house (stinking kitchen and disgusting dormitory), he extracted passages from the diary for the article 'Hop Picking' (by Eric Blair) that appeared in the *New Statesman and Nation* of 17 October 1931, nine days after the last entry in the diary. During the week that the article was current, it dispensed its quota of information capably enough – how hops are picked, and who picks them, and what the work pays – then sank from view, never to reappear: the common fate of most casual journalism from which it was not rescued even by the Collected Edition.

What makes the diary exceptional among Blair's writings is the sense of happiness that pervades it. There are the squalid details as before, the bugs in the beds, the faecal stink, the vile food, the grime and poverty in London, the exhausting, ill-paid work in the hop fields, the sordid living conditions on the farm, the latrine too filthy to be used, etc. etc. And yet. On the road (for example) he and Ginger are caught in a rain storm and take shelter in a lych-gate outside a church. Their clothes are drenched through; they have nothing to smoke; they had walked twelve miles that day – 'yet I remember that we were quite happy and laughing all the time'. One takes away the impression, as one does so seldom in Orwell, that this is the record of a joyful not a miserable experience. And when he draws upon it for that generally bleak, sad novel *A Clergyman's Daughter*, he allows Dorothy, his heroine, to reflect after an exhausting day in the hop fields: 'Yet you were happy, with an unreasonable happiness.'

It had been a kind of rough idyll, full of camaraderie and adventure and the smell of hops like a wind blowing from an ocean of cool beer. But like any idyll it could not be prolonged indefinitely. The nastiness of life in the kip when he and Ginger were back in London began to get on Blair's nerves. Mornings they would spend helping the porters in Billingsgate; and in the afternoons, Eric (we learn from the diary that on this expedition he had been using his own Christian name) would go into the reading-room of the public library in Bermondsey: there he wrote up the notes for his diary, and the article for the *New Statesman*. When he had been at the Fierzes', he had met a man who was starting a new paper, *Modern Youth*, who had asked him to send him some stories, and he felt that he should get to work on them. But he couldn't, not in those surroundings. He wrote to South-wold for money, which his mother sent him, enough so that he could take a room of his own in Windsor Street, Paddington. Then, on 8 October, the two friends parted, Ginger back to the road again, and Eric Blair back to the literary life.

It was in Windsor Street later in the month that he heard from Jonathan Cape. The letter has not survived; Blair's summary of it is laconic and to the point. The book was rejected.

Part Five
Becoming Orwell

The first letter from Cape, upon which he placed the most favourable construction possible, had inspired a period of optimistic activity during which he revised, lengthened, and completed the book they had now rejected. The effect upon him of the second letter was equally powerful: optimism, pitched too high before, gave way to an unwarranted pessimism, activity to a paralysing diffidence. So far as the fate of his book was concerned, thereafter he resigned it to his friends, allowing it to become their concern, not his.

He had always been fearful of failure or rejection; indeed, the two were synonymous in his eyes. The next eight months, between November 1931 and June 1932, comprise a period so dispiriting, so negative, so unmitigated in its gloom, that in his memory he chose to let it infect all the years before he was Orwell. In 1946 he asserted that until he was thirty he had always expected that whatever he attempted would fail. Passing silently over the rebuffs and frustrations that marked his struggle to become a writer, he attributed the attitude to his experience of St Cyprian's (as though he had actually failed there). The psychological mechanisms that determine his ways of dealing with failure and rejection are unmistakable in these eight defeated months: passivity, diffidence, and self-devaluation. The simplest, least humiliating course was to stand still: if one did not put oneself forward, offering one's manuscript, say, then one did not run the risk of rejection – not having tried, one could not be said to have failed. But if one had made the offer and it was rejected, the proper response was indifference, to behave as though it did not matter. Or else, dangerously attractive to someone of his temperament, there was agreement, a devaluation of the self: to accept that one (or one's manuscript) deserved to be rejected. It was as though he were to say, if I am not loved it is because I am unworthy, I smell, I am ugly, I don't have money or a handle to my name, I don't wear kilts to church on Sunday, I have written a fairly trivial book that doesn't begin to do justice to its subject, I am a failure.

Paradoxically, but not unusually, defeatism was paired to the will to succeed. In the end, it was the latter that triumphed: as Richard Rees would remark to Rayner Heppenstall in 1934, Blair was 'doomed to success'.[1] Cape's rejection of *Down and Out* did not swerve him from his determination to become a writer: the sense of vocation was as formidable as ever. If he were no more than the 'defeatist' he represents himself as being at the time, surely he would have acknowledged that the career upon which he had embarked in 1927 had come to nothing, and turned to something else. Instead, within a few weeks he began writing *Burmese Days*.

But his faith in *Down and Out* had evaporated. He was all too ready, given his tendency to expect the worst, to accept Cape's verdict as the final word, and, unlike most beginning writers, he was unwilling to make the rounds with the manuscript. Having once been rejected, the work in which he had invested so much emotion, experience, and effort was to be written off as a failure. Here, fortunately, his friends intervened. Rees, when Blair some weeks later told him what had occurred, pointed out that it was not unusual for a book to be turned down by one publisher and accepted by another. Casually, for he did not want to seem to be patronizing him, he suggested that he might be able to help and asked if he might see the manuscript. To this Blair agreed, but he added, as one would expect, that it was not much good really. Rees had already read 'The Spike', and he had allowed Blair to use his flat when he changed into tramp's clothing, so to some extent the subject matter came as no surprise. Even so he was unprepared for the breadth and depth of experience that the book disclosed – neither then nor later was theirs a friendship that depended on intimate confidences. For Rees, the effect was disturbing, and difficult to reconcile with Blair as he knew him, though it added to the fascination of what he read. But summoning up as much detachment as he could, putting himself in the position of a reader who knew nothing about the author but what was revealed in his book, he felt certain that *Days in London and Paris* ought to be published, and with Blair's permission gave it to his friend T. S. Eliot, who was a reader for Faber & Faber (and later became a director of the firm).

Sometime earlier, Rees had already spoken to Eliot about Blair, as a young writer who was having a hard struggle, and who would welcome any sort of editorial odd job. On the strength of this, Blair wrote to him on 30 October to ask if Faber might be interested in his undertaking a translation of a recent French novel, *A La Belle de Nuit* by Jacques Roberti. Realistic in style, operatic in situation, it tells of a prostitute's life and death – in love with a criminal, she is killed by the simple fisherman who loves her. Later Blair would describe it as 'appallingly indecent'.[2] Eliot replied promptly and asked that he send the novel, which he did on 4 November. But the project came to nothing – unpublishable by reason of obscenity, Blair thought – and nothing came of his request that he be considered as a French translator if Faber might need one in the future. (As for *A La Belle de Nuit*, it was published without incident in 1933 by T. Werner Laurie as *Houses of the Lost* in a translation by Mary Ford.)

Everything seemed to be going wrong for him at this time. Even *Modern Youth*, the new publication for which he had concocted two short stories, went out of business for lack of funds before its first number could appear. He had money enough to live on, thanks to what his mother sent him from Southwold, but her cheques, though essential, heightened his sense of guilt and failure: he asked for less and less, claiming to have something coming in from literary odd jobs, until he allowed himself to take only barely enough for survival. He was at a point in his life when he did not have to go very far down and out to know what poverty was like.

The down-and-out expeditions were still going on intermittently and would continue into the autumn of the next year. The last of them for which a record survives seems to have been made a short time before Christmas 1931. It began at Rees's flat, where Blair arrived and 'asked if he might change his clothes. Having left his respectable suit in the bedroom, he went off again dressed more or less in rags.' His aim was to be put in prison – to know what it was like to be a prisoner – but the provocation he decided upon, to be drunk and disorderly, was even less likely to produce the result he desired than to light a bonfire in Trafalgar Square. He did get drunk, having put down four or five pints of beer and finished off with a quarter of a bottle of whisky, and he did get picked up by the police – literally so, for he was falling down in the street. He was held at the Bethnal Green police station from Saturday to Monday morning, when he was taken before the magistrate and fined six shillings for drunkenness (which he refused to pay and so was returned to the jail for another few hours) but this was not the imprisonment he had hoped for. When he told the story to Rees he was prepared to alter the actual facts a bit (as he later recorded them in 'Clink') to emphasize the absurdity of the outcome: 'he had received a fatherly talk, spent the night in a cell and been let out next morning with a cup of tea and some good advice'. Like so much else in his life in these months, even the attempt to go properly to prison – to be taken seriously at what he wanted to do – had ended in failure.

He made no effort to conceal his discouragement from Mabel Fierz, and she, quick to sympathize and eager to help, suggested that what he must do now was entrust his future to a literary agent – as all professional writers did – someone who would know to whom a particular manuscript should be offered and how to obtain the best price for it. And of course it was very like her to know just the man, her friend Leonard Moore, of the firm of Christy & Moore. Late in the year, obedient to Mrs Fierz's advice, Blair wrote to him, saying that he was sending him four stories (two new ones, and the two survivors from the *Modern Youth* débâcle), and mentioned as it were in passing the book that was then at Faber & Faber.

In January Moore replied to him at his parents' house in Southwold that he was doubtful that he could place two of the stories; about the others he would see; and he wondered if Blair had yet had any word of the book. No, came the answer, he had not; it was still at Faber – on the recommendation of a personal friend of Eliot's – they, he felt, were likely to be the only publisher who might do it. (It is unclear why he should have thought it was particularly *their* book; perhaps he was already so discouraged he wanted to close off the possibility of Moore offering it round.) He went on to ask that the story 'The Idiot' be sent back to him, as he said that the *Adelphi* would take it. (Apparently the magazine must have changed its mind – Rees had no recollection of the story at all – for it never appeared there or elsewhere, nor did the other three stories fare any better.) Finally he asked if Moore might be able to get him some work as a translator, either in French which he knew thoroughly, or Spanish which he knew pretty well. A relationship, however tenuous, had been established between author and agent.[3]

In February he was back in London, living in lodgings in Westminster Bridge Road. It was there at the end of the month that he finally heard from Faber & Faber. The letter, written by T. S. Eliot, was brief, courteous, and disheartening.[4] It began with an apology for having kept the manuscript, went on to praise it, and then to reject it, and concluded with an expression of thanks for having been allowed to see it. In April Blair would tell Leonard Moore accurately enough that Faber had found the book interesting but too short. He passed over the perhaps more disquieting, because not wholly unjustified, of their objections: that the construction of the book was too loose, and the Paris and London episodes were only slightly connected. For Eliot the episodes in London evidently held the greater promise; and he suggested in a final sentence that Blair might be able to make a book of considerable interest if he were to limit himself to down-and-out life as he had known it in England. However well meant, it was a suggestion more easily made by a reader in a publishing house than accepted by a writer in a lodging-house down to his last shilling.

The impact of this second rejection was decisive. Although he left no later record of what he felt at the time, his actions speak eloquently for him. It was as though all the illusions by which he had been living until then were stripped away, and he saw himself and his situation clearly for the first time.

He began by rejecting the book itself. When the manuscript was in his hands again, he carried it off to Golders Green, and left it with Mabel Fierz, telling her to read it or not as she pleased, and then to destroy it. 'Burn it and keep the clips,' he said.[5]

Next he rejected the life dedicated to writing that he had pursued without interruption (save for the down-and-out expeditions that essentially were a part of it) since he had come back from Paris, and that he had allowed his mother, on however small a scale, to subsidize. If he meant to go on writing – and he did – and to go down-and-out – about which he was less certain – then the cost henceforth would have to be borne by himself. What this meant, in the immediate practical sense, was that he would have to take a job. After five years he had arrived at the point where the greater number of young writers traditionally begin. From there his next step was traditional with young writers too, for he put on his respectable suit and went round to Truman & Knightly Associates to see if they might find him a place as a schoolmaster. They were not discouraging. Admittedly, his qualifications were not all they might be – he had not been at one of the ancient universities, which rather limited the possibilities, and he could hardly expect something of the first class. Still, he was an old Etonian who had been in College (which could be translated as good at classics) and he had served in the Indian Imperial Police (good at games). Though it was an awkward time in the academic year to be starting out, a vacancy might unexpectedly come up, something might be found for him and, in fact, in remarkably short order, something was. In April he was to begin teaching at Evelyn's School, a prep school for boys in Hayes, on the out-skirts of London. With his fate thus decided, he went down to Southwold to wait for the beginning of term, to listen to the approving comments of his parents, to begin work on a long poem about a day in London that occupied him for the next few months (no trace of it survives), and to go for walks, separately, with his friends Eleanor Jaques and Brenda Salkeld.

Then came April, to a reader of *The Waste Land* inevitably 'the cruellest month', and one ventures to think that the phrase would have occurred to Blair, for more than one reason, arriving at a waste land of his own: a dreary prep school in a dreary suburban town. So at least he found them on first acquaintance, and his view of them did not perceptibly brighten over the fifteen months that he was at Evelyn's. The school was like St Cyprian's in its academic objective – to prepare boys for Public Schools – though a day school and less grand in its social pretensions, and much less secure in its financial aspect. (As business enterprises schools such as these had to make a profit or close down. The Depression was a perilous time for them, especially for those on the fringes, and in the end it forced Evelyn's to close. It collapsed after the academic year 1933-4, and Blair's first experience of schoolmastering was at an end. Unlike Evelyn Waugh, who had also been a prep-school master, he would never say 'It was very jolly and I enjoyed it very much.'[6] But he went on with hardly a pause to a much more solid and imaginative school, Frays College in Uxbridge, making the transition along with some of the physical effects of Evelyn's itself, which the Principal of Frays had bought when the contents were put up for sale.)

After so many years to be back again in the ambience of St Cyprian's darkened his view of everything: the school was 'foul', the boys 'brats', and Hayes 'godforsaken'. His only friend was the local curate. At night he would go home to the genteel dinginess of The Hawthorns, a house in the Station Road where he rented lodgings, and in his room he would try to work at his long poem or to evoke for his novel the flamboyant landscape of Upper Burma, while outside grey rain fell, and downstairs a woman banged hymn-tunes on the piano. He had entered a world of gentility at the end of its tether, that he had not known at first hand before, though he had read of it in Gissing and some of Lawrence's stories (such as 'Daughters of the Vicar') and that in due course would be revealed to him as a subject for *A Clergyman's Daughter*. But that was still in the unforeseeable future, Orwell's future as a recognized, published author. In Hayes, at the beginning of April 1932, even the idea of Orwell did not yet exist; he was Eric Blair, stalled in an apprenticeship that had no successful end in sight, the unrecognized author of a twice-rejected and now abandoned manuscript.

Fortunately he had left the manuscript in good hands. This was the opportunity that Mrs Fierz had been waiting for for more than a year, to read Eric's book, and once she had done so there was no question of her following his advice and burning it. True, it was not the book she had imagined him to be writing, for his reminiscences of Paris in their conversations tended to be more romantic than sordid, and it was hard to believe that the charming, attractive, sensitive young man who would go with her one night to an aesthetic drawing-room in Chelsea to hear T. Sturge Moore read his poetic plays was the same young man who, perhaps a night later, would be sinking down into the squalor of a down-and-outer's life in the East End. But how remarkable a book it was, even so. Blair – diffident, passive, eager to believe the book a failure – had felt that the rejection by Faber & Faber settled its fate; Mrs Fierz, blazing with enthusiasm, was determined that the book must be published. She now proceeded, in effect, to launch George Orwell. She took the manuscript herself to Leonard Moore and, over a cup of tea in his office, spoke enthusiastically of Blair and his work. Moore, who had had no success with any of Blair's stories, may well have identified the book as the one that had been offered to Faber & Faber with a personal recommendation to Eliot from a friend. He glanced at the manuscript – awkward length, difficult subject, unknown author – and said no. But Mrs Fierz was not to be so easily put off. Here was a remarkable book – would she have brought it to him if it were not? – by a young author in whose future she believed, and so must he. She had a second cup of tea, and a third, and badgered him until, in order to get rid of her (as she later said), he agreed to keep the manuscript and give it a proper reading.

Suddenly, and unexpectedly, we have arrived at the end of the unknown period of his life. Until April, there had been no reason not to expect that the apprenticeship might extend itself interminably and inconclusively: Blair one more failed writer with a closet stacked high with unpublished novels. Now, thanks to Mabel Fierz, and Leonard Moore, and presently Victor Gollancz, he was propelled forward towards a goal that had been continually receding as he approached it. Within eight months he was to be a published author, a name to be taken into account. Yet the writer who emerges at the end of the five years of apprenticeship is not to be Eric Blair, as one might logically have assumed, but George Orwell. That he should have decided to take a pseudonym is perhaps the most singular aspect of a literary history ('Becoming Orwell') that by contrast to the history of abrasive struggle preceding it ('Becoming a Writer'), seems mysteriously negligent and non-committal.

Blair, sunk in depression in his first weeks at Evelyn's, had not been in touch with Mrs Fierz since the afternoon he had left the manuscript with her, and so had no knowledge of her activities on his behalf. Towards the end of April he was surprised by a letter from Leonard Moore. It was very much the kind of letter that earlier would have stirred up a blaze of optimism such as had occurred with the first letter from Cape, for here was Moore saying that he had read *Days in London and Paris* and liked it and thought he might be able to place it, and asking for its history – had it been offered anywhere but at Faber? Blair was polite but depreciatory: the fires had been banked and he had no wish to be burnt again. He supplied Moore with an account of the manuscript: first to Cape, then to Cape again, then to Faber, and so to Mrs Fierz, whom he had asked to destroy it, for it was not, in his opinion, 'a good piece of work'. Nor had his opinion of it changed. He was pleased of course that Moore should like it, and he was grateful that he should want to try to sell it, and of course he hoped that he would. But in the unlikely event of the book's being accepted, he would want to have it published pseudonymously as he was 'not proud of it'.

Here, in April 1932, five years after Eric Blair had embarked upon his literary career, is the first mention of a pseudonym, and it comes, significantly, at the first hopeful sign that his book – the most ambitious undertaking that he had attempted thus far – might finally be published. Until then, as we have seen, whatever he had written had appeared under his own name, even 'Hop Picking' and 'The Spike' (which had been incorporated into the book) whose subject-matter he might have thought would reveal too much (to his parents) of his life away from Southwold, and cause them anxiety or embarrassment. Yet now he proposed to remove his name altogether from his work and replace it with an invention. Eliot's rejection, which really was not very damning, weighed upon him, and deepened his own conviction of the book's inadequacy: that it was not a good piece of work of which he could be proud. This is the sole explanation he resorted to. As a connoisseur of failure, he seemed to be preparing for the worst: if he was to fail in public, he preferred to do so under a *nom de plume*. It would not be inconsistent with his psychology, of course, but would this be sufficient cause for so dramatic a decision? Or was it (at first) perhaps no more than a gesture to prove to himself as well as to Moore how little he cared whether the book was accepted or not?

But the diffident role was difficult to sustain as the weeks passed and he heard nothing further from his agent. He taught; he reviewed *The Spirit of Catholicism* by Karl Adam for the *New English Weekly*; he worked at his poem; he planted marrows in a small square of garden behind the house; he went fishing. But he grew increasingly restive and, early in June, devising a pretext that would not suggest impatience, he wrote, not for news of the book, but to ask if Moore might be able to get him work as an 'annotator' (Blair's word) from the Clarendon Press. An odd request, and Moore very likely recognized it for what it was, for when he did reply a fortnight later he made no reference to it: he had more important news. At the top of the letter Blair had sent him in April, Moore had scribbled in pencil the notation 'Gollancz'; and it was there, astutely, with a successful agent's sense of matching house to manuscript, that he had sent *Days in London and Paris*. Now he could report to Blair that Victor Gollancz liked the book and wanted to publish it.

The question of a pseudonym became a practical rather than a theoretical concern. Blair met with Gollancz at the end of June to discuss minor alterations in the text (swear words to be taken out, and certain names changed for fear of libel) which were easily dealt with. And Gollancz asked for a new title. It would have seemed an appropriate time for Blair to mention to him that he would be using a pseudonym, but he did not. He waited another week until he wrote again to Moore: in that letter, even more diffidently than before, he remarks that he thinks, if no one objects, he would prefer to have the book come out pseudonymously. And he asked Moore to tell Gollancz this. The tone is oddly uncertain and self-effacing: after all, he had no reputation, and if this first book had any kind of success, the pseudonym would have some value, and he could use it for future books. But he gives no reason, and he had no particular name in mind, or none that he was ready to disclose: he found it easier to invent a new title (*The Lady Poverty*, a phrase from a poem of Alice Meynell's) than a new name. So far as publisher and agent was concerned, the book's author, with whom the contract was being made, was still Eric Blair. His tone at this time is such as to leave one uncertain as to how deeply the question mattered to him. It seems fair to say that if Gollancz had insisted upon the name of Eric Blair on the title page, he would have yielded.

At the end of July, he went down to Southwold for the summer holiday. His mother not long before had bought Montague House in the High Street, but the family had not yet moved in. Three Queen Street had been let to summer visitors and Mr and Mrs Blair had gone to spend six weeks with the Dakins. Eric and Avril took possession of Montague House, where, in effect, they camped out for the month. The house 'had very little furniture in it', Avril remembers,[7] 'because most of our furniture was in the other house. Eric was writing away hard all day, and I was out. I was at that time working in a tea-shop in the town and came back pretty late at night. For some unknown reason, we only had two electric-light bulbs. I don't know why we didn't buy more, but we each had one, and we used to take them round from room to room plugging them in wherever we wanted them.'

At this time Eric told her that he thought he might have a book coming out soon, and that he had decided to publish it under a pen-name because he was 'ashamed' of it: he meant, he explained, that he thought their parents would be upset by it, it was all about his life in Paris. She felt that he must decide such things for himself; at the same time she was certain he exaggerated the effect the book might have upon either Mr or Mrs Blair, who were a good deal more worldly than Eric seemed willing to admit, and not, as Avril says, 'easily shockable, although my father was Victorian'. But his mind was made up, except for one important detail: he did not know what the name was to be.

From Southwold he sent the signed contract to Moore to send on to Gollancz (who had not yet commented either on the change in title or the proposed use of a pseudonym) and he offered another title: *In Praise of Poverty*. The pseudonym was left up in the air. It was six months since he had first mentioned it to Moore, but he still had no definite suggestion to offer: the important thing, he emphasized, was a name that would be easy to remember. Even after he went back to Hayes, to resume his dreary life as a schoolmaster, he could not reach a decision. The book was being set in type, and its title page was still blank.

In November, by which time it was already in proofs, Gollancz, growing impatient, proposed that it be called *Confessions of a Down and Outer*, and that the author's name be given simply as 'X.' Blair was not happy with either proposal. As a pseudonym for a young man passionately determined as Blair was on a literary career, and not merely the authorship of a single volume, 'X' would not do at all. On 15 November he reminded Moore that the pen name must be one that he could use again, which 'X' obviously was not. Yet even then, at virtually the last possible moment, he had not brought himself to the point of suggesting an alternative either to 'X' or to Eric Blair. Apparently he was willing to leave the matter to Moore and Gollancz to decide.

Four days later, he finally produced a list of possible pseudonyms. The first was his old tramping name, P. S. Burton. The second was Kenneth Miles. The third was George Orwell. The fourth was H. Lewis Allways. He himself admitted to a slight preference for George Orwell.*

For the title, he now offered *Confessions of a Dishwasher*.

Moore hastily forwarded the suggestions. Time was running out, the book was scheduled for publication two months hence; there could be no further hesitations. Gollancz conflated the various suggestions he and Blair had put forward for a title, and he chose from among the four names Blair had offered him for a pseudonym.

Seldom can a man have shed one identity and taken another with less concern as to who he was finally to be. But it was not the name that mattered: it was the self, the essential second self, under the name, which had been set free.

Down and Out in Paris and London by George Orwell was published by Gollancz on 9 January 1933. For a first book by an unknown author it did unusually well. The first edition had been sold by the end of the month, and a second impression was ordered. Reviews were plentiful, prompt, and favourable. His career had been successfully launched.

* As to the name itself, Anthony Powell, who became a friend of Orwell's in 1941, has written in a memoir of him: 'The Orwell is a river in Suffolk, "George", the most characteristically English Christian name. I once asked him if he had ever thought of legally adopting his *nom de guerre*. "Well, I have," he said slowly, "but then, of course, I'd have to *write* under another name if I did." '[8]

'The family, of course, read it with great interest,' Avril recalls. 'It almost seemed as if it had been written by a different person.'

A week or so after publication, returning from Southwold to Hayes, Blair met Mrs Fierz in London. They paused outside a shop where a window was filled with copies of the book, his book, his name, George Orwell, again and again: a promise for the future.

Notes

Many of the source books we have consulted have been in the American Edition, and these are the Editions acknowledged.

Part One: *From Bengal to St Cyprian's*

1 For Charles Blair's will, see Kenyon 522, Somerset House; for the exchange of deeds, see V. L. Oliver, *Caribbeana*, London, 1910.

2 Avril Dunn, 'My Brother, George Orwell', *Twentieth Century*, March 1961, p. 255, and interviews.

3 For Dorset and the Blair family: Hutchins, *History and Antiquities of the County of Dorset*, London, 1863; The Assistant Archivist, County Record Office, Dorset to authors; The Rev. J. L. Baillie, Milborne St Andrew to authors, and interview; *The Gentleman's Magazine*, 1867, II, 542.

4 For R. W. Blair, see *History of Service*, *Opium Department*, India Office Records; for Limouzins, see R. R. Langham Carter, *Old Moulmein*, Moulmein, 1947, copy courtesy of Mrs M. Lecky-Thompson.

5 Richard Rees, Afterword, *Burmese Days*, Signet Classics Edition, New York, 1963, p. 248.

6 Ruth Pitter, interview.

7 Humphrey Dakin to authors.

8 Cyril Connolly, *Enemies of Promise*, revised edition, New York, 1948, p. 160. Copyright 1938, 1946, 1952, © 1960 by Cyril Connolly.

9 Cecil Beaton, *The Wandering Years*, Boston, 1961, p. 29.

10 Connolly, *Enemies*, pp. 146-7.

11 Beaton, *Wandering*, p. 30.

12 Gavin Maxwell, *The House of Elrig*, New York, 1965, p. 83. See also E. H. W. Meyerstein, *Of My Early Life*, London, 1957.

13 Beaton, *Wandering*, p. 31.

14 Connolly, *Enemies*, pp. 146–7.
15 *The Collected Essays, Journalism and Letters of George Orwell*, London and New York, 1968, Vol. I, pp. 362–3, Vol. IV, p. 422.
16 Avril Dunn, 'My Brother . . .', pp. 255–6.
17 Beaton, *Wandering*, p. 32.
18 Eton examination based on Philip Brownrigg, 'College', in Bernard Fergusson, *Eton Portrait*, London, 1937, pp. 38–57.
19 Philip Magnus, *Kitchener : Portrait of an Imperialist*, London, 1958, p. 379.
20 Letter and poem, courtesy of Cyril Connolly.

Part Two: *Eton*

1 About Wellington, Graham Stainforth to authors.
2 Quotations from Eton contemporaries come from Cyril Connolly, interviews, and as cited; Denys King-Farlow, interviews, and 'College Days with George Orwell', unpublished manuscript; George Wansbrough to authors; Sir Maurice Whittome to authors; Francis Cruso to authors; James Gibson to authors; R. M. Cazalet to authors; W. C. A. Milligan to authors; Sir Steven Runciman, interviews; Christopher Hollis, interview, and as cited.
3 C. A. Alington, *Edward Lyttelton : An Appreciation*, London, 1943, p. 18. *The Times*, 5 June 1916.
4 Christopher Hollis, *Eton*, London, 1960, pp. 297–8.
5 Richard Rees, *George Orwell: Fugitive from the Camp of Victory*, London, 1961, p. 154.
6 *The Observer*, 1 August 1948. The piece has not been reprinted. Two paragraphs are quoted in Christopher Hollis, *A Study of George Orwell*, London, 1956, pp. 18–19. By permission of the Bodley Head.
7 Rees, *Orwell*, p. 42.
8 Hollis, *Orwell*, p. 13.
9 Avril Dunn, 'My Brother . . .', p. 256.
10 See Cyril Connolly's 'Theory of Permanent Adolescence', *Enemies*, p. 253, and Orwell's comment on it 'Inside the Whale', *The Collected . . .*, Vol. I, p. 517.

11 Malcolm Muggeridge, Introduction, Orwell, *Burmese Days*, London, 1967, pp. viii–ix. By permission of Heinemann Educational Books.

12 Hollis, *Orwell*, pp. 13–15, and interview. Sir Steven Runciman, interviews.

13 Connolly, *Enemies*, p. 187.

14 Marie-Jacqueline Lancaster, *Brian Howard*, London, 1968, p. 21.

15 As quoted in Eric Parker, *College at Eton*, London, 1933, p. 216.

16 Ibid., pp. 239, 250.

17 Hollis, *Orwell*, p. 15.

18 Connolly, *Enemies*, pp. 215–17.

19 Hollis, *Orwell*, p. 23.

20 Elizabeth Bowen in Oliver Stallybrass, cd., *Aspects of E. M. Forster*, New York, 1969, p. 1.

21 Cyril Connolly, *The Condemned Playground*, London, 1945, p. 62.

22 Samuel Hynes, *The Edwardian Turn of Mind*, Princeton, 1968, p. 14.

23 Connolly, *Condemned*, pp. 140–41.

24 Rayner Heppenstall, *Four Absentees*, London, 1960, pp. 20–21.

25 J. D. R. McConnell, *Eton – How It Works*, London, 1967, pp. 61–2.

26 Connolly, *Enemies*, pp. 204–5.

27 Ibid., p. 251.

28 McConnell, *Eton*, pp. 136–7.

29 Jack London, *The People of the Abyss*, London, 1926, p. 11.

30 A. S. F. Gow to Jeffrey Meyers, 1 January 1969, quoted in Jeffrey Meyers, 'George Orwell, the Honorary Proletarian', *Philological Quarterly* XLVIII, October 1969, p. 531.

Part Three: *Burma*

1 T. R. Fyvel, 'George Orwell and Eric Blair', *Encounter*, July 1959, p. 62.

2 Sir Steven Runciman, interviews.

3 *The Collected . . .*, Vol. I, p. 1.

4 As Orwell wrote in 'My Country Right or Left' (1940), his early world was 'tinged' with militarism, compounded by the five 'boring' years he spent in Burma 'within the sound of bugles', *The Collected . . .*, Vol. I, p. 540.

5 Information about Blair's application and examination: India Office Records: Judicial and Public Department file for 1922 (J & P 6079/22 vol. 1806).

6 *The Collected . . .*, Vol. IV, p. 266.

7 Roger Beadon, 'Burma 1922–1927'. We are very grateful to Mr Beadon for this memoir (from which subsequent quotations are taken) and for his assistance and advice. See also 'With Orwell in Burma – Roger Beadon talks to Pamela Howe', *The Listener*, 29 May 1969, p. 755.

8 Orwell, 'Notes on the Way', *Time & Tide*, 30 March 1940.

9 The details of Blair's work in Burma is based on interviews with Roger Beadon and on letters from contemporaries of his in Burma. R. G. B. Lawson to authors, also quoted pp. 152-3, 163, 165, 167, 169.

10 Blair to Henry Miller, 26 August 1936, *The Collected . . .*, Vol. I, p. 229.

11 J. G. Scott, *Burma: A Handbook of Practical Information*, 3rd edition, London, 1921, p. 146. See also J. S. Furnivall, *Colonial Policy and Practice*, New York, 1956; H. Tinker, *The Foundations of Local Self-Government in India, Pakistan and Burma*, London, 1954; also Annual *Report on the Administration of Burma*.

12 For Orwell's later views, see *The Lion and the Unicorn*, London, 1941, p. 45.

13 Anthony Powell, 'George Orwell', *Atlantic Monthly*, October 1967, p. 63.

14 A. Dunbar to authors.

15 A. L'e Brownlow to authors.

16 *Horizon*, Vol. IV, p. 201.

17 W. Somerset Maugham, *The Gentleman in the Parlour*, New York, 1930, pp. 7–8.

18 Maung Htin Aung, 'George Orwell and Burma', *Asian Affairs*, February 1970, p. 23.

19 For Robinson, see George Orwell, 'Portrait of an Addict',

The Observer, 13 September 1942, and also the book itself,
Captain H. R. Robinson, *A Modern DeQuincey*, London,
1942.

20 'Lawrence' to authors, and interview; Hollis, *Orwell*, p. 27,
and interview.

21 Harold Acton, *More Memoirs of an Aesthete*, London, 1970,
pp. 152–3; Orwell to Gorer, *The Collected . . .*, Vol. I, p. 382.

22 C. B. Orr to authors.

23 R. Gordon, B. Prescott to authors. Also quoted p. 182.

24 Orwell to Connolly, *The Collected . . .*, Vol. I, p. 329.

25 Sir Richard Rees, interviews.

26 For Orwell's reading, see *New Statesman*, 25 January 1941;
also *The Collected . . .*, Vol. III, pp. 105, 187–9; Vol. IV, pp.
3 33.

Part Four: *Becoming a Writer*

1 Avril Dunn, 'My Brother . . .,' p. 257.

2 Rees, *Orwell*, p. 145.

3 A. S. F. Gow, interview; also *The Collected . . .*, Vol I, p. 225.

4 Ruth Pitter, broadcast, 3 January 1956, and interview, also
quoted pp. 200–201, 240–41.

5 *The Collected . . .*, Vol. III, pp. 155–6.

6 I. O. Evans, Introduction, London, *Abyss*, pp. 9–11.

7 Brenda Salkeld, interview.

8 *La Vache enragée*, Paris, 1935, pp. 7–9.

9 Bailey to Blair, 29 April 1929, Berg Collection, New York
Public Library.

10 'A Farthing Newspaper', *The Collected . . .*, Vol. I, pp. 12–15.

11 *Progrès Civique*, 28 December 1928, 4 January, 11 January
1929. For Blair's Paris publications, we are indebted to the
Library of the Hoover Institution, Stanford University.

12 *The Listener*, 4 February 1971, p. 144.

13 Loelia, Duchess of Westminster, *Grace and Favour*, London,
1961, p. 225.

14 On the Dakins: Humphrey Dakin to authors; Fyvel, 'George
Orwell and Eric Blair', pp. 60–65.

15 Professor Richard Peters, interview and broadcast.

16 Mabel Fierz, interview.
17 Michael S. Howard, *Jonathan Cape, Publisher*, London, 1971, p. 133.
18 London, *Abyss*, p. 23.
19 Brenda Salkeld, interview, and broadcast, 2 November 1960.
20 Jack Common broadcast, 6 July 1958.
21 Rees, *Fugitive*, p. 141, also p. 318, as well as interview.

Part Five: *Becoming Orwell*

1 Heppenstall, *Four Absentees*, p. 46.
2 *The Collected . . .*, Vol. I, p. 78.
3 Letters to Moore, in part unpublished, Berg Collection, New York Public Library; see *The Collected . . .*, Vol. I.
4 We wish to express our gratitude to Mrs Valerie Eliot for sending us a copy of this letter.
5 Mabel Fierz, interview.
6 Evelyn Waugh to Julian Jebb, *Writers at Work*, New York, 1967, p. 108.
7 Avril Dunn, 'My Brother . . .', pp. 257–8.
8 Powell, 'George Orwell', p. 63.

Index